KNQ
470
.A67
C497x
2002
c. 2

AF865082

China's Legal Reforms and Their Political Limits

English-language Series of the Institute of Asian Affairs, Hamburg

VERBUND STIFTUNG
DEUTSCHES ÜBERSEE-INSTITUT

The Institute of Asian Affairs forms, together with the Institute of Comparative Overseas Studies, the Institute of African Affairs, the Institute for Ibero-American Studies and the German Oriental Institute, the Foundation German Overseas Institute in Hamburg.

The object of the Institute of Asian Affairs is to promote research on contemporary political, economic and social developments in the various Asian countries.

In so doing, the Institute endeavours to encourage the expression of various opinions. The reader should note, however, that the views expressed are those of the authors and not necessarily those of the Institute of Asian Affairs.

East Asia by the Year 2000 and Beyond
Edited by Wolfgang Pape

China's Economic Security
Edited by Werner Draguhn & Robert Ash

French and Japanese Economic Relations with Vietnam
Henrich Dahm

Tourism and Local Economic Development in China
Gang Xu

China's Legal Reforms and Their Political Limits
Edited by Eduard B. Vermeer & Ingrid d'Hooghe

China's Legal Reforms and Their Political Limits

Edited by

Eduard B. Vermeer
and
Ingrid d'Hooghe

CURZON

First Published in 2002
by Curzon Press
Richmond, Surrey
http://www.curzonpress.co.uk

© 2002 Eduard B. Vermeer and Ingrid d'Hooghe

Printed and bound in Great Britain by
IBT Global, London

All rights reserved. No part of this book may be reprinted or reproduced or utilised in any form or by any electronic, mechanical, or other means, now known or hereafter invented, including photocopying and recording, or in any information storage or retrieval system, without permission in writing from the publishers.

British Library Cataloguing in Publication Data
A catalogue record of this book is available from the British Library

Library of Congress Cataloguing in Publication Data
A catalogue record for this book has been requested

ISBN 0–7007–1423–5

Contents

Introduction

Cooperation in the field of law between China and the European Union has grown in recent years. There were close to 100 Chinese jurists at the China-Europe Legal Alliance Symposium held in Beijing at the end of 1997. The foci of this symposium were on the functions of legislation in economic development in four areas: administration, environmental protection, arbitration, and economic crime. At times, fundamental discussions have been held on human rights which are significant because they concern citizens' rights and the essential elements of Chinese communist rule. Independent reflection on the present nature and development of the Chinese legal system can make an important contribution to the European understanding of contemporary China. For that reason, the Sinological Institute of Leiden University organized a workshop on legal developments in China within the framework of the ECAN (Europe-China Academic Network) in October 1998. We are grateful to the European Commission for providing financial support for this workshop. The contributions to this volume, based on the six papers presented at that workshop, reflect a diversity of issues confronting China: human rights, administrative law-making, central versus local law-making, criminal justice, foreign investment authorization and shareholder rights in privatized collective industries. However, many similar underlying structural and political problems were identified, and this led to common conclusions about the nature and capacity for development of the present legal system in China.

The law in China, whether imperial or communist, was a flexible tool, not an absolute, independent standard. Laws were and are embedded in, and often subservient to, societal norms and values and the ruling elite. Traditionally, the legal code of China was primarily an instrument of punishment in the hands of government. Though under the Republic and the People's Republic a Western legal system was gradually introduced which included civil laws and courts which were separate from government, the role of law in government and society remained very limited. The constitution and some of the laws of the new communist government followed the Soviet model closely. Law became an instrument in the hands of the Communist Party, and was a means to further its political interests.[1] After a decade, China split with the Soviet Union, and efforts to build up a legal system were discontinued.[2] Instead, China relied on norms and sanctions imposed by the Communist Party and other authorities, and (during the Cultural Revolution) by Maoist leaders of mass movements. The court system, which never handled anything but the most serious cases, ceased to function for almost a decade.

In 1979, a new leadership under Deng Xiaoping undertook political and legal reform in an effort to catch up with the rest of the world and restore legitimacy to China's ruling party. The establishment of 'socialist legality' became a cornerstone of the policy to remove the Maoists from power and to end the privileged position of Party leaders at all levels. No longer should Party members be above the law. The 1982 constitution endowed the National People's Congress (NPC) with legislative powers, including amendments to the constitution, and the NPC became increasingly active, even if it never managed to shake off Communist Party control. Anthony Dicks, in an overview of the first decade of PRC legal reform, noted very significant achievements, all the more admirable as China had to start from scratch again and without trained lawyers. Yet the political system itself stood in the way of the protection of civil liberties by law and an independent judiciary.[3] The early milestones – the criminal law, criminal procedure law, and economic contract law – drew on enactments from the 1950s, which in turn were based on Soviet experience and on Republican statutes. The civil procedure law (draft) and subsequent administrative litigation law restrained bureaucratic power, as people could now appeal decisions by state agencies. However, these laws could not be used to question discretionary decisions, the regulations on which administrative decisions were based or Party decisions.[4]

The repression of civil liberties at Tiananmen in 1989 marked a temporary end to the reform movement in China. Whilst economic

---

[1] Cohen, J.A. (1969), 'The Chinese Communist Party and "Judicial Independence", 1949-1959', *Harvard Law Review*, No. 82, p. 967.

[2] Li, Victor H. (1971), 'The Evolution and Development of the Chinese Legal System', in John M.H. Lindbeck (ed.), *China: Management of a Revolutionary Society*, Seattle: University of Washington Press.

[3] Dicks, Anthony (1989), 'The Chinese Legal System: Reforms in the Balance', *The China Quarterly*, No. 119 (September).

[4] Potter, Pitman B. (1999), 'The Chinese Legal System: Continuing Commitment to the Primacy of State Power', *The China Quarterly*, No. 159 (September), pp. 673–683.

reforms regained momentum after 1992, driven not so much by Deng Xiaoping as from below – by local administrations and companies and foreign investors – political and legal reforms were stalled much longer. In the 1990s, the developmental and cultural gap between coastal and inland China became wider and wider. The functions of central government were affected by a general disillusionment with politics and the rise of localism, which became particularly strong among the rapidly developing, business-oriented Cantonese and Fujianese, and also in Shanghai. The Chinese Communist Party was not ready for federalism, and clung to a one-party, centrally controlled unitarian state. Under such circumstances, adoption of new laws which satisfied different local needs and could be implemented effectively throughout China became a daunting task – yet one taken up with much vigor by Chinese law-makers.

Recent academic publications on Chinese law stress the significance and scope of reforms.[5] Indeed this is an area of frenzied activity. Every year a dozen or more new laws are passed, and others are revised, as they are too general and unspecific to be of much use, or pertain to a planned economy which has already transformed into a market economy. As the deputy-general of the NPC Standing Committee Liu Zheng once remarked: 'Some legal measures are irrational, and some rational measures are illegal.'[6] Chinese politicians claim they want to build a socialist country ruled by law. But Chinese reformists have gone further, and professed that instead of rule *by* law, one should strive after the rule *of* law.

An important milestone was the Administrative Litigation Law passed in 1989. It gave Chinese citizens a legal instrument with which to defend themselves against the abuse of state power by government agencies and officials; it also strengthened the position of the judiciary.[7] A Chinese lawyer claimed it to be 'the most distinctive and powerful law for the protection of human rights'.[8] However, it has its limitations. For instance, in April 1998 the *International Herald*

[5]E.g. Potter, Pitman (ed.) (1994), *Domestic Law Reforms in Post-Mao China*, New York: M.E. Sharpe; Lubman, Stanley (1996), *China's Legal Reforms*, New York: Oxford University Press.

[6]Xinhua News Agency (in Chinese), 16 March 1998, as quoted in *BBC Far East*, No. 3180 S1/11.

[7]Potter, Pitman (1991), 'The Administrative Litigation Law of the PRC: changing the relationship between the courts and administrative agencies in China', *Chinese Law and Government*, Vol. 24, No. 3, pp. 3–21.

[8]Ying, Songnian (1999), 'China's Administrative Procedural Legal System – Present and Future', *China Law*, No. 3, pp. 74–76.

Tribune carried a story about a woman who sued her employer for imposing a huge penalty (three months' wages, and no reimbursement of medical costs) after she had a baby without prior approval from her employer. So far, two Beijing courts have upheld the employer's right to do so, in spite of the absence of legal grounds. The *International Herald Tribune* gave an optimistic spin to the story, saying it showed that many Chinese are no longer afraid to sue the authorities. Indeed there is a growing number of tried cases, tripling between 1993 and 1998 to almost 100,000, or 40 per cent of all court cases. Public security and land use were the most common tried cases. About half of the plaintiffs were enterprises, the other half private persons. The province with the largest number of cases was Hunan, maybe reflecting a Hunanese tradition of revolt against authority. In a third of the cases, rulings were in favor of plaintiffs, and in one-sixth, the government. Interestingly, almost half of all cases were withdrawn by the plaintiff, usually after government agencies gave in and settled out of court.[9] It seems the same mechanism is applicable here as that which Philip Huang has demonstrated was true of the late imperial government.[10] Many suits were filed only in order to influence ongoing informal mediation.

There have been positive developments in China's criminal justice system: the increasing professionalism of judicial personnel, the separation and mutual supervision of the public security bureau, the procurate and the courts, and the growing role of defense lawyers. Even so, interference by the Communist Party remains strong. Moreover, the legal apparatus is still extremely underdeveloped. China could be one of the few countries which has fewer lawyers than judges: 100,000 lawyers against 170,000 judges. Judges are appointed by local people's congresses, and such political appointees cannot be independent. With the growing corruption in government – in the past five years, over 300,000 cases were investigated by the procurates – political ties pose increasing threats to the functioning of the courts.

Economists have shown growing interest in the development of property rights in China under privatization. Most believe that a market economy requires property rights that are defined with sufficient clarity, and enforced with sufficient predictability, to encourage

[9] Pei, Minxin (1997), 'Citizens v. Mandarins: Administrative Litigation in China', *The China Quarterly*, No. 152 (December), pp. 832–862.

[10] Huang, Philip C.C. (1996), *Civil Justice in China: Representation and Practice in the Qing*, Stanford: Stanford University Press.

people to work, plan, invest, and take risks. Therefore, China's economic reform towards a market economy has much to do with changes in property rights, and how to set up institutions which ensure the clarity and predictability of those rights. A big question is whether it is possible to have effective transitional substitutes for Western-type civil law and for independent courts and regulatory agencies; if so, will China be capable of forming such transitional institutions?[11] Some people question whether clear property rights are really necessary: the fuzziness of 'collective' rights in rural industries has not prevented their obvious success. The bundle of property rights as distinguished by Demsetz – control, income and transfer – shows that most rights are partial only, and shared with others. Such rights are enforced in a variety of ways, ranging from formal law to social custom. My own research in this volume showed that privatization of Chinese companies has created shareholders with very diverse, but usually rather limited and ill-defined rights – often not unlike those in family firms in the West.

Jan-Michiel Otto and Yuwen Li provide an overview of law-making organs at central and different local levels. They note that provincial and lower levels of government, which are entitled to pass local regulations and rules, play an important role in adapting national laws to local circumstances. Local regulations cannot be applied to criminal offenses, the rights and duties of citizens, and the state organs, but beyond those, limits are not always clear. However, because of the principle of 'non-contravention' local regulations are still subject to formal approval from above. That holds for the so-called 'autonomous regions' as well. So as long as national legislation is wanting, local regulations may fill in the void, but once national laws have been passed, they take precedence. Otto and Li note a tendency for national laws to become more comprehensive and detailed, thereby leaving less room for local adaptation to specific circumstances. The drafting process of national bills often includes the consultations and solicitation of opinions of various departments, legal specialists, and also the central Communist Party organs. Once a draft bill has been put on the agenda, the legislative affairs committee of the National People's Congress will review it until it becomes acceptable for an NPC (or its standing committee) vote. As regards regulations, only the State Council has a standard procedure, whereas ministries and lower government organs do not. In terms of quantity, quality and

[11] Oi, Jean C. and Walder, Andrew (eds) (1999), *Property Rights and Economic Reform in China*, Stanford: Stanford University Press.

transparency, Otto and Li see enormous progress in law-making over the past two decades. However, the rapid and many legal revisions threaten legal stability and certainty, and some laws leave too much room for different interpretations by lower organs. The division of legislative powers is also unclear and inadequate.

Jean-Pierre Cabestan is less positive about administrative law-making in his contribution. Admittedly this is a highly politically-sensitive area. In 1987, its importance was belatedly recognized by the authorities. The National People's Congress has had considerably less input in this area than in others, as most laws and regulations were issued jointly with the Communist Party Central Committee or by the State Council. The 1993 regulations for public servants have suffered from resistance by the Communist Party Organization Department and the lack of public participation in the drafting process; the concept developed by Zhao Ziyang and his reformist legal advisers was diluted and marginalized after his downfall. Foreign examples of administrative laws have been used, but selectively and with the insertion of many restrictions. Severe administrative sanctions such as 'sheltering for examination' and 're-education through labor' circumvent the procurate.[12] Cabestan carefully distinguishes between laws, decrees and other regulations. The CCP Central Committee Political and Legal Commission plays a major coordinative role in law-making. The decrees emanating from the State Council may prepare the ground and collect the necessary experience for subsequent laws. The other regulations vary greatly in status. The example of the adoption of the Administrative Litigation Law shows that the central government is willing to wait and compromise whenever it meets with opposition from local authorities or departments. Cabestan notes that provincial governments enjoy great freedom in passing administrative regulations, freedom which may be at the expense of their legality; and that harmonization of local rules remains difficult to achieve.

Geor Hintzen argues that China's resistance to Western human rights is not just political, but firmly rooted in Chinese culture and societal values. He believes that a 'collective redefinition' in line with traditional Confucian values would constitute a more credible basis for the human rights dialogue with the West than a poorly understood idea of the Western concept. The latter evokes immediate

[12]Wong, Kam. C. (1997), *Sheltering for Examination (Shoushen) in the PRC: Law, Policy and Results*, Occasional Papers/Reprint Series in Contemporary Asian Studies, No. 3, School of Law, Baltimore: University of Maryland.

negative responses and would only serve to destabilize China's political system and society. While maintaining a principled approach, European Union members should de-ideologize the issue and clarify the practical meanings of human rights by long-term engagement in various forms of legal support and training. With Marxism-Leninism as the normative 'default mode' in contemporary China's political culture, Chinese scholars and politicians are unfamiliar with human rights concepts, yet want to engage in the international debate for foreign policy reasons. China has joined, but not yet ratified, most UN treaties on human rights. The crux lies with different concepts of the nature of man, which in the Chinese view includes correct social behavior. Human rights are a political gift from above rather than an innate dimension of man. Therefore, concretization of these rights in everyday life, whether by individuals or by social groups, can occur only within political and social limits. Hintzen distinguishes ethical, Marxist and legalist views of Chinese intellectuals, and his discussion seems to suggest that while in the 1980s instrumental and moral legal views of the role of human rights coexisted, later a combination of traditional and socialist values became paramount. The 'civil society' debate was carried on mainly in the West. After an overview of the growth of civil associations in China, Hintzen concludes that most autonomous groups have been marginalized or pushed into illegality. The recent official campaign against the Falungong confirms the determination of the Chinese authorities to stamp out any movement, political or not, which they do not control.

The criminal justice system in China has seen a major overhaul in 1996-1997. Jianfu Chen finds the changes to the criminal law wanting in many respects, but is much more positive about the Criminal Procedural Law. Compromises struck between scholars, lawyers and officials in the process of drafting these laws did remedy a number of deficiencies. Provisions on analogy (for which there was a long Chinese tradition) were finally abolished, and the principle of 'no crime without definition by law' accepted. Equality before the law was mentioned explicitly. A new element was introduced with the recognition of crimes by corporations and other legal units. The new criminal law did not provide much guidance in the matter of proportionality and still allows for an extremely wide range of punishments for specific crimes, with seventy-six articles allowing the death penalty. 'Counter-revolutionary' crimes and the death penalty which had drawn most international and some domestic criticism were not changed in any fundamental way, though the former were reworded as crimes 'endangering state security'. Most disappointing was the silence of the new law on the legality of the administrative sanction of re-education through labor. The Criminal Procedural Law fared better, and Professor Chen traces carefully how various compromise solutions were found. The presumption of innocence, though not accepted, was at least brought nearer by explicit rejection of the presumption of guilt. The right to counsel was strengthened, and defense lawyers given greater powers. Sufficiency of evidence became a matter of determination not before, but during the court session. Trial judges have been relegated to a much more modest role, as the prosecutors and lawyers battle their case. But the issue of judicial independence remained unsolved, and ultimately depends on changes in the political system. Chen ends with the cautionary remark that the practical significance of the revisions will depend on their adoption by the law enforcement agents and lawyers, something which requires an attitudinal change.

The negative trade balance for the EU (imports being twice as large as exports) has been a factor in the EU anti-dumping cases against Chinese companies. In 1997, there were eight such cases. Now that China has been taken off the non-market economies list – a gesture which was greatly appreciated by Chinese politicians – it is no longer necessary to select a third country to establish a proper price. In China's view, such selection was often arbitrary. Moreover, China felt that whether the EU industries suffered losses or not was not always decided in an even manner. Anti-dumping measures remain a sensitive issue, but are overshadowed by the larger, intractable problem of World Trade Organization (WTO) participation.

Jan Holthuis's contribution on direct investment authorization touches on the essence of China's foreign investment policies. It is well known that even before the Asian crisis – in 1997 and again in 1998 – direct foreign investment in China decreased for several reasons, an important one being the abolition of preferential policies for import of equipment in 1996. Though only a quarter of investment has come from outside the region, a major part of China's technology imports came from the EU, particularly Germany. China's primary objective in directing foreign investment is economic modernization, mainly through the introduction of advanced technology. Moreover, it stresses a foreign exchange balance and the fact that there are actual surpluses which bolster native and foreign confidence in the currency (and perhaps the regime). Holthuis rightly points out that there is confusion about which government agency is authorized to approve projects. The central government has a long-term view: it wants to prevent cut-throat competition between local governments in their attempt to attract foreign investment, and costly duplications which might reduce overall profitability. The transparency of Chinese regulations remains a problem, and many are not even publicly available. The 1995 'Interim Provisions guiding the direction of foreign investment', and the appended list which classifies several hundred categories of investment which are encouraged, more or less restricted (A and B), or prohibited, have been superseded by the more restrictive 1998 Catalogue. The categorization of the Catalogues, and their effective enforcement, is not too clear; moreover, there are other catalogues: one on key sectors, products, and techniques supported by the state, and another on foreign investment items which will not be granted tax exemption on imported goods.

Restrictive foreign investment rules are only one method of supporting domestic industries and services. Since 1996 many factories have been idle, leading to huge losses, and industrial restructuring programs (in steel, textiles, car manufacturing, household appliances, and other sectors) implemented since 1997 have cost millions of jobs in the old industrial cities of China. The call for protection of China's own industries has become louder recently. China has imposed limited market shares on foreign Joint Ventures (JVs) in some sectors (e.g. in breweries). It still favors its state-owned enterprises (SOEs) with cheap loans, lower tariffs, less stringent environmental demands, and lower social security bills. SOEs are allowed to copy foreign technology without strict enforcement of copyright and patent rights. Nevertheless, some progress has been made in this field. The 1997 Criminal Law contains seven articles on the protection of intellectual property. In the event of infringement, a penalty of up to seven years' imprisonment may be imposed. Foreign copyright owners may bring complaints to the local copyright administration. Amendment of the 1991 Copyright Law in the near future should bring greater compliance with the TRIPS (Trade-Related Aspects of Intellectual Property) Agreement and the Berne Convention.

One may conclude that the class nature of Chinese socialist law still prohibits genuine independence of the legal system. Even if most of the newly passed laws are 'technical', their application and implementation rests with a hierarchy of Chinese political structures dominated by the Communist Party.[13] Political and institutional reforms

[13] Senger, Harro von (1994), *Einführung in das chinesische Recht* (Introduction to Chinese Law), München: Verlag C.H. Beck.

have lagged behind economic and social reforms.[14] The defense of the rights of citizens and private organizations against the (often combined) authorities of state, party, employer and other authorities ultimately rests on the capacity to use the civil law – of which there is no tradition. Moreover, the increasing participation of private and foreign companies in the Chinese economy creates a great need for civil dispute resolution. Though rapidly improving, the Chinese courts are poorly equipped, and the execution of civil judgments leaves much to be desired.[15] Cooperation between the European Union and China in legal and other fields should contribute not just to drawing China closer into the international community, but also to reinforcing civil rights in China and creating greater mutual understanding of the lessons and limits of the European tradition.

Eduard B. Vermeer
Sinological Institute, Leiden University

[14] Shih, Chi-Yu (1999), *Collective Democracy: Political and Legal Reform in China*, Hong Kong: The Chinese University Press.
[15] Clarke, Donald C. (1995), 'The Execution of Civil Judgments in China', *The China Quarterly*, No. 141 (March).

1

Central and Local Law-Making: Studying China's Experience

*Yuwen Li and Jan-Michiel Otto**

Contrary to the situation in the 1960s and 1970s – a period during which there was hardly any law to rely upon in China[1] – in the 1980s and 1990s such a large quantity of legislation has been issued that even keeping track of it is proving difficult. Between 1978 and the end of 1998, the National People's Congress (NPC) – China's highest legislative body, and its Standing Committee (SC) has passed and issued 339 laws and decisions relating to legal issues. The State Council, China's highest executive body, has promulgated approximately 750 administrative regulations. People's congresses at provincial level have adopted about 5,800 regulations.[2] These pieces of legislation, although sometimes inconsistent and of a short-term policy character, have to a large extent met the country's urgent need for economic and social development. One may say that in today's China as far as written law is concerned, the aspiration that 'there must be laws to be relied upon' (*youfa keyi*) has largely been achieved. In this chapter

* The authors would like to express their appreciation to the Dutch Ministry of Education and Culture for funding the Leiden-Beijing Legal Transformation Project which is conducted at the Van Vollenhoven Institute.

[1] From 1957–1976, the NPC only adopted the National Outline for Agricultural Development (1958–1967) and the 1975 Constitution. The SC-NPC issued seven regulations concerning public order, household registration and agricultural tax. Local legislation did not exist. Chen 1995, p. 151.

[2] *Renmin ribao* (*People's Daily*), internet edition, 9 December 1998 and 3 February 1999.

we will explore some aspects of law-making in China at both national and local levels.[3] It is common knowledge that economic and social development can be harmed, not only by extreme centralization, but also by extreme decentralization. Moreover, any evaluation of decentralization should take the effectuation of specific developmental goals as a standard.[4]

In the common type of decentralization which is often called devolution,[5] the legal power of local law-making bodies has always been a prominent element. The idea is that the lofty goals of democracy and authenticity require that people make their own regulations at local levels. However, other development goals such as nation-building, stability, distributive justice and, to some extent, economic growth have motivated national governments all over the world to keep policy and legislation in central hands.

It seems that the experience of China confirms an observation common to most studies of decentralization in developing countries: while certain legal powers and administrative tasks have been shifted to lower levels, the corresponding transfer of resources and decision-making power is mostly lacking.[6] The legal transfer of law-making powers to local populations is often half-hearted, incomplete or even deceptive.[7] Chinese jurists and political scientists have conducted intense discussions about the desirable type, degree and scope of local law-making.[8]

In order to maintain a balance, one must be aware of the strengths and weaknesses of both central and local law-making. This requires a thorough interdisciplinary study of legal texts, as well as of actors, institutions and processes at various levels. A general overview of national law-making in China and its problems can be constructed on

[3]Local level refers to provinces, national autonomous areas, special economic zones, capitals of provinces and autonomous regions and other large cities designated by the State Council. According to Chinese law, people's congresses, their standing committees, and governments at the above-mentioned levels have legislative powers and functions.

[4]Frerks and Otto 1996.

[5]In this respect, we follow Rondinelli, Nellis and Cheema 1984. They use the term decentralization in a broad sense, as an umbrella concept covering different types of transfers from a central level, downwards or sideways. It includes devolution, deconcentration, delegation and privatization.

[6]An interesting case study about local law-making and autonomy in Asia is the (1999) Ph.D. thesis of Nicole Niessen about the city of Bandung, Indonesia. This research was carried out from 1993–1998 at the Van Vollenhoven Institute and the Research School CNWS of Leiden University.

[7]Phan 1996, pp. 83–108.

[8]Li 1998.

the basis of available legislation and literature.[9] However, it is more difficult to produce an overview of local law-making. This chapter is thus of an exploratory nature only. Issues addressed include law-making organs and the types of legislation at central and local levels, the process of national and local law-making, the division of legislative power between central and local organs, and finally, the main functions and features of local law-making.

Legislators and legislation at central level

Chinese positive law is formed primarily through the products of legislation. At the national level, we can distinguish three categories based on the Constitutional provisions: national law enacted by the National People's Congress and its Standing Committee, administrative regulations (*xingzheng fagui*) promulgated by the State Council, and ministerial rules (*buwei guizhang*) issued by ministries and commissions under the State Council.

The NPC and SC-NPC

According to the Chinese Constitution (Art. 58), legislative power lies with the NPC and its SC. The NPC is the highest organ in the Chinese state system. It consists of around 3,000 deputies who are chosen by provincial people's congresses and by the army. The NPC's plenary session convenes only once a year (usually around March) for about two weeks. A single term for a deputy of the NPC is five years. The legislative powers of the NPC include the power to amend the Constitution, to enact and amend basic laws (*jiben falu*) (sometimes translated as 'basic statutes') concerning criminal offenses, civil affairs, the state organs and other matters (Constit. Art. 62).

When the NPC is not in session, it functions through its Standing Committee and nine special committees.[10] The SC-NPC, the permanent organ of the NPC, consists of about 150 members and meets every two months. The SC has independent legislative competence.

[9] Otto and Li 1998. In this paper the work of important authors such as Albert Chen, Perry Keller and Murray Scott Tanner is summarized.

[10] The Committee of Nationality, the Committee of Law, the Committee of Finance and Economy, the Committee for Education, Science, Culture and Health, the Committee of Foreign Affairs, the Committee of Overseas Chinese, the Committee for Internal and Judicial Affairs, the Committee for Environmental and Resources Protection, and the Committee on Agriculture and Rural Areas.

Not only can it 'interpret' the Constitution and laws promulgated by the NPC, but it can also enact and amend laws, except for those which should be enacted by the NPC (Constit. Art. 67). Under the SC, the Legislative Affairs Commission (*fazhi gongzuo weiyuanhui*) (occasionally translated as the Legal System Work Committee) conducts legal research and drafts some laws. This commission is a working unit of the SC, and its members are not deputies of the NPC. This distinguishes them from the members of the Committee of Law of the NPC, in which all members are deputies.

The State Council

The State Council, the Chinese 'cabinet', is the highest administrative organ in China. It is composed of a premier, vice-premiers, state councillors, the auditor-general, the secretary-general and a number of ministers and commissioners. These ministers and commissioners head the large central government institutions, the ministries and commissions (Constit. Art. 86). According to the Constitution and Chinese legal theory, the State Council is not meant to be a legislative body. However, in practice the State Council fulfils important legislative tasks. Some of these tasks are based on the Constitution and the laws, while others were delegated to the State Council by the NPC. The State Council's legislative acts are generally referred to as administrative regulations, according to Article 89 of the Constitution. These regulations have an important impact given their general scope, and are used as the legal basis for lower-level decisions.

The Legislative Affairs Office (LAO) of the State Council is responsible for the State Council's legislative work, which is of the greatest importance as regards both policy and legal-technical matters. Its 250 or so employees assess draft legislation from the ministries, revise it if necessary, and draft important regulations themselves. The LAO is also involved in the drafting of laws, of which the SC-NPC is in charge. Moreover, it is responsible for *inter alia* 'law-interpretation', the verification of the implementation of laws by the administration, inter-departmental co-ordination in the implementation and evaluation of laws, the registration of central and local laws and rules, as well as the publication of legislation and the authorized translations thereof.[11]

[11] Bureau of Legislative Affairs of the State Council of the People's Republic of China, Beijing, 1996, pp. 8–13.

Ministries and commissions

The ministries and commissions under the State Council may, in their own policy fields, make administrative rules in accordance with the Constitution, laws, and administrative regulations of the State Council (Constit. Art. 90). Such rules are generally referred to as ministerial rules. This form of national administrative rule-making is in principle concerned with the implementation of higher regulations of the State Council, since the latter often contain quite general provisions. In addition, it is often the case that there are no administrative regulations on a particular subject. In such a situation, ministerial rules become an important source of law. Apart from making their own rules, ministries and commissions also draw up drafts of administrative regulations and laws to be enacted by the State Council and the NPC respectively. Keller observes that 'whilst it is true that these drafts are frequently amended by the NPC, the ministries are still able to set the primary agenda and often control implementation'.[12]

Legislators and legislation at local level

Based on the Constitution, the 1995 Organic Law of the PRC on Local People's Congresses and Local People's Governments (hereafter simply referred to as the Local Organic Law (LOL)),[13] the Law on Regional National Autonomy (LRNA),[14] and the decisions of the NPC and SC-NPC to delegate legislative powers to Special Economic Zones (SEZs), we can distinguish four categories of local law-making, to wit: law-making at provincial level, law-making in national autonomous areas, law-making in special economic zones, and law-making by capitals of provinces and autonomous regions, and other large cities designated by the State Council.[15]

Provincial level

This level includes twenty-two provinces, five autonomous regions (border provinces populated with non-Han ethnic groups) and four

[12] Keller 1994, p. 739.

[13] The text can be found in the *1996 Law Yearbook of China*, pp. 207–214.

[14] The English translation can be found in The Legislative Affairs Commission of the SC-NPC 1987, pp. 87–101.

[15] The return of sovereignty over Hong Kong to China has added a new type of local legislation: The Basic Law. However, legislation in Hong Kong is not within the scope of this paper.

municipalities directly under the central government. People's congresses (PCs) and their standing committees (SCs) at this level may enact 'local regulations' (*difang fagui*) in the light of the specific conditions and actual needs of the areas under their respective jurisdictions. Such regulations must not contravene the Constitution, the laws or administrative regulations and they must be reported to the SC-NPC.[16] Provincial governments may adopt 'local rules' (*difang guizheng*) in accordance with the laws, administrative regulations, and regulations of their respective provincial legislatures. Such local rules should be reported to the State Council and its respective SC-PC so that records may be kept.[17]

Both the 1954 and 1978 Constitutions provided that legislative power was exercised exclusively by the NPC. The 1979 LOL, for the first time, extended legislative competence to PCs and their SCs at provincial level. This was confirmed in the 1982 Constitution. Most local legislation is made at this level. The most sensitive issue of law-making at this level is how to interpret the principle of 'non-contravention' mentioned above.

National autonomous areas (NAAs)

'National autonomous areas'[18] include: autonomous regions, autonomous prefectures, and autonomous counties (Constit. Art. 112). They are equivalent to provinces, prefectures and counties, respectively. People's congresses, their SCs, and governments in the autonomous areas enjoy specific legislative powers based on the right of autonomy.

Four types of legislation can be distinguished in this category: autonomous regulations (*zizhi tiaoli*), specific regulations (*danxing tiaoli*), flexible provisions (*biantong guiding*), and supplementary provisions (*buchong guiding*).

An autonomous regulation is the most general type of regulation of the NAA: it may deal with political and economic affairs as well as cultural and social life. To date, 123 autonomous regulations have become effective in NAAs and they are all reflections of the 1984 Law on Regional National Autonomy. Specific regulations refer to specific, sectoral affairs within the autonomous areas, such as the local lan-

[16]Article 100 of the Constitution. The reporting system is only for keeping records at central level.

[17]Article 60 of the LOL.

[18]The term 'national autonomous areas' is used in Chinese official translation. However, we feel that 'autonomous nationality areas' is clearer.

guage and culture, economy, education, health, natural resources and the environment. About 113 such regulations have been approved.[19] Both autonomous and specific regulations should be made in accordance with 'the political, economic and cultural characteristics of the nationality or nationalities in the areas concerned' (Constit. Art. 116). Moreover, those regulations enacted by autonomous regions must be submitted to the SC-NPC for approval before they can become effective. Those made by autonomous prefectures and counties must be submitted to the standing committees of the people's congresses of the respective provinces or autonomous regions for approval before they come into effect (Constit. Art. 116).

According to Article 115 of the Constitution, the organs of self-government of the autonomous regions, prefectures and counties (including people's congresses and people's governments, (Art. 112 Constit.) can implement the laws and policies of the state in the light of the 'existing local situation'. Article 20 of the LRNA provides: 'If a resolution, decision, order or instruction of a state organ at a higher level does not suit the conditions in a national autonomous area, the organ of self-government of the area may either implement it with certain alterations or cease implementing it after reporting to and receiving the approval of the state organ at a higher level'. Based on these provisions, flexible provisions and supplementary provisions can be made for NAAs, which means that national laws and administrative regulations are applied after appropriate adaptation. There are now fifty-nine such provisions, related to the Criminal Law, the General Principles of Civil Law, the Law of Civil Procedure, the Law on the Protection of Old People's Rights and Interests, the Law on Forest, etc.[20]

In addition, a number of national laws contain specific provisions entrusting autonomous areas to exercise their rights of autonomy, including for instance, Article 36 of the Law on Marriage, Article 25 of the Law on Inheritance, Article 31 of the Law on Adoption, Article 53 of the Law on the Protection of Women's Rights. The various NAAs have issued supplementary provisions to these Laws.[21]

It should be noted that even though local regulation and rules in NAAs can be made to a certain extent to deviate from national law, such legislation is subject to an approval procedure of higher

[19]Li and Wang 1998, pp. 254 and 259.
[20]Li and Wang 1998, p. 254.
[21]Phan 1996, pp. 103–104.

organs. This may be an indication of the limited nature and scope of legislation at the level of the NAAs.

The SEZs

Law-making in SEZs differs from other local law-making, because it is based entirely on the delegation of legislative power by the NPC and SC-NPC. From 1981 to 1996, the NPC and its SC have issued five decisions delegating legislative powers to people's congresses, their SCs, and the governments of the provinces of Guangdong, Fujian and Hainan, and the cities of Shenzhen, Xiamen, Shantou and Zhuhai.[22] The motivation for the central organs of power to delegate legislative power to SEZs is closely linked with the open-door policy and with attracting foreign investment. An essential part of this policy has been to establish a few SEZs along China's coastline, where new economic policies and systems could provisionally be experimented with before being applied nationwide.

Some of the delegating decisions restrict legislative power in SEZs to specific economic regulations. In practice, most legislation in SEZs is in the area of economic policy. However, other decisions do not limit legislation to the economic field, and instead only require that legislation in SEZs must comply with the Constitution, the basic principles of the law and the administrative regulations. As a result, in some SEZs legislation covers a wide range of subjects. At present, two models of SEZ legislation can be identified. One is the Shenzhen model, which is characterized by a comprehensive scope of legislation covering almost every area of law. Another is the Shantou model (a much smaller SEZ), which emphasizes actual needs in specific fields.[23]

[22]The Decision of the SC-NPC on Delegating the People's Congresses and Their Standing Committees in Guangdong and Fujian Provinces to Enact Specific Economic Regulations for Special Economic Zones under Their Jurisdiction (26 November 1981). The Decision of the NPC on Establishing Hainan Special Economic Zone (1998). The Decision of the SC-NPC on Delegating Shenzhen People's Congress and Its Standing Committee and Shenzhen People's Government to Enact Regulations and Rules Respectively within the Shenzhen Special Economic Zones (1 July 1992). The Decision of the NPC on Delegating Xiamen People's Congress and Its Standing Committee and Xiamen People's Government to Enact Regulations and Rules Respectively in Xiamen Special Economic Zones (22 March 1994). Decision of the NPC on Delegating Shantou and Zhuhai People's Congresses and Their Standing Committees, and People's Governments to Enact Regulations and Rules Respectively in Their Special Economic Zones (17 March 1996).

[23]Qiu 1997, p. 39.

Legislation is generally referred to as regulations made by the SEZs (*jingji tequ fagui*) and rules of the SEZs (*jingji tequ guizhang*).

Capitals and large cities

According to Articles 7(2) and 43(2) of the LOL, people's congresses and their standing committees of capitals of provinces, autonomous regions and large cities determined by the State Council (hereafter 'capitals and cities') may enact local regulations in the light of the specific situations and actual needs of their respective cities, provided that they do not contravene the Constitution, the law, the administrative regulations, and local regulations of their respective provinces and autonomous regions. They become effective upon approval by the people's congress standing committees at provincial level, who will report those regulations to the SC-NPC and the State Council. Under Article 60 of the LOL, the governments of 'capitals and cities' may adopt rules in accordance with the law, the administrative regulations and local regulations of their respective provinces and autonomous regions. Such rules must be reported to the State Council, SCs of PCs and governments of respective provinces and autonomous regions, and SCs of PCs at the same level ('capitals and cities').

At the present time, competent organs in twenty-seven capitals and nineteen large cities enjoy such legislative power. Legislation at this level is generally referred to as local regulations and local rules. In recent years, a general trend is that local authorities in 'capitals and cities' have been demanding more independence in exercising legislative power. Some of them consider the approval procedure for local regulations too time-consuming. Sometimes, a regulation is not approved for two or three years without any reasons being given. In addition, if a local regulation concerns the power, interests and administration of both a provincial government and of a 'capital or city', and the two sides cannot easily reach agreement, then the regulation in question will not be approved. Therefore, the leadership of 'capitals and cities' has called for a change from the system of approval by higher level organs to a system of reporting, i.e. a local regulation should become effective after it has been reported to competent organs at provincial level. However, at this moment the authorities of some of the provinces and autonomous regions consider the approval procedure to be necessary to ensure the legality, feasibility and consistency of local regulations. In their view, the quality of local regulations made by 'capitals and cities' is usually low because of a lack of legislative experts at that level.[24]

Processes of national law-making by the NPC and SC-NPC

There is no one single piece of law which provides a detailed procedure on how to conduct the process of law-making at national level. Based on the Organic Law of the NPC,[25] the Rules of Procedure of the NPC[26] and the Rules of Procedure of the SC-NPC,[27] the process of law-making by the NPC and SC-NPC can be divided into six stages: making a legislative plan, drafting a bill, introducing the draft bill, reviewing the bill, passing the bill, and the promulgation and publication of the enacted law.[28]

(1) The making of a legislative plan as the first step of the law-making process is a rather recent phenomenon in China. The first such plan was made in 1991 by the 7th SC-NPC. In 1993, the 8th SC-NPC started to draw up the five-year legislative plan (1993–1998). The plan contained the legislative subjects which were to be drafted and reviewed, the organs which were to take charge of the drafting work, the proposed time for review, etc. Based on the five-year plan the SC-NPC then decided its annual legislative work. This pattern has now been followed by the 9th NPC.

(2) Drafting a bill. In the absence of a written law which provides concrete steps for bill drafting, the practice of the NPC and SC-NPC can been summarized in five steps.[29] First, the drafting bodies must

[24] Zhou 1996, p. 85.

[25] Arts. 9, 10, 31, 32 and 37 of the Organic Law of the National People's Congress. The English translation of this law can be found in the Legislative Affairs Commission of the SC-NPC 1987, *The Laws of the People's Republic of China 1979–1982*, pp. 334–342.

[26] Arts 5, 21, 22, 23, 24 and 25 of the Rules of Procedure of the National People's Congress.

[27] Arts. 12, 13, 14, 15, 16, 17, 18, 20, 30 and 33 of the Rules of Procedure of the National People's Congress Standing Committee.

[28] Some contributions in English have provided insightful analysis on the process of national law-making in China, such as Keller 1994; Clarke 1991; O'Brien 1994; and Tanner 1996. In this chapter our information is largely based on Chinese legal documents and literature, especially 'Chapter VI: Legislation of the Central Organs of Power' in Li and Wang 1998, written by Wang Wenyou, who is the Head of the Office on Research under the General Office of the SC-NCP.

[29] Li and Wang 1998, pp. 149–152.

be determined. In the NPC and SC-NPC, the Legislative Affairs Commission drafts most bills. A Special Committee of the NPC can also act as a drafting body. Deputies of the NPC and members of the SC-NPC can also make draft proposals. Sometimes, special drafting committees are set up by the NPC or SC-NPC to undertake specific drafting work, such as the drafting committee on the Basic Law of the Hong Kong Special Administrative Region.

A bill which is put forward by the State Council to the SC-NPC can be drafted either by the Legislative Affairs Office of the State Council or by ministries or commissions under the State Council. In addition, the Supreme People's Court and the Supreme People's Procuratorate are competent in the drafting of laws concerning adjudicative and procuratorial work respectively. The Central Military Committee is in charge of drafting laws on military matters. Some central government organs, such as the All China Trade Union and the All China Women's Association, have also taken charge of drafting some bills. If a proposed piece of legislation covers a broad range of jurisdictions, joint drafting is organized. For example, the draft work of the Marriage Law was headed by the All China Women's Association, with participation by the Supreme People's Court, the Supreme People's Procuratorate and the Ministry of Civil Affairs.

The second step is to set up a drafting team. Each drafting body usually forms a drafting committee which consists of legal as well as technical experts. Sometimes, external experts are invited to sit on the committee.

Third, the drafting committee undertakes research and investigation, determines the purposes of the draft bill, the major problems to be resolved, collects and studies the relevant laws, documents, books and information, organizes seminars to discuss and gather the opinions of experts, and finally makes a research report to be approved by the head of the drafting body.

Fourth, based on the approved report, the drafting committee draws up an outline and then puts this into concrete form by drafting individual articles. At the same time, the drafting committee should write an explanation of the draft, which indicates the detailed drafting process, the legal basis, the necessity and feasibility of the draft as well as the opinions given by any relevant government organs.

Finally, after a draft is made, it is sent to the relevant government bodies. A series of meetings are then organized by the drafting committee to collect different opinions and allow different bodies to reach compromise solutions. After this, a draft is made for submission to the head of the drafting body. If the draft is made by the Legislative Affairs Commission of the SC-NPC, it should be discussed and approved by the Council of Chairpersons (*weiyuanzhang huiyi*), which consists of the Chairman, a number of Vice-Chairmen and a Secretary-General of the SC-NPC. The Council acts as an executive committee leading the work of the SC.

It should be noted that during the process of drafting, especially of important laws, the Legislative Affairs Commission, the Legislative Affairs Office, and the relevant departments of ministries and commissions cooperate closely. Distinguished scholars in particular fields are also deeply involved. And moreover, the draft will be sent to the relevant organs of the Central Communist Party for approval (this is an informal but inevitable procedure). The drafting of the 1997 Criminal Code is a typical example.[30]

(3) Introducing a bill. The competent organs and persons who can propose a bill to the NPC include: the Presidium of the NPC, the SC-NPC, the Special Committees of the NPC, the State Council, the Central Military Committee, the Supreme People's Court, the Supreme People's Procuratorate, a delegation (*daibiao tuan*, deputies elected by a provincial PC), deputies of the NPC (at least thirty acting jointly).

Apart from the Presidium and a delegation of the NPC, the abovementioned organs and persons, together with the Council of Chairpersons of the SC-NPC, can also introduce a bill to the SC-NPC. In practice, however, most bills are presented to the NPC either by the SC-NPC or the State Council.[31] Nevertheless, in recent years the number of bills and draft law proposals submitted by delegations and deputies has increased. In March 1999 during the second session of the 9th NPC, 759 draft proposals were put forward, nineteen by delegations and 740 by deputies. This created a record number of proposals in the NPC.[32]

Whether a bill can be listed in the agenda of the congress is a key issue. According to Article 21 of the Rules of Procedure of the NPC, if a bill is put forward to the NPC, the Presidium is to determine whether a bill is to be included in the agenda. However, in reality it is somewhat different, for the agenda of the NPC is passed by the preparatory meeting of the plenary meeting organized by the

[30]Lang 1997, pp. 54–57.
[31]Chen 1993, p. 80.
[32]*Renmin ribao* (*People's Daily*), internet edition, 15 March 1999.

SC-NPC before a Presidium is composed. Thus, the Presidium can only determine whether to put a draft proposal on the agenda if it is presented when the NPC is in session. In such a case, the Presidium usually decides to leave the matter to be handled by the SC-NPC. For instance, of the 759 draft proposals mentioned above, 229 were passed to the Special Committees of the NPC: the committees are expected to provide assessments on whether to include a draft proposal in the agenda of the NPC or the SC-NPC. The SC-NPC makes its decision based on those assessments. The rest of the 530 proposals were taken as opinions of deputies, and were passed by the General Office of the SC-NPC to the relevant government organizations: the latter are expected to take decisions upon proper evaluations.[33]

If a bill is put forward to the SC-NPC by the Council of Chairpersons, it will be reviewed directly by the SC. If it is put forward by other organs, the Council of Chairpersons will decide whether or not to include it in the agenda. In reality, all bills presented to the NPC are first put forward to the SC-NPC. The Council of Chairpersons decides whether the draft bill is to be reviewed by the NPC or SC-NPC. Even if it is decided that a bill is to be submitted to the NPC, the bill will preliminarily be reviewed at least once by the SC-NPC before a decision is made to put it on the agenda of the NPC. Thus, whether a bill can be included in the agenda of the NPC or SC-NPC is determined mainly by the Council of Chairpersons.

(4) The review process also contains a number of stages. One month before a draft bill is to be reviewed by the NPC, the General Office of the SC-NPC should send the draft bill to all deputies. When the NPC is in session, deputies will first hear an explanation of the bill by a representative of the body presenting the bill. The bill is then examined by each delegation and by the Special Committees of the NPC. Responses to the bill are reported to the Committee of Law. This Committee then produces a report of the review to the Presidium and a revised bill. The Presidium examines the revised bill and determines whether to agree with it or to return it to the Committee of Law for further amendment. After a draft bill (the revised draft) is passed by the Presidium, the report on the review of the draft by the Committee of Law will be given to all deputies. The review procedure is then at an end. The review of a draft bill is usually finished at one session of the NPC. If this cannot be achieved,

[33] *Ibid.*

the NPC may delegate the SC to conduct a further review or the NPC may decide to review it at its next session.

The review procedure of the SC-NPC is similar to that of the NPC as described above. The difference is that the Legislative Affairs Commission plays an important role in the SC-NPC's procedure. This Commission collects the review assessments of the SC and the Special Committees, sends bills to the relevant government departments at national and provincial level, organizes investigation teams to collect local opinions, and discusses the draft bills with scholars and experts. Based on all the feedback, the Commission revises the draft, article by article. In the past, a draft was usually reviewed twice by the SC, and in exceptional cases three or four times.

Since the 9th SC-NPC in 1998 a 'three review' procedure has been set up. At the first review, a representative of the drafting body provides an explanation of the bill and then members of the SC conduct the preliminary review. After two months or more, members conduct the second review focusing on significant, difficult provisions and the provisions on which opinions differ most greatly. The third review takes place after a Special Committee of the NPC has revised the bill based on the opinions of the members of the SC and has delivered a review report. If views do not differ greatly, then the bill is put forward to be voted on.[34] A new development in 1998 was that the SC-NPC divided its members into six groups for reviewing a bill, instead of four groups as in the past. Since members of Special Committees of the NPC, persons in charge at provincial people's congress standing committees and some deputies of the NPC are also invited to participate at its review proceeding, each group has around forty-five people (instead of the sixty previously). The aim of this reduction in the number of people in a group is to give members more opportunities to express themselves during the review process.[35]

In order to illustrate the review procedure in a concrete manner, one can take a recent example. At the second session of the Ninth NPC in March 1999, the draft contract law was reviewed by the NPC. The bill was first introduced by Gu Angran who is the Director of the Legislative Affairs Commission of the SC-NPC. He explained the purposes and the process of drafting the new unified contract law, and the main content of the law to the plenary meeting. The delegations took three days (9–11 March) to review it. Based on suggestions made by delegations, the Committee of Law reviewed the

[34] *Renmin ribao* (*People's Daily*), internet edition, 11 March 1999.
[35] *Ibid.*

draft and made concrete revisions. A few substantive revisions were made which relate to the scope of the law to be regulated, the enforcement of contracts, *rebus sic stantibus*, construction contracts and technology contracts. In addition, there were also about 30 changes in the wording of the draft. The Committee then suggested that the Presidium should review the revised draft and make the decision to put the revised draft forward for voting at the plenary meeting. On 15 March, the Contract Law was passed by the NPC.[36]

(5) Voting. A bill is passed by the NPC or the SC-NPC if the majority of the deputies present votes in its favor. In practice, if a bill is put to the vote it is always passed. This is because 'if sharp differences of opinion emerge in the course of consideration of a bill, the usual practice is not to put it to the vote immediately but to conduct further research and suggest amendments for the purpose of reaching a higher degree of consensus before actual voting'.[37]

(6) Promulgation and publication. The President of the country promulgates the laws passed by the NPC and the SC-NPC. The laws are then published in the *People's Daily* and in the *Gazette of the SC-NPC*.

The process of regulation-making by the State Council

The process by which the State Council enacts administrative regulations follows stages similar to that of the SC-NPC, except that there is no voting. Of course, at each stage the key players are different, and the time needed for making a regulation is in most cases shorter. Five-year plans and annual legislative plans of the State Council are drawn up by the Legislative Affairs Office in consultation with the ministries and commissions and subject to the approval of the State Council.[38] In most cases, about fifty legislative items are listed in an annual legislative plan. However, the leaders of the State Council

[36] *Renmin ribao* (*People's Daily*), internet edition, 15 and 16 March 1999.

[37] Chen 1993, p. 81.

[38] According to Li Shishi, the Deputy Director of the Legislative Affairs Office of the State Council, in the past the legislative plans were made in this way: the various ministries and commissions put forward their respective legislative items to the Bureau of Legislative Affairs (the predecessor of the LAO), the latter compiled them and gave a report to the State Council for examination and approval. Since 1998, much of the initiative for drafting legislative plans seems

can always add new items to the plan if they consider them necessary. As far as drafting work is concerned, it can be undertaken either by the relevant ministries or commissions or directly by the LAO. The draft will then be reviewed by the LAO before it is submitted to the Executive Meeting of the State Council.[39] The LAO, together with other relevant departments, revises the draft according to the recommendations of the Executive Meeting and then submits it to the Premier for signature. The Premier takes the final responsibility for the promulgation of administrative regulations. Once enacted, they are published in the *Gazette of the SC-NPC.*

The process of rule-making by ministries and commissions

Even though rule-making at this level follows stages similar to those mentioned above, at each stage the procedure is simpler and faster. Within most ministries and commissions there is a division in charge of legal affairs which is the main player in rule-making. The division draws up a legislative plan based on the proposals of other divisions of the ministry. The plan can be either on an annual or a five-year basis, and is to be approved by the minister. Drafting work can be conducted either by the relevant division or by a drafting team led by the division of legal affairs. The final draft is submitted to the executive meeting of the ministry for review, and if it is passed, then the minister signs it. In addition, all ministerial rules must be reported to the State Council to be recorded within thirty days of their enactment.[40]

Since there are numerous bodies which are authorized with the power to issue ministerial rules, and such rules are often made to resolve urgent practical problems (which means that they have to be issued in something of a hurry), the standardization of such rule-making is rather important. So far, there is no one single law in this respect. The 1990 Decisions Concerning the Registration of Regul-

to have been invested in the LAO. See Li Shishi (1998), 'The State Council and Law-making', paper presented at the Leiden Conference on Law-making in China, 26–28 October 1998, p. 7.

[39]'The Interim Regulations on Procedure for Formulating Administrative Regulations', issued by the General Office of the State Council in 1987. The text can be found in the *1988 Law Yearbook of China*, pp. 138–139.

[40]Art. 4 of the Decision Concerning the Registration of Regulations and Rules, *1991 Law Yearbook of China*, pp. 173-174.

ations and Rules (DRRR)[41] deal only with the recording of regulations and rules by the State Council.

The process of local regulation-making

There is no national law which provides detailed rules of procedure for enacting local regulations. Instead, many people's congress standing committees at provincial level, and Shenzhen SEZ have made their own rules of procedure. Some of those which were made in the 1980s, are generally simple, while the more recent ones are more detailed. However, they all bear a more or less similar structure and provide stages of regulation-making similar to those at national level.[42]

Comparable to the NPC, people's congresses at provincial level convene only once a year for about two weeks and they do not have sufficient time to examine regulations in depth. Consequently, most local regulations are examined and passed by SCs of PCs. The following is a summary of the Rules on Regulation-making by the Standing Committee of the Shenzhen People's Congress (hereafter the Shenzhen Rules), which can be used as an example to illustrate the general process of local regulation-making.[43]

(1) Making a legislative plan. The legislative affairs commission of the people's congress standing committee in Shenzhen (a local level version of the Legislative Affairs Commission of the SC-NPC) makes a legislative plan in the first quarter of the year and submits it to the chairmen's meeting (*zhuren huiyi*) of the SC for approval.[44] The chairmen's meeting has the same status as the Council of Chairpersons at the SC-NPC.

(2) Drafting. A regulation item which has been included in the annual plan should be drafted by the unit which puts forward the proposal. A regulation which is put forward by the chairmen's meeting or by a group of more than five members of the SC jointly should be drafted

---

[41] *Ibid.*

[42] Chao 1994, pp. 96–104.

[43] The Rules were passed on 15 October 1992. The text can be found in *The Collection of Shenzhen SEZ Regulations (1992-1993)* (1995), compiled by the General Office of the Shenzhen People's Congress Standing Committee, Haitian publisher, pp. 1–9.

[44] In some places, SCs-PCs operate in a manner similar to that adopted by the SC-NPC by making five-year, biennial and annual legislative plans. Such plans are usually made by the Department of Legislative Affairs of the government, in consultation with the SC of the PC and other departments of government.

by the relevant working committee of the SC, or the general office, or the unit entrusted with the task by the chairmen's meeting. Before a proposed draft regulation is submitted to the SC, the unit in charge of the drafting should consult the relevant departments, and study relevant laws and regulations at national level.[45]

(3) Introducing a draft regulation. Qualified organs and persons which can present draft regulations to the SC are: the chairmen's meeting, the people's government of Shenzhen, members of the SC (at least five jointly), and the intermediate court and procuratorate in Shenzhen. A draft regulation must be submitted with the necessary supplementary material, such as an explanation, and the legal and policy basis of the draft.

The general practice is that most of the regulations passed by PCs and their SCs are put forward by local government, second by the chairmen's meeting, special committees of the PC, or working commissions of the SC-PC, and a few by the courts or procuratorates. Draft proposals made by delegations (deputies, at least ten jointly) and members of SCs (at least five jointly) are numerous, but they are hardly ever put into the review agenda. This is because most of these drafts are incomplete and lack explanation and reference materials. Thus, these proposals are integrated into draft regulations made by the government organs.[46]

(4) Review of a draft regulation. A draft submitted to the SC will first be examined by a working commission of the SC, which will then report its findings to the chairmen's meeting. If a draft is submitted by the people's government, the SC will review it. If a draft is introduced by members of the SC, the court or the procuratorate, then the chairmen's meeting should, according to the preliminary assessment of the relevant working commission of the SC, determine whether it should be reviewed by the SC. The chairmen's meeting can require the working commission or the unit which drafted the regulation to conduct further investigation and consultation, and propose a revised draft. After the SC has reviewed a draft, if it considers it necessary to revise the draft, then the legislative affairs commission should work together with the other relevant commissions and units to make the

[45] It is not mentioned in the Shenzhen Rules, but as a general practice if a regulation concerns significant issues then the draft must be submitted to the Communist Party at provincial level and the Party's amendments should then be incorporated into the draft.

[46] Li and Wang 1998, p. 242; Chao 1994, pp. 98-99.

change, and report to the chairmen's meeting. The chairmen's meeting can then give the revised draft to the SC for the second review. Thus, a draft regulation is usually examined twice by the SC before it is put to the vote.

(5) Voting, promulgation, publication and keeping record. As at the NPC and the SC-NPC level, a regulation can be passed by the majority vote of all the deputies. It should then be published in the *Gazette of Shenzhen PC-SC*, the *Journal of Shenzhen PC-SC*, the *Shenzhen SEZ Daily*, the *Shenzhen Commercial Daily*, and the *Shenzhen Legal Daily*. The regulation should also be reported to the NPC-SC, the State Council and the PC-SC in Guangdong province.

The process of local rule-making

Similar to the local regulation-making process, the local rule-making process can also be divided into the five stages mentioned above. However, some different elements of rule-making should be noted.[47] First, local rules are often made to supplement local regulations or to meet urgent needs. Thus, legislative planning by the government is not as essential as it is for the SC-PC, although most local governments do make an annual plan. Second, local rules of a comprehensive nature are usually drafted directly by the office of legal affairs of the local government, while rules which relate only to the administration of certain departments of the local governments are drafted by the relevant departments. Since most local rules deal with very concrete issues, the relevant departments of local governments play a major role in rule-drafting. Third, rules drafted by the departments must be submitted to the office of legal affairs of the local government for examination. During the process of examination, the office can conduct its own investigation, and solicit general feedback. The office then presents the revised draft to the executive meeting for approval. Fourth, there is no voting procedure for passing local rules: instead, the decision of the head of local government is sufficient. A local rule is signed by the provincial governor, the chairman of the autonomous region, or the mayor, and is published in the government gazette and the local newspaper.

[47] Li and Wang 1998, pp. 246–249.

The division of central and local legislative power

The division of central and local legislative power is a core issue, as well as an issue of considerable difficulty in the improvement of China's legislative system. Even though there are some general basic rules in dividing central and local legislative power, their practical utility is much less clear than was intended.

The first rule is that according to Articles 62 and 67 of the Constitution, the NPC has the exclusive power to amend the Constitution, to enact and amend 'basic laws concerning criminal offenses, civil affairs, the state organs and other matters'. In these fields, local legislation cannot be made. However, a difficult question is how to understand the words 'other matters'. Based on the functions and powers of the NPC and SC-NPC as provided in the Constitution, some Chinese scholars have tried to enumerate specific national legislative powers in a list. These powers relate to the following categories: basic political, economic and social systems, the basic rights and duties of citizens, principles concerning the structure and power of state organs, basic laws on criminal, civil and litigation matters and judicial principles and system, defense, foreign affairs, nationality, state territory and other affairs where the sovereignty of the state is at stake, financial and taxation systems, the basic administrative systems on postal services, telecommunication, railways, civil aviation, space and nuclear technology and other public utilities, the calendar, weights and measures, and other matters for which the Constitution provides that legislation should be made at the national level.[48] Such a list provides a general picture of the scope of national legislation, although it is by no means exhaustive.

For the last few years, the Legislative Affairs Commission of the SC-NPC has taken the responsibility of drafting a law on legislation. Some have proposed that this law should contain a detailed list of legislative fields which are under the absolute power of the NPC and SC-NPC. However, for the time being this may not be feasible. In modern China, legislation remains at an early stage of development. In order to meet actual needs – particularly in economic and commercial fields – both national and local legislation is needed, and each is dependent upon the other. By providing areas of exclusive legislative power for the central organs, the result could be to limit local legislative power.

[48]See Li and Wang 1998, pp. 231-232; Guo 1998, pp. 50-51.

The second rule is that local regulation must not contravene national law. Article 100 of the Constitution states that the PCs and their SCs at provincial level may adopt local regulations, which must not contravene the Constitution, the laws and administrative regulations. The 'non-contravention' rule can have two implications. The first is that local regulation must not conflict with the Constitution, the laws and administrative regulations. The second is that where certain matters are not yet regulated by central law, local regulations can be made because of an absence of conflict in such situations. However, when central law in that field is made, it then prevails over the local regulations. In such cases, if the latter conflict with the national law, then they must be annulled.

In connection with this issue, it should be noted that a different principle applies in cases of rule-making by local government. According to Article 60 of the LOL, a people's government at provincial level may enact administrative rules 'in accordance with' the laws, the administrative regulations, and local regulations of the respective province. Here, the principle of 'in accordance with' has a different connotation from the principle of 'non-contravention' i.e. provincial governments are not allowed to issue rules on matters for which the laws, the administrative regulations, and the local regulations do not yet exist. In other words, the law-making power of local PCs and their SCs is wider than that of local governments.

The third rule is that local law must be made according to actual needs. Articles 7 and 38 of LOL provide that PCs and their SCs at provincial level may enact local regulations in the light of 'the specific conditions and actual needs within their jurisdiction'. This can be called the principle of 'need'. However, this is an open-ended norm and in practice it is difficult to follow. Local authorities can always substantiate a local 'need'. In legislative practice, where sensitive and important issues are concerned, if the central law is absent or lacking, then local authorities often ask for the opinion of the relevant organs at central level so as to avoid or reduce the risk of local law contradicting national law. Of course, in some cases this has also led to the postponement or cancellation of local law-making.

Despite the above-mentioned statutory rules, in practice the division of central and local legislative powers is sometimes provided for in individual laws. For instance, the Administrative Punishment Law provides that the '[l]aw may impose various administrative punishments', and that '[a]dministrative punishment concerning the restriction of personal freedom can only be made by law' (Art.9). Further, it states that '[l]ocal regulations may provide administrative punishments except the restriction of personal freedom and the revocation of enterprise business licenses', and that '[w]here law and administrative regulations have provided administrative punishment provisions on illegal acts, while local regulations need to provide concrete provisions, such provisions must be within the scope of the types and limits of administrative punishments provided by law and administrative regulations' (Art. 11). Another example is the Budget Law promulgated by the NPC in 1994. In Chapter Two, seven articles give a detailed division of functions in the administration of budgetary affairs between the NPC, SC-NPC and local people's congresses at county level and above.

Functions and features of local law-making

The primary function of local legislation is to implement national laws and regulations which, in many cases, contain only general principles and provisions which cannot always provide answers for everyday legal problems. Consequently, local legislative organs and governments have played an important role in making concrete regulations and rules to ensure the implementation of national law. In so doing, a basic principle is to adapt national law in the light of actual situations and practical need. For instance, according to the Economic Contract Law, bureaux of industrial and commercial administration at various levels are responsible for contract administration. But in some remote rural areas, such bureaux exist only at and above county level, and most township governments do not have such organs. If one merely applied the Economic Contract Law, the administration of land contracts in these rural areas would be problematic. Under such circumstances, regulations are required to add new provisions which befit the local situation.

However, a serious problem is that local regulation often reiterates provisions of national law, rather than simply making the necessary additions. This has serious negative effects. For instance, local regulation mixes those newly added provisions in a long and repetitive text, so that the specifics of local regulation cannot easily be identified. Consequently, the actual purpose of local laws is often not as obvious as it should be. In addition, provisions of national law are copied in local law which downgrades the authority of national law provisions.

It should be noted that a recent trend is that laws and regulations made at central level are becoming more comprehensive and detailed, which leaves increasingly less room for local authorities to enact local laws. This is true for the Company Law, the Securities Law, the bank laws and tax laws and regulations. This is owing partly to the fact that local law and practice have accumulated a lot of experience, enabling the central organs to make more extensive laws, and partly owing to the central government's decision to emphasize centralized control over the market economy. Local bodies, especially local governments, sometimes complain that the space in which they can make local rules is being narrowed down.

The second function of local legislation is to fill in legal lacunae. Economic reform in China has resulted not only in an increasingly complicated economic system but also in many changes in social relationships. Disputes and conflicts have increased in number, and they often require legal resolution. In some cases and some legal fields, national laws are not enacted quickly enough. This is particularly true in commercial law: local laws are sometimes the first to be issued before national laws are enacted. For instance, in February 1985 the Shenyang City Government had already issued the 'Provisions on Bankruptcy of Urban Collective Industrial Enterprises (for trial use)'. The National Bankruptcy Law was promulgated in December 1986 and became effective in November 1988. Another example is in the field of company law. The Company Law of the PRC was promulgated in December 1993 and became effective in July 1994. But in September 1986, the People's Congress Standing Committee in Guangdong province had already issued the first local regulation on companies: 'Regulations on Foreign-Related Companies in Special Economic Zones in Guangdong Province'. In April 1993, the Shenzhen People's Congress issued the first regulation on the limited liability company. Another example is the 'securities boom' in China since 1991. In April 1994, Hainan province issued 'Administrative Regulation on Securities in Hainan Province'. The Securities Law of the PRC was only enacted by the SC-NPC in December 1998.

Sometimes, national law-makers postpone the regulation of practical but rather delicate issues. This subsequently leaves local authorities free to make local regulations. Family planning is a typical example. It is common knowledge that family planning is a basic state policy in China, but so far there is no national law in this field, while the coverage of local regulations is ample. Other typical examples are in social security law and the law relating to real estate.

Another phenomenon is that the contents of local laws are sometimes more progressive than those of national law. For instance, the Regulations on Lawyers in Shenzhen Special Economic Zones which became effective on 1 May 1995, define a lawyer as a legal practitioner who has obtained a legal qualification and holds a certificate to practise law and who provides legal services to society. This definition was also used in the Law of the People's Republic of China on Lawyers passed in May 1996, which became effective on 1 January 1997. Before this date, the national law on lawyers was the Provisional Regulations of the PRC on Lawyers adopted in August 1980 by the SC-NPC. The Provisional Regulations defined lawyers as 'state legal workers', who enjoyed civil servant status. Another example is the 1986 Bankruptcy Law which applies only to enterprises owned by the whole people, namely state-owned enterprises. But the Rules of the Shenzhen Special Economic Zone on Enterprise Bankruptcy, issued in November 1993, apply to all enterprise legal persons registered in Shenzhen SEZ or registered outside but having their domicile in Shenzhen SEZ. In addition, under the national bankruptcy law an application for bankruptcy is an absolute precondition for the involvement of a court. In other words, a court is not empowered to declare a debtor bankrupt without a prior application. But the 1993 Shenzhen Rules provide that a court may *ex officio* declare a debtor company bankrupt, if it establishes, during a civil action or execution proceedings, that the debtor is unable to discharge mature debts or does not meet settlement requirements.

In addition, sometimes local commercial law has adopted more of international practice than has national law. Again, taking bankruptcy law as an example, the national bankruptcy law provides that the criteria for bankruptcy are 'poor operation and management that result in serious losses and inability to repay debts that are due'. The 1993 Shenzhen Rules provide that a company may be declared bankrupt if 'it is unable to pay its debts as they fall due'. This latter criterion is the one most often used by industrialized countries. In connection with this, one may note that the foreign input in local law-making is receiving more attention, especially in SEZs, and that may to some extent improve local law-making.

Local regulations are often focused on economic affairs, physical planning, resource management and social security.[49] Economic affairs is the main area of local regulations. Such regulations account for about 50 per cent or more of the total of local regulations. For

[49]Interviews with civil servants at Beijing Municipality, September 1998.

instance, in 1996, among the twenty-seven local regulations enacted and approved in Inner Mongolia, thirteen deal with economic matters. In Shanghai, fifteen local regulations were enacted or revised, seven relating to economic affairs. In Anhui Province, twenty-three local regulations were promulgated, including thirteen on economic affairs. In Fujian province, twenty-eight local regulations were enacted or revised, fourteen of which concerned economic affairs.[50]

Concluding remarks

Over the last two decades, legislation in China has made dramatic progress in several respects. First, the number of competent organs in law-making has been expanded. Initially, legislative power was completely centralized in the NPC. The 1979 LOL for the first time entrusted people's congresses and their standing committees at provincial level with the power to enact local regulations. The power of law-making by the SC-NPC was confirmed in the 1982 Constitution, although in practice laws and amendments to NPC-enacted laws were already issued by the SC during the period of 1978–1982. The law-making function of the State Council and ministries and commissions under it was resumed in the 1982 Constitution. The 1986 amended LOL expanded rule-making power to local government at provincial level, and people's congresses, their standing committees and governments of capitals of provinces and autonomous regions and other large cities designated by the State Council. Local law-making in SEZs started in 1981 and gradually expanded in the 1990s. Generally speaking, a multi-level and multi-dimensional legislative structure has been established. Initiative and enthusiasm in law-making at both national and local levels have been on the increase.

Second, the quantity of legislation (in terms of the total number of laws passed) is rather impressive. As far as quality is concerned, the increase of provision and detail in legislation is also obvious. For instance, the 1979 Criminal Code contained only 192 Articles, while the 1997 Criminal Code consists of 452 Articles. The 1996 Lawyers Act has fifty-three Articles, while the previous law had only twenty-one Articles. As far as law concerning economic entities is concerned, the 1979 Sino-Foreign Equity Joint Venture Law contains fifteen Articles, while the 1994 Company Law includes 230 Articles. The increased number of articles makes the law more detailed and concrete which provides better chances for implementation.

[50] *1997 Law Yearbook of China*, pp. 744–761.

Third, law-making procedures have become more systematic and transparent. In the early 1980s, the law-making process was treated more like an internal working procedure, kept secret and involving only a very limited sphere of persons. Gradually, it has been developed into a kind of publicly-known legal procedure. In recent years, both government officials and academics have been strong advocates of making the law-making process more democratic, more open to groups having specific interests and to the public as a whole. In 1998, the draft law on land administration (revised), the draft organic law on village committees, and the draft contract law were published in newspapers in order to generate public opinion. It is reported that from June to August 1998 the Legislative Affairs Commission of the SC-NPC received 541 letters concerning the draft organic law on village committees.[51]

However, all this progress cannot be looked at in absolute terms because tension and problems have also occurred and developed at the same time. In the first place, the expansion of the number of organs involved in law-making also causes the problem of 'law coming out of various doors' (*fachu duomen*), which to a certain extent affects the unity of law, and the consistency of law, which definitely affects the certainty of law and renders implementation more difficult.[52] It has also caused the problem of overstepping one's power (*yuequan lifa*): i.e. some laws which should be enacted by the NPC and its SC, have been issued by the State Council or local organs and some regulations which should be made at national level, have been issued at local level. Another problem is departmentalism (*bumen zhuyi*), in the sense that authorities compete with each other to have the rules reflect their own interests in law-making. In addition, the hierarchical order of laws is also not always clear. For instance, whether a ministerial rule precedes a local regulation and rule remains unclear. The relationship between the regulations and rules of provinces and those of the SEZs within those provinces also remains unclear. Since regulations and rules in the SEZs are enacted according to legislative power delegated by the NPC and SC-NPC, one may assume that they belong to a higher level, but this has not been established firmly.

---

[51] *Renmin ribao* (*People's Daily*), internet edition, 10 March 1999.

[52] Keller observes that '[t]he disparate mass of laws and regulations which makes up the formal written resources of Chinese law does not possess sufficient unity to be regarded as a coherent body of law'. Keller 1994, p. 711.

Second, laws are constantly being modified. One of the guiding principles of China's legislation is to issue a piece of law as soon as the time to enact it is ripe. Thus laws are made quickly, and when new developments take place, laws are revised correspondingly. As a principle this seems rather natural in any country's legislative experience. However the problem in China is that the speed of change is so frequent that legal stability and certainty are being diminished. In addition, in most cases national laws are still filled with general provisions, and a great deal of room is left to the administrative organs to issue implementing regulations and rules. The latter rules are often made in a haphazard manner, in the sense that they may clarify some issues but leave others for later implementation, or they change too frequently to adapt to the policy shifts or short-term needs. It is a common complaint both within and outside China that it is difficult to keep track of which laws are in force when legal issues are handled. This problem is particularly obvious where foreign trade, investment, and the administration of foreign currency are concerned.

In connection with the frequent changes of law, one should note that Chinese legal draftsmen not only have legal issues to deal with, but also have to take into account government policies and politics. Politics puts constraints on law-makers because legal issues sometimes cannot be ideally resolved by legislation. In view of the remaining ideological limits and the fact that China's economic reforms are being undertaken in phases, it can be very difficult indeed in some cases for legal draftsmen to determine how far the law can be made to meet practical needs, without it becoming rapidly outdated or too liberalized.

Third, in spite of the improvement of the legislative process, the transparency of and public participation in law-making in China both remain at a rather low level. Stages and steps of law drafting and reviewing still need to be laid down by law and strictly followed. The democratization of the law-making process in administrative organs is an area in particular need of being strengthened. Efficient and feasible rules and measures remain to be found in this regard. In addition, the position of the Communist Party in terms of political leadership is not apparent in any of the written laws relating to law-making. But in reality, this invisible hand enjoys a special position. Important laws, regulations and rules all need to have the approval of the party leadership. This may be an unfortunate but inevitable phenomenon in today's China where the country's political system still remains under the Party's supreme control.

One must admit that most of these problems have been recognized by the Chinese authorities, and efforts have also been made to tackle them. Making a law on legislation is a major step towards resolving these problems. However, some issues cannot be resolved by law itself. For instance, the division of legislative power between central and local levels, and between state legislative organs and administrative organs, does not seem likely to be resolved by the law on legislation. This is because the issue touches the division of powers which has wide implications and is deeply rooted in the complex of China's political system. Over the last two decades, China's economic, legal and social systems have undergone tremendous transformation, but the same degree of change has not been evident in the political sphere. Even though the power distribution between the central and local levels has been modified to the extent that more power has been allocated to the local level (such as in the fields of taxation and finance), a clear-cut division of powers by law is still well behind schedule. According to Article 3 of the Constitution, '[t]he division of functions and powers between the central and local state organs is guided by the principle of giving full play to the initiative and enthusiasm of the local authorities under the unified leadership of the central authority'. This general but basic principle may be a long-lasting one in directing central and local law-making in China. In practice, this implies that there will always be some grey areas in which national and local legislation overlap.

After weighing the pros and cons of China's legislative practice, one final observation is that the progress made is remarkable and has been much appreciated both domestically and abroad. Problems have also been recognized by the central and local governments and critically studied by Chinese scholars. In China's legislative agenda, the target is to establish a comprehensive legal system with Chinese characteristics by 2010.[53] This involves enacting new laws, revising existing laws and abolishing some laws. One may only hope that the envisaged process both at national and local levels will make Chinese law more consistent, stable, transparent and certain.

[53] Tang 1998, p. 58.

References

Chao, Chien-min (1994), 'The Procedure for Local Legislation in Mainland China and Legislation in National Autonomous Areas', *Issues & Studies*, Vol. 30, No. 9 (September), pp. 96–104

Chen, Albert H.Y. (1993), *An Introduction to the Legal System of the People's Republic of China*, London: Butterworths

Chen, Jianfu (1995), 'China: Constitutional Changes and Legal Development' in Tay, Alice E-S. and Leung, Conita S.C. (eds), *Greater China: Law, Society and Trade*, Sydney: The Law Book Company Limited

Clarke, Donald C. (1991), 'What's Law Got to Do with It? Legal Institutions and Economic Reform in China', *UCLA Pacific Basin Law Journal*, Vol. 10, No. 1 (Fall), pp. 1–76

The Collection of Shenzhen SEZ Regulations (1992-1993) (1995), compiled by the General Office of the Shenzhen People's Congress Standing Committee, Haitian publisher

Frerks, G. and Otto, J.-M. (1996), *Decentralization and Development: A Review of Development Administration Literature*, Research Report 1996/2, Leiden: Van Vollenhoven Institute for Law and Administration in Non-Western Countries

Guo Yan (1998), 'Cong "Buxiang dichu" yuanze tan woguo difang lifa tizhi de wanshan' (From the 'non-contravention' principle to discussing the perfection of China's local legislation), *Ningxia shehui kexue* (Ningxia Social Sciences), No. 1, pp. 50-51

Keller, Perry (1994), 'Sources of Order in Chinese Law', *The American Journal of Comparative Law*, Vol. 42, pp. 711–759

Lang, Sheng (1997), 'On the Conception and Birth of the New Criminal Code of the People's Republic of China', *China Law*, No. 2, pp. 54–57

The Legislative Affairs Commission of the SC-NPC (1987), *The Laws of the People's Republic of China 1979–1982*, Beijing: Foreign Language Press

The Legislative Affairs Commission of the SC-NPC (1987), *The Laws of the People's Republic of China 1983–1986*, Beijing: Foreign Language Press

Li, Buyun (1998), 'Several Issues Related to the Drafting of the Legislative Law of the People's Republic of China (Drafted by Experts)', Paper presented to the Conference on Law-making in the People's Republic of China, 26–28 October 1998 at Leiden Univers-ity, Netherlands

Li, Buyun and Wang, Yongqin (eds) (1998), *Zhongguo lifa de jiben lilun he zhidu* (Basic Theory and System on China's Legislation), Beijing: China Legal System Publisher

Li, Shishi (1998), 'The State Council and Law-making', paper presented at the Conference on Law-making in the People's Republic of China, 26–28 October 1998 at Leiden University, The Netherlands

Niessen, Nicole (1999), *Municipal Government in Indonesia: Policy, Law, and Practice of Decentralization and Urban Spatial Planning*, Leiden: Researchschool CNWS

O'Brien, Kevin J. (1994), 'Chinese People's Congresses and Legislative Embeddedness: Understanding Early Legislative Development', *Comparative Political Studies*, Vol. 27, No. 1, pp. 80–109

Otto, J.M. and Li, Yuwen (1998), 'An Overview of Law-making in China', Occasional Paper C98/4, Leiden: Van Vollenhoven Institute for Law and Administration in Non-Western Countries

Phan, Binh G. (1996) 'How Autonomous Are the National Autonomous Areas of the PRC? An Analysis of Documents and Cases', *Issues and Studies*, Vol. 32, No. 7 (July), pp. 83–108

Qiu, Lufeng (1997), 'Guanyu tequ lifaquan ruoqan wenti de tantao' (Discussion of Several Issues on Legislative Power of Special Economic Zones), *Fashang Yanjiu* (Journal of Commercial Law), No. 6, pp. 36–41

Rondinelli, D.A., Nellis, J.R. and Cheema, G.S. (1984), *Decentralization in Developing Countries. A Review of Recent Experience*, Washington: The World Bank

Tang, Dehua (1998), 'The Transformation from Focusing on Legal Systems to Emphasizing on Administration by Law', *China Law*, 15 September, No. 3, pp. 57–60

Tanner, Murray Scot (1996), 'How a Bill Becomes a Law in China: Stages and Processes in Law-making', in Stanley Lubman (ed.), *China's Legal Reforms*, Oxford: Oxford University Press

Zhou, Wei (1996), 'Shenghuishi ji jiaodashi difang lifa de lishi, xianzhuang yu qianzhan' (History, Current Situation and Future Perspective of Law-making at Capitals of Provinces and Large Cities), *Xiandai Faxue* (Modern Legal Science), No. 3, pp. 83–86

2

Administrative Law-Making in the People's Republic of China

Jean-Pierre Cabestan

Although China has a rich bureaucratic tradition, administrative law constitutes one of the most recent and underdeveloped aspects of the legal system of the People's Republic of China (PRC). This is not to say that law-making had no influence whatsoever on the organization and the functioning of the administration before the promulgation of the much publicized Administrative Litigation Law (ALL, *xingzheng susong fa*) in 1989. We will see that, on the contrary, as soon as legal reforms were introduced in the early stage of the Deng Xiaoping era, the bureaucracy had to gradually readjust the way it was used to operating externally and even internally. However, it was only in the late 1980s that the concept of administrative law received a clearer definition, its scope was clarified and, more importantly, the first administrative norms were drafted.[1]

Many factors explain why the drafting of administrative laws has been so slow. The Maoist legacy, the priority given after 1979 to the construction of a legal framework aimed primarily at attracting foreign investments, the overwhelming role of the Chinese Communist Party (CCP) in the administration and the political sensitivity of any reform directly touching upon the heart of the system have postponed, at least for a decade, attempts to draft any specific administrative law.

These are some of the reasons why administrative law-making is and will probably remain quite different from law-making on civil or economic matters. It is contended that political factors and CCP

[1] This contribution is scheduled to be included in a conference-volume to be published by Kluwer and the Van Vollenhoven Institute of Leiden University.

intervention in administrative law-making are stronger, that while the Supreme People's Court may play some supplementary role, the National People's Congress (NPC) seems to have less say than on other law projects, local input or initiatives are weaker, foreign influence instilled by law experts is uneven and direct public participation quasi-non-existent.

Yet, administrative law-making is certainly not less complex and less decentralized, nor less disorganized in practice than law-making in other areas. The lingering debate about political reform at the top of the CCP hierarchy, constant conflicts of competence or interests among the various central and local government agencies involved and growing pressures both from the Chinese society and part of the world community have influenced, sometimes in opposite ways, the process of administrative law-making.

In order to better understand the specificity of administrative law-making, a definition of the uncertain and changing scope of administrative law will be given; then the respective role of the main Party and state organizations in administrative law-making will be discussed; and finally, one case of administrative law-making will be briefly presented, viz. the Provisional Regulations on State Civil Servants of 1993.

I The uncertain and changing scope of administrative law

In China, as in most countries, administrative law is defined as the set of legal norms and procedures which organizes the ways the administration and its working staff operate both within the boundaries of the bureaucracy and in their relations with society and the political authorities. Nevertheless, this definition does not fully apply to the PRC for four reasons:

1) There is no clear line separating the administration from the political power, the government from the CCP. For instance, many important decisions are jointly issued by the CCP Central Committee and the State Council, PRC's central government. And numerous regulations and circulares concerning state-leading cadres or functionaries are drafted both by the CCP Organization Department and the Ministry of Personnel.[2] Are these norms political or administrative ones?

[2]See for instance the 'Rules on the Obligation for Leading Cadres to Report their Major Personal Properties' (*guanyu lingdao ganbu baogao geren zhongyao shixiang de guiding*), jointly published in March 1997 by the CCP Central Committee General Office and the State Council General Office, *Renmin ribao* (*People's Daily*), 25 March 1997, p. 1.

2) Administrative law is an area of Chinese law which has been defined *ex post facto* or retroactively. Though between 1950 and 1956, Soviet-type administrative law was introduced in the PRC (870 regulations concerning the organization and the management of administrative institutions were then promulgated), as soon as the late 1950s, this discipline gradually disappeared before being totally abrogated during the Cultural Revolution in order to grant the administration – and actually the Party – boundless powers. After 1979, administrative law was not immediately 'rehabilitated'. Though the 1982 Civil Procedure Law (Interim) in its Article 3 gave for the first time some legal basis for administrative litigation cases (*xingzheng anjian*), no working law nor specific procedures (except the ones applying to civil cases) allowed private citizens to sue government agencies or their officials. And it was 1983 before the first textbook of administrative law was published.[3] Actually, in those years, administrative law overlapped a great deal both with constitutional law and criminal law:

a) Constitutional law: the main administrative law was 'organic law' (*zuzhifa*) concerning the organization of central (State Council, NPC) and local state powers (people's congresses and governments), the judiciary (people's courts and procuratorates) and mass representative bodies (villagers' and residents' committees). However, before the late 1980s, these texts were not yet clearly qualified as administrative laws.

b) Criminal law: only breaches of law legally defined as 'crimes' (*zui*) were dealt with by the courts according to the 1979 Criminal Law and Criminal Procedure Law. Numerous offenses were – and are still today – dealt with directly by the Public Security and the 're-education through labor' Committees according to published or non-published (*neibu*) administrative regulations. The much criticized 'Sheltering for examination' (*shourong shencha*) and re-education through labor (*laojiao*) are probably the best-known examples of 'administrative sanctions' (*xingzheng chufa*) that the public security could – and still to a large extent can – take without the approval of the procuratorate.[4]

[3] Liang 1996, p. 708.
[4] Wong 1997.

Actually, the true emergence of administrative law was directly linked to the first reform plan of the political structure (*zhengzhi tizhi gaige*). Discussed by scholars and CCP leadership advisers in the years 1986–1987 and presented by Zhao Ziyang, the then General Secretary of the Party to the 13th CCP Congress in October 1987, this plan included two key reforms: (1) the transformation of state cadres (*guojia ganbu*) into public servants (*guojia gongwuyuan*) and (2) the establishment of administrative chambers (or tribunals, *xingzheng shenpanting*) in every people's court, in charge of settling legal disputes involving the administration. Although Tiananmen put aside until 1993 the approval of the (provisional) regulations on state public servants (*guojia gongwuyuan zanxing tiaoli*), it could not slow down the introduction of the ALL. Passed in April 1989, the ALL began to be implemented, as initially decided, in October 1990.[5] And after 1992, the drafting of a more comprehensive set of administrative laws and regulations was initiated. These law-making activities included the State Compensation Law (*guojia peichangfa*) in 1994; the Law on People's Police (*renmin jingcha fa*) in 1995; the Law on Administrative Punishments (*xingzheng chufa fa*) in 1996; and the Law on Administrative Supervision (*xingzheng jianchafa*) in 1997.

In other words, it was only in late 1987 that administrative law was recognized by the PRC's highest authorities as an important area of law. Then every earlier law and regulation concerning the administration was included in this new discipline and a clearer line began to emerge between administrative law on the one hand and constitutional and criminal law on the other.

3) However this redefinition of administrative law raises a third question: Does administrative law include administrative regulations? Most Chinese scholars give a positive answer to this question. In the early 1990s, administrative laws and regulations (*xingzheng fagui*) were still considered one and the same.[6] And as we have already seen, new administrative norms do not necessarily have the status of a law: some major texts in this area are decrees (*tiaoli*) or orders (*banfa*) passed by the State Council. But the problem is that the codification of administrative law is a very recent process which remains far from completion. Plenty

[5] Pei 1997, pp. 832–862.

[6] *Zhongguo sifa da cidian* 1991, p. 809.

of remaining regulations are no longer in accordance with the administrative legislation promulgated in the last decade. Are these regulations part of the new administrative law the PRC authorities are building? Probably not.

4) This last point actually raises a final problem. As, in China, the role of the administration in the economy and the society is rapidly changing, the scope of administrative law must be constantly redefined. Today, its scope is closer to the scope of administrative law in Western countries. However, it still includes a larger area. Indeed, in spite of recent streamlining, PRC's government organs are today involved not only in public security, re-education through labor, diplomacy, defense, administrative supervision, state auditing, fiscal and monetary affairs, customs and judicial administration but also in banking, public transportation and communications, public construction and environmental protection, education, science and technology, management of natural resources, culture and information, not to mention the grain trade and industry. And though a number of ministries and bureaux have been turned into state companies or independent institutions, it is not always clear whether these new entities are ruled by civil and economic law or by administrative law.[7]

Thus, in spite of the huge administrative law-making work which has been completed in less than ten years, the scope of administrative law remains to some extent uncertain and changing.

II Main official agencies involved in administrative law-making

As seen above, administrative law still covers a wide area of activities and administrative law-making therefore involves numerous agencies. The formal process of administrative law-making is not particularly different from the one followed by other laws. As in other areas, we first have to distinguish the central and the local levels of government. However, the role played by various 'informal' actors (CCP, law scholars), for the reasons indicated above, is quite peculiar.

[7]This ambiguity may also persist in some European countries, in particular those, like France, which still have an important share of their economy controlled by the government.

1. *Central administrative law-making*

Here a clear distinction must be made between three sets of norms: laws, decrees and other regulations.

a) Administrative laws

The first set of administrative norms remains quite limited: it is made up of a dozen key general laws (the most important have been mentioned above) which have been passed after having gone through a long and arduous procedure. It remains difficult to identify a standard procedure since the drafting work, depending on the matter, can be assigned either to government agencies, the NPC, CCP Central Committee departments or a joint working group of these three institutions. A very powerful body should be mentioned beforehand: the CCP Central Committee Political and Legal Commission (*zhengfa weiyuanhui*) (PLC). As we will see, the CCP organizations take part in the drafting of administrative laws in various ways and at various stages of the process. However, now chaired by Luo Gan, a key member of Li Peng's faction, this commission plays a crucial coordinative role, e.g. in initiating and approving major legal reforms and laws. Administrative law is of course no exception. On this commission are, ex officio, the President of the Supreme Court (Xiao Yang), the Procurator General (Han Zhubin, who is also deputy secretary of the CCP Central Discipline Inspection Commission) and three ministers, those of Public Security (Jia Chunwang), State Security (Xu Yongyue) and Justice (Gao Changli). Of course, since it has only a small staff, the PLC relies on the preparatory work conducted by the various drafting groups. But the PLC plays a crucial role in many ways: for instance, it approves the namelists of these drafting group members and settles or arbitrates the possible conflicts or differences of views among agencies involved in the drafting or concerned by the promulgation of a new law or regulation.

- If the area of a new administrative law draft is specialized enough to be drafted by a ministry, the procedure will be, at least formally, clear: once the draft elaborated by this ministry is ready, it is passed on to the State Council's Bureau of Legislative Affairs (BLA) which checks whether the text is in accordance with existing laws and regulations and whether its promulgation requires some adaptation of the existing set of laws and regulations. Then the draft is approved by the State Council and transmitted to the NPC for promulgation. The Law on Education, which was mainly drafted by the then State Commission on Education, is a good example of this procedure.

The drafting of the Law on Administrative Supervision followed a similar pattern. However, instead of one formal agency, two closely related organizations were involved in the drafting work: the Central Discipline Inspection Commission (CDIC) of the Party and the Ministry of the Supervision of the State Council. But one may question how distinct these two institutions are in view of a merger of their working organs in 1992. An illustration of these close links is the fact that the Minister of Supervision, He Yong, is Deputy Secretary (and only number 4) of the CDIC. Any administrative regulation related to an issue as sensitive as the drive against corruption has to be directly drafted by the CCP top organizations.

However, the NPC specialized bodies are usually involved much earlier in the drafting work. Here the division of labor among two committees has to be emphasized: the Legislative Affairs Commission (LAC) of the NPC Standing Committee (*changwuwei fazhi gongzuo weiyuanhui*) and the Law Committee of the NPC. The former is a true working body including a large number of full-time law specialists and has in general a much greater influence on the drafting process than the latter, a prestigious group of well-known but older officials and law experts who meet much less often and usually take part only in the last stage of the drafting work, e.g. before the law is submitted for approval to the NPC (which meets once a year, in March-April) or, more often, the plenary session of the NPC Standing Committee (which meets every two months or six times a year). However, if this first type of procedure is followed, the government agency which drafts the law maintains a key influence upon the global content of the text.

- If the topic of a proposed administrative law draft partially overlaps the responsibilities of several agencies or cannot be drafted by a single organ, the highest authorities of the PRC (the CCP Politburo, the General Secretariat, the State Council or the PLC) can either set up an *ad hoc* drafting committee made up of representatives of the major 'departments concerned' (*youguan bumen*) or ask a department in charge of legal affairs to take responsibility for the drafting work. The former option is used more rarely, and is in general reserved for important laws such as the establishment of Hong Kong Special Administrative Zone's Basic Law. In this instance, the working committee (which is still in operation today) was set up under the umbrella of the NPC's Standing Committee. The latter option is more frequently used but also often leads to the creation of a cross-agency drafting committee. That was the case with the drafting of the ALL, which was assigned to a group of legal scholars under the auspices of the NPC Judiciary Committee.[8] However, as a sign of the NPC's growing intervention in the drafting process, a third option is increasingly being preferred: the establishment of a joint drafting group under the co-sponsorship of the State Council's BLA and the NPC's LAC.

b) Decrees (*tiaoli*)

The second set of administrative norms is made up of a larger number of texts. These decrees (or statutes) can have a general and sometimes critical impact on the functioning of the bureaucracy (e.g. the Provisional Regulations on Civil Servants). However, only endorsed by the State Council (and most often by its Standing Committee during its weekly session) and formally signed by the Premier, these *tiaoli* are often provisional regulations tested for a number of years before being turned into formal laws. A good illustration of this is again the Law on Administrative Supervision promulgated in May 1997. This text was a (substantially) revised version of the December 1990 Regulations on Administrative Supervision (*tiaoli*).[9] This is to say that *tiaoli* are a convenient type of legal norm which have been used extensively by the Chinese government, particularly during reform and transitional periods. *Tiaoli*, therefore, are well adapted to the needs of PRC's burgeoning administrative law.

Most decrees originated from a specialized government agency. However, the majority of *tiaoli* related to administrative matters (such as the one we have just mentioned or the Regulations on State Civil Servants) is jointly drafted by CCP and State Council departments. When the decree concerns cadres and personnel affairs, the Central Committee's Department of Organization and the Ministry of Personnel set up a joint working group. Other key organs such as the General Offices (*bangongting*) of both the Central Committee and the State Council are also usually involved.

c) Other regulations

The third set of administrative norms consists of more technical regulations which sometimes must be approved by the Standing Committee of the State Council but more often are promulgated by a specific ministry with the approval of, or after having been reported (*bei'an*) to, the government's Bureau of Legislative Affairs for registration.

[8] Potter 1994, pp. 274–276.

[9] *Renmin ribao*, 10 May 1997, p. 4; cf. Also, Wu 1998. The Regulations were published in a bilingual edition by the Ministry of Supervision in 1991 (34 pp.).

For instance, while the 'Order (*banfa*) on the use of the national emblem in activities relating to foreign affairs' was promulgated (*fabu*) in September 1993 by the Ministry of Foreign Affairs with the approval (*bizhun*) of the State Council, the 'Order (*banfa*) of the judicial organs on compensation in administrative and criminal cases' was simply published by the Ministry of Justice in September 1995. Actually the first type of norms belongs to the administrative regulations (*xingzheng fagui*) category while the second type refers to statutes published by the ministries, commissions and bureaux of the State Council (*Guowuyuan ge bu, wei, ju guizhang*). Though decrees and decisions (*jueding*) clearly belong to the former and statutes to the latter. In actual fact, orders, circulars (*tongzhi*), rules (*guiding*) or detailed application of rules (*shishi xize*) can apply to both categories of regulations.[10]

However, for any of these central administrative norms, depending on the issue and its sensitiveness, CCP departments and in particular the PLC can be involved in the drafting work. That is the case in particular for regulations related to personnel (organization), culture, education and media (propaganda) or public security when it involves the Central Committee for Comprehensive Management of Social Security, a body whose membership partially overlaps with the PLC).

d) Local level input

It is particularly difficult to assess the influence of local governments upon the drafting of administrative laws and regulations. On the whole, local bureaucracies seem to remain an obstacle to the introduction of laws which would limit their powers. But their attitude largely varies depending on the issue, and from one region to another.

The best example of the effect of a negative attitude was the drafting work of the Administrative Litigation Law. In 1986, an NPC-sponsored group of legal experts began drafting this law. The first draft was completed in 1987. Then a poll was organized among 80 municipal, county and district departments which reflected a very negative response from the interviewees; the overall majority of the officials polled (95%) considered the ALL 'premature' and asked the promulgation of the law to be delayed.[11] Was their request heard? Only temporarily. As mentioned earlier, in October 1987 the CCP 13th Congress approved the introduction of administrative laws and

---

[10]Cf. For example, *Zhongguo falü nianjian 1993* 1994, pp. 363–752. *Fazhi ribao* (*Legal System Daily*), 19 October 1995, p. 3.

[11]*Liaowang* (Perspectives), 29 October 1990, p. 14.

the establishment of administrative tribunals. Passed in April 1989, the ALL came into effect in October 1990.

Actually, this compromise allowed the central authorities to test this reform for a few more years and, in so doing, step by step win over the local bureaucrats. This gradualist approach which Deng Xiaoping favored so many times – *mo shitou guo he* (cross the river in touching the stones) – was eased by the passing in 1986 and the implementation in January 1987 of the Decree on Penalties Imposed in the Course of Maintaining Public Order (*zhi'an guanli chufa tiaoli*). For the first time, this decree allowed private citizens to question public security decisions (e.g. penalties) not only before the public security organs of the upper level but also before the court and in particular the administrative tribunals already in place (only around 1,400 in 1988). Though, at that time, in most cases, the courts turned down the request of the plaintiff and confirmed the decision of the Public Security, this decree was a genuine testing ground for the ALL.[12]

In October 1988 the draft version of the ALL was submitted to the NPC Standing Committee, and was at the same time circulated to local government agencies and courts. One hundred and thirty of them submitted commentaries.[13] Though it remains hard to evaluate the impact of these commentaries, the ALL was implemented on an experimental basis in several provinces. This testing period did not alter the law but allowed the judiciary and the government to supplement the ALL with useful regulations and interpretations (see below).

e) The role of the judiciary

In administrative law-making as in law-making in other areas, the judiciary and in particular the Supreme Court, which provides a guide to every court in the implementation of a new law, play an increasing role. For example, in May 1991, just a few months after the ALL came into effect, the Judicial Committee of the Supreme Court made public a long explanation of every major point (115) of this law. Adopted on a trial basis, this 'opinion' (*yijian*) helped to ease the work of the newly set-up administrative tribunals. It also lead to an increase in the number of administrative cases.[14]

[12] *Falü yu shenghuo* (Law and Life), No. 82, October 1990, p. 20.
[13] *Xinhua yuebao* (New China Monthly Magazine), No. 534 (April 1989), p. 36.
[14] Ma 1994, pp. 362–381.

f) The contribution of academics

The contribution of academics remains very uneven. Academics and law experts tend to be associated with the drafting of major administrative laws or regulations such as the ALL or the State Civil Servant Regulations. But as we will see below, such a participation is subject to variations. Here political factors play a critical role: in periods of opening up and reform, more scholars are able to participate in administrative law-making while in times of repression their influence is generally marginal.

2. Local administrative law-making

Today, the official hierarchy of legal administrative norms is as clear as in most countries: rules (*guizhang*) approved by local governments are subordinate to local regulations (*fagui*) passed by the People's Congress at the same level and these regulations are themselves subordinate to State Council regulations which must be in accordance with the laws promulgated by the NPC or its Standing Committee. Similarly, the scope of central legislative powers is well established: it includes 'the basic political, economic and cultural systems, the fundamental rights and duties of the citizens, the overall system of governmental structures, the judicial system, national defense and foreign policy'.[15] Any other matter can be subject to local regulations. Nevertheless, the *de facto* legislative powers that local authorities enjoy are not without problems of coordination and consistency.

There is an old tradition in China, much older than the PRC, pertaining to adapting national decisions and laws to local realities. In the realm of administrative law, this is particularly obvious. For instance, in the years after the State Civil Servants Regulations were promulgated, most provinces drafted local recruitment and examination rules.[16]

The major difficulty here is the possible distance such local legislative powers may create between the original administrative law and the actual implementation. The case of the Law (for trial implementation) on Villagers' Committees (1987) is worth mentioning as an example. It shows how a lack of sufficient guidelines from the Ministry of Civil Affairs and the fact that the law's implementation was

[15] Jiang, Xiao and Guo 1994, p. 33.

[16] See for example, 'Shaanxi Province Order on the Recruitment of State Civil Servants' (*Shaanxi sheng guojia gongwuyuan luyong banfa*), adopted on 7 June 1997 by the Standing Committee meeting of the Provincial Government, *Shaanxi ribao* (*Shaanxi Daily*), 7 July 1997, p. 7.

stalled, allowed the emergence of numerous types of election systems and organizational structures, even within the same province.[17] To limit such deviations, the central authorities have spent much time summoning local officials to Beijing where they have been regularly briefed about the real meaning of the new laws and the ways to harmonize their local regulations with these (superseding) norms. Here two agencies appear to play a crucial coordinative role: the NPC Standing Committee's LAC and the State Council's BLA. For instance, in June 1996, these two agencies organized a conference to 'sum up and exchange rudimentary experiences in enforcing the Law on Administrative Punishments' and to prepare its implementation, in October of the same year. Officials of every provincial government's LACs and BLAs attended the meeting where they were told that 'they still had to do tremendous work in revising local laws and statutes ... which were inconsistent with the stipulations in the Law on Administrative Punishments'.[18] It remains to be seen if such instructions are fully carried out by these officials once they return to their region. In some areas, the work of stabilization of the local regulations or *li, gai, fei* (law-making, reforming and abolition) can take many years.[19]

One obstacle to the harmonization between central and local administrative norms is the large 'proto-legislative' powers enjoyed by the people's congresses and, actually, governments of the provincial level (and of a few major cities of sub-provincial level). The administrative regulations they pass only have to be reported to the NPC and the State Council for registration (*bei'an*) and no real check on the legality of these regulations is carried out on a regular basis.

But at a lower level, within the boundaries of a single province, conflicting administrative regulations often coexist. In order to reduce such a risk, most provincial authorities have centralized the drafting work of local rules (*guizhang*) in the hands of legal departments (*fazhi bumen*).[20] But no unified system of local administrative law- and regulation-making has yet been introduced. Thus, coordination and harmonization seem to be harder to achieve at the local level, both provincial and **sub**-provincial levels, than at the national level.

---

[17] *Zhongguo nongcun cunmin weiyuanhui huiyi zhidu* (The Report on the Villagers' Representative Assemblies in the System of Village Committees in China), 1994.

[18] Xinhua, 22 June 1996.

[19] Cf. note 14, p. 34.

[20] *Ibid.*

III The Case of State Civil Servant Provisional Regulations: A highly politicized drafting process

One key area of administrative law has been the establishment of a modern civil service system, but one 'with Chinese characteristics'. For the moment, this reform has not given birth to a comprehensive set of laws but to several, still often experimental, regulations. The State Civil Servant Provisional Regulations are the most important of them. The history of the drafting of these regulations underlines the close connection between administrative law-making and politics. It also shows to what extent reform-minded scholars can influence the drafting work.[21]

As we have seen, the transformation of the Soviet-inspired state cadre system into a public servant system was decided in 1987 by the 13th Party Congress. However, the origins of this reform go back to August 1980 when Deng Xiaoping put the reform of the cadre system on the Party's agenda. A year later, the Chinese Academy of Social Sciences (CASS) was asked by Premier Zhao Ziyang to study this reform. Then the CASS convened a series of conferences which favored a dialog between scholars and officials on this sensitive matter.

In 1984, the reform of the cadre system was taken into the hands of the Party, just after CCP General Secretary Hu Yaobang and Premier Zhao Ziyang, with the support of Deng Xiaoping, launched the industrial reform process. But the dialog with the scholars went on. In November of that year, the CCP Central Committee's Department of Organization and the then Ministry of Labor and Personnel set up a drafting working group made up of senior officials of both agencies and academics. This group was chaired by Cao Zhi, one of the deputy directors of the Organization Department and deputy secretary general of the NPC Standing Committee. The choice of this close associate of Qiao Shi, then head of the Organization Department, is interesting: though the NPC did not formally participate in the drafting of these regulations, Cao Zhi could act as a bridge between both institutions.

Between November 1984 and December 1986, this working group not only studied various foreign service systems but also successively prepared ten drafts of regulations. The first draft was a set of 'Regulations Concerning Workers in the State Organs' (*guojia jiguan gongzuo renyuan tiaoli*) while the drafts produced after January 1986 referred only to the personnel of the administrative state organs (*guo-*

[21]This section is inspired by the following publications: Burns and Cabestan 1990–91; Cabestan 1992; and *China News Analysis*, No. 1507, 1 April 1994, p. 6.

jia xingzheng jiguan): the cadres of the organs of state power (the people's congresses), the judicial bodies and the leading cadres of various levels of governments were then excluded from the scope of the draft. This was a clear move toward a narrower and more standard (or Western-type) definition of the civil service.

Nevertheless, a crucial conceptual change occurred in April 1986 when Deng Xiaoping pushed the debate on the reform of political structures. Then the concept of 'state administrative personnel' was replaced with 'civil servants' and the reform work was taken over by the highest authorities of the PRC. In July 1986, a Central Committee's Reform of the Political Structures Research Group (*zhongyang zhengzhi tizhi gaige yantao xiaozu*) was established, composed of Zhao Ziyang, Politburo members Hu Qili and Tian Jiyun, Peng Chong and Bo Yibo. In December 1986, this powerful body formed a Leading Group on the reform of the cadre and personnel system still headed by Cao Zhi. Though the Organization Department and the Ministry of Labor and Personnel remained closely associated with the drafting work, the input of academics became stronger. In March 1987, the thirteenth draft was approved 'in principle' by the Small Group. This draft constituted the basis of the section of Zhao Ziyang's Work Report to the 13th CCP Congress related to the civil service.

The major point of this reform was then to create two categories of civil servants: on the one hand, the 'political civil servants' (*zhengwulei gongwuyuan*) recommended by the CCP and formally elected by the people's congresses and on the other hand, the 'professional civil servants' (*yewulei gongwuyuan*) entirely recruited through open examination. But Zhao's reform plan even went further: its ambition was to separate the activities of the CCP and the government (*dangzheng fenkai*). This implied that gradually the 'political civil servants' (e.g. the leading members of each level of governments) would have been really, and not only formally, appointed by the people's congresses, themselves elected in a more pluralistic way.

However, this reform plan was rapidly perceived by the conservatives of the Party as jeopardizing the CCP's leading role and the PRC's political stability. After the 13th Congress, Zhao Ziyang transferred the responsibility for drafting the regulations from the Organization Department to the newly created Ministry of Personnel. However, this did not last long. In January 1988, the more centrist number three in the Politburo's Standing Committee, Qiao Shi set up a Central Group in charge of Personnel Affairs consisting of officials from both agencies, including the conservative head of the Organization Department, Song Ping. Scholars were then clearly relegated to a secondary role. This is the reason why the following drafts fell short of the political reform planned by Zhao. For instance, approved by the Ministry of Personnel in June 1988, the fifteenth draft 'Provisional Regulations Concerning State Civil Servants' (*guojia gongwuyuan zanxing tiaoli*) partially questioned the principle of recruitment through open examination for senior executive posts.[22] This category of 'professional civil servants' (no regulations concerning the 'political civil servants' were drafted at the time) was to be recruited through 'special examination' in which recommendation by recruiting bodies (e.g. CCP organization departments) or by their unit of origin would have played a crucial role.

In any case, this fifteenth draft constituted an important stage in the reform process since, for the first time, the new regulations were put on trial in several central and local government agencies. Based on these experiments, a sixteenth draft, which contained no major change compared to the preceding text, was framed in April 1989.

Tiananmen not only slowed down for another four years the adoption and the promulgation of the Civil Servants Regulations but also contributed to reverse the reformist dimension of these regulations. After June 1989, the sixteenth draft was tested in just six central departments and two local governments. Though in 1990, the deputy Minister of Personnel Cheng Lianchang announced the promulgation of these regulations before the end of the year, under the pressure of the Organization Department and the Party leadership, this was postponed until after the 14th CCP Congress (1992). Zhao's basic ideas could not remain the political framework of the civil service that Jiang Zemin and Li Peng wanted to establish. A change of approach was needed. The CCP leadership (Qiao Shi, but also Song Ping, who was promoted in June 1989 to the Standing Committee of the Politburo) and Lü Feng, the new Organization Department director, became the major leaders supervising the drafting: they harshly criticized any attempt to separate the Party and the government, dropped the distinction between political and professional civil servants and, thus, extended the reform to all kinds of government cadres. The August 1993 Regulations are the result of this new swing.

So the Regulations which came into effect on October 1, 1993 concern all public servants under the same fifteen-grade scale from the Prime Minister (grade 1) down to the ordinary clerk (grades ten to fifteen). Only two positions, included in the March 1992 draft, are

[22] Burns and Cabestan 1990–91, pp. 10–23.

no longer in the final text: the PRC President and Vice-President. Functionaries now come under two categories: officials in leadership positions (*lingdao zhiwu*: grades one to thirteen) and officials in non-leadership positions (*feilingdao zhiwu*: grades nine to fifteen). Moreover, recruitment through examination or assessment is limited to non-leading positions at or below the level of senior section staff (*zhuren keyuan*).

The drafting of the State Civil Servant Regulations offers a clear example of the gradual marginalization – under the constraints of both the sensivity of this reform and the time-frame for its introduction – of the academics and the reform-minded experts in the law-making process.

Conclusions

Of course, without additional research, the conclusion that we have just drawn cannot be applied to the law-making process of all administrative laws and regulations. However, it appears sensible to conclude that administrative law-making is more sensitive to political and bureaucratic factors than law-making in other areas. In the case of the Civil Servant Regulations, the two main obstacles to the achievement of any dramatic change have been: (1) The counter reform political environment triggered by Tiananmen and (2) the very resistance of the CCP Organization Department which has always been reluctant to relinquish or even to transfer part of its power to the Ministry of Personnel. But this example also underlines the fact that any law-making work which involves a change in the relationship between the administration and society or even a redistribution of power inside the bureaucracy is highly sensitive and may be more easily slowed down and sometimes thwarted by political factors.

Not mentioned in this chapter is the possible role of the public. The direct participation of the public is quasi-absent. When drafting the ALL, the NPC asked commentaries from private citizens: it received a total of only 300 replies.[23] This is not to say that the Chinese society cannot influence administrative law-making. The public's pressure to enjoy some judicial relief from official abuse of power certainly contributed to the drafting and the relatively rapid promulgation of the ALL. Similarly, society's growing resentment of official corruption has accelerated the elaboration of numerous laws and regulations aimed at cleaning up the administration (*lianzheng*). But this participation remains marginal and mostly indirect.

[23] *Xinhua Yuebao*, No. 534 (April 1989), p. 36.

Foreign inputs in administrative law-making are also rather difficult to trace. The Chinese law experts and Party officials have studied the administrative systems of many countries. They have appraised the advantages and drawbacks of each system and more importantly the adaptability of foreign administrative law experience to the Chinese political and economic environment. For instance, though the 1993 Civil Servant Regulations were partially inspired by the Singaporean civil service legislation, the two systems remain different in many respects. The ALL was also based on the administrative procedures developed by various Western countries but the scope of the Chinese law is much narrower: it only gives the court the power to revoke 'concrete administrative actions' (*juti xingzheng xingwei*). It does not allow the plaintiff, as in France and most Western countries, to question the legality of an administrative regulation.[24]

Finally there are law-making institutions more reform-minded than others in the realm of administrative law-making. One may be tempted to qualify the NPC and its LAC or the State Council's BLA as playing a more reformist role in comparison to the Party organizations which would act as obstacles to change. However, such a line is hard to draw, partly because, as in other areas of law-making, drafting work is often conducted by cross-agency working groups. In the final analysis, administrative law-making accelerates when the supreme leadership of the CCP becomes politically more reform-oriented and slows down when tensions appear between the state and the society or when conservative forces become stronger.

References

Burns, John and Cabestan, Jean-Pierre (eds) (1990-91), 'Provisional Chinese Civil Service Regulations', *Chinese Law and Government*, Vol. 23, No. 4 (Winter), pp. 3–9

Cabestan, Jean-Pierre (1992), 'Civil Service Reform in China: The Draft "Provisional Order Concerning Civil Servants"', *International Review of Administrative Sciences*, Vol. 58, pp. 423–426

Jiang Mingli, Xiao Zucai and Guo Wanbo (1994), 'Shilun difang xingzheng lifa' (About Local Administrative Law-Making), *Guizhou shehui kexue* (Guizhou Social Sciences), No. 3, p. 33

[24] Potter 1994, pp. 282–287.

Liang Jinming (1996), 'Nouveau développement du droit administratif en Chine' (The New Development of Administrative Law in China), *Les Cahiers du Droit*, Vol. 37, No. 3 (September), p. 708

Ma Shaobin (ed.) (1994), *Xingzheng susong zhishi yu anli* (Explanation and Cases of Administrative Litigation), Beijing: Falü chubanshe, pp. 362–381

Pei Minxin (1997), 'Citizens v. Mandarins: Administrative Litigation in China', *The China Quarterly*, No. 152 (December), pp. 832–862

Potter, Pitman (1994), 'The Administrative Litigation Law of the PRC: Judicial Review and Bureaucratic Reform', in Pitman Potter (ed.),*Domestic Law Reforms in Post-Mao China*, Armonk, N.Y.: M.E. Sharpe, pp. 274–276

Shaanxi sheng guojia gongwuyuan luyong banfa, (Shaanxi Province Order on the Recruitment of State Civil Servants), adopted on 7 June 1997 by the Standing Committee Meeting of the Provincial Government, *Shaanxi ribao* (*Shaanxi Daily*), 7 July 1997, p. 7

Wong, Kam C. (1997), *Sheltering for Examination (Shoushen) in the People's Republic of China: Law, Policy, and Practices*, Occasional Papers/Reprints Series in Contemporary Asian Studies, No. 3, (140), School of Law, University of Maryland, 53 pp.

Wu Xiuling (1998), 'Zhonggong "xingzheng jiancha fa" pingxi' (Analysis of Communist China's Law on Administrative Supervision), *Zhongguo dalu yanjiu* (Studies on Chinese Mainland), Vol. 41, No. 4 (April), pp. 39-48

Zhongguo falü nianjian 1993 (1993 Legal Yearbook of China) (1994), Beijing: Zhongguo falü nianjianshe

Zhongguo nongcun cunmin weiyuanhui huiyi zhidu (The Report on the Villagers' Representative Assemblies in the System of Village Committees in China) 1994, Beijing: Zhongguo shehui chubanshe

Zhongguo sifa da cidian (Dictionary of China's Judicial Activities) (1991), Changchun: Jilin renmin chubanshe

3

To Have One's Cake and Eat It? Human Rights in Chinese Culture

Geor Hintzen

Few problems between China and the West are both as sensitive and as persistent as human rights issues. In part, this is due to the ideological nature of these issues. Over the past fifty years, human rights have increasingly become a fundamental element in the secular and liberal democratic ideologies of Western nations. Formal adherence to human rights by all governments is slowly but surely becoming a minimal criterion for acceptance by the West. In China, by contrast, Western demands that human rights be observed are viewed as attempts to further Western 'bourgeois' interests. Western calls for adherence to human rights often lead to the opposite of what they seek to bring about. Stung by renewed 'attempts at interference' in its internal affairs, the Chinese authorities adopt a 'principled' (*yuanzexing de*) stance and reject these calls. Behind this public and highly predictable ritual, however, the sensitivity and persistence of human rights issues in China is also prolonged by deep-seated cultural differences and misunderstandings.

This chapter will attempt to offer an outline of the place that human rights hold within the culture of the PRC's politics and society. A basic assumption behind this approach is that the problems surrounding human rights issues in China are not merely political ones that may be solved by a change of heart in the Chinese elite, but constitute culturally - and socially - rooted issues, which require an insight into some of the values and practices that structure Chinese society itself. I do not believe that the severe differences in viewpoints on human rights may be overcome in this way. Nor do I think that Chinese culture makes the introduction of human rights impossible. The example of Taiwan is a case in point. I am convinced, however, that a better understanding of the way human rights are viewed in the PRC will improve the prospects for human rights in China. For example, by 'placing' human rights issues within the Chinese cultural context, it will become considerably easier to gauge the changes that take place in this field. I say this, because I believe that often changes in the Chinese political system or in Chinese society are misinterpreted from a Western cultural perspective. An approach is needed that recognizes the way Chinese act and think amongst themselves.

To this end, I will propose a cultural framework that is based on Clifford Geertz's view that,

> culture is best seen not as complexes of concrete behavior patterns – customs, usages, traditions, habit clusters – as has, by and large, been the case up to now, but as a set of control mechanisms – plans, recipes, rules, instructions (what computer engineers call 'programs') – for the governing of behavior.[1]

Culture, in this view, is not to be observed from the outside, but from the inside. It does not consist of specific opinions and values, but serves as a framework within which such opinions and values are placed. In other words, culture is not a factor that serves primarily to distinguish certain groups of people from others, but as an internal form of communication among the members of a group. It is acquired through informal socialization and – more formally – education. Culture in this sense is very elusive because often similar social events may be interpreted differently (but no less coherently) according to different cultural rules. In the past, it has even been denied that there is such a dimension of communication. Many other scholars, who admit that there is something like culture, hasten to add that it changes both easily and constantly, and thereby attempt to downplay its role. It is ventured here, that although it is far less structured and explicit than language, culture as a form of social communication may possess remarkably persistent and formative features.[2] As the issue of human rights in China over the past century reveals, in spite of the huge socio-economic changes that the country has undergone, some Chinese cultural premises have remained remarkably stable.

[1] Geertz 1973, p. 44.

[2] This is one of the main theses of my Ph.D. thesis, Hintzen 1998.

The main object of this chapter is to gain an overall insight into some of the main views and social conditions that are related to human rights issues in the PRC today. Through the cultural approach I will try to show that the official redefinition of human rights seeks to combine two mutually exclusive aims in the interests of the Chinese party-state. On the one hand, it allows it to partake of the Western discourse of modernity. On the other, it provides a justification for its authoritarian rule. Internally, the definition of human rights may be placed within the framework of the political culture of the establishment. In its redefined form, it serves to fit the authoritarian policies of the party-state. This leads to the overall question, which this contribution seeks to highlight: are human rights issues in the PRC a matter of being able 'to have one's cake and eat it'?

An outline of cultural control mechanisms

In simple terms, the idea behind the existence of control mechanisms is that all human beings undergo a positive process of socialization and education, during which they are 'programmed' to function within their society. Different societies have their own rules.[3] Knowledge of these rules increases understanding of the way in which a society is meant to operate. Of course, things may take an unexpected turn or go wrong, but these rules, or control mechanisms, precisely serve to 'place' such unexpected events and possibly to qualify them as 'right' or 'wrong'.[4] This makes for a 'healthy' society.

Control mechanisms, however, are not merely about right and wrong. It is important to distinguish between some of the main kinds of cultural control mechanisms. These include such notions as 'arena', 'normative and traditional default modes', and 'taboos'. Finally, control mechanisms may be 'inherently variable'. The meaning of each of these notions will be described.

The mental space within which different kinds of views on an issue are appraised is called an 'arena'.[5] This is the vaguely conceived mental space within which one may say a topic and its associated notions are to apply. Within the arena of human rights all the different views

[3]These rules lay down values, but also serve as control mechanisms to regulate and 'place' behavior.

[4]The fact that I believe that persons belonging to other groups may behave according to other criteria of right and wrong than mine, should not be interpreted as moral relativism. Although I still believe my values to be the best, this should not stop me from taking seriously and 'thinking through' the values of others.

[5]A good example of such a 'projection' is the modern state, with its imagined, but very real boundaries.

are placed in a general and often vague relation to each other. In any society, both in free and open ones and in closed and authoritarian ones, there is always a range of views about any given issue. In fact, individuals themselves may change their views. This is called the inherent variability of control mechanisms. In China, where public expressions of one's views are closely monitored, the extent of the inherent variability of such topics as human rights and democracy offers an insight into the permissible range of ideas.

Within the arena, the rules for right and wrong are called default modes and taboos. In a sense, the arena may be pictured as an extended mental space around its default mode, that is bordered by taboos. The default mode is the view about a topic that is socially presented as correct. Because it is usually the control mechanism one has been brought up with, it is the rule one falls back on when in doubt. I distinguish between traditional and normative default modes. The traditional default mode is the one that is informally transmitted and is used in society. In China the traditional default mode may still be said to be overwhelmingly Confucian, although different default modes are clearly present in the cities. The normative default mode is the 'politically correct' control mechanism. It is the Marxist-Leninist set of social rules. Although these two share a considerable number of features, they also stand at odds on a number of important issues. Moreover, because the normative default mode is far more explicit, its arena is more restricted and formal than that around the traditional default mode. Finally, taboos mark the point where control mechanisms cease to be socially acceptable.

Behind the notions of normative and traditional default modes the assumption is made that elites try to steer society in a certain direction. They do this amongst other things by putting forward normative default modes. In the process, it is in their interest to deny the existence or the continuity of a traditional default mode in society. Such a concession would only make their task less acceptable. Society, nevertheless, does have its own habitual way of conducting affairs. These are the traditional default modes, which may differ amongst regions and social groups, but which are never so different as to impede a degree of mutual understanding. Knowledge of the different default modes that characterize different groups within a culture, in fact, is instrumental in 'placing' persons in social contacts. Between the two kinds of default modes there is an interaction, in which the two are influenced by each other. Logically speaking, if a normative default mode is too different from the traditional ones, it will be accepted less easily than one that is more in tune.

Since the normative default mode is the most visible control mechanism, the development of the official view of human rights in the PRC will be discussed further. Then, some of the inherently variable views about human rights within the elite will be outlined. Finally, the interplay of normative and traditional default modes and some of the resulting taboos will be illustrated through an overview of the functions and nature of social groups in Chinese society.

The official view of human rights in the PRC

It has been a little noted fact that Jiang Zemin's political report at the 15th Party Congress was the first such document to refer to the term 'human rights' (*renquan*) in a positive way.[6] In fact, since the Tiananmen Incident, human rights have increasingly become a part of the official political discourse of the PRC. It is likely, however, that only since Deng Xiaoping's death has a more positive view towards human rights become possible.[7] Deng's views represented an earlier rejection of 'bourgeois' conceptions of rights that was typical of orthodox Marxist-Leninist ideology. By the early 1980s, this ideological stance had led to a general lack of familiarity with debates about human rights in the Chinese political elite. Although in the late 1970s and the 1980s, there were some early articles on human rights by establishment intellectuals these were usually written in the context of domestic issues, such as the campaign against the 'Gang of Four' and the discussions on the new Constitution.[8] Until the 1990s, no serious research was conducted on human rights.[9] External factors, however, served as an important catalyst for attention

[6]Jiang Zemin 1997, p. 3, where Jiang calls the Party to 'respect and guarantee (*baozhang*) human rights'. Since many rights are only protected (*baohu*) in the Constitution, one may wonder whether Jiang's remark constitute an 'upgrading' of the importance of human rights in the PRC.

[7]A glance at a number of references by top leaders to human rights reveals that Deng never said anything positive about the topic; see Jiang and Duan 1991, pp. 3–9.

[8]For a list of human rights articles between 1979 and 1992, see CASS Law Department 1992, pp. 448–468.

[9]A good indication of this is the complete absence of human rights in the list of favored research topics of the seventh Five-Year Plan (1986–1991); see *Beijing shelian tongxun* 1987(2), pp. 57–58. The only topic that may be associated with human rights is the item 'research of Marxism concerning the development of man', which is to be found not under law or political science, but under philosophy.

on human rights. China's will to play a larger role in international affairs, and especially within the United Nations, forced it to deal with human rights. It is probable that initially some fundamental assumptions behind UN documents on human rights presented Chinese officials and scholars with embarrassing problems.[10] Clearly, the PRC has been torn between its reticence about human rights ideas and its will to partake of the standards of international organizations. Although China has recently joined the two main UN covenants on human rights, it still has not ratified them.[11]

In recent years the PRC has sought for ways to reconcile these conflicting aims. Official support for research on human rights only came in the wake of the Tiananmen Incident. Typically, the international – that is, foreign – condemnation of the PRC sparked off a series of academic conferences on human rights,[12] which resulted in an official White Paper on human rights and an academic handbook.[13] Ideologically, however, the PRC did not budge one inch.[14] The White Paper redefined human rights to fit the pre-existing ideology and policies of the Marxist-Leninist party-state. The handbook provided an informative overview of the world's human rights legislation, but clearly mapped out China's principled position. Still, both proved to be important documents because they formally stipulated the official Chinese view on the matter, thereby making it impossible for establishment intellectuals to continue to debate freely.[15] What, then, is the officially sanctioned definition of human rights?

In general terms, depending on the different political views within the Chinese elite, several views are possible. There is even room for

[10] Among these assumptions the legitimate right of individuals to question the actions of their states and the individualism behind many rights may be cited. UN Secretary-General Kofi Annan's remarks that 'It is never the people who complain of human rights as a Western or Northern imposition. It is too often their leaders who do so' does not fit into the normative default mode of human rights that the Chinese authorities would want to propagate; quoted in Baehr 1998, p. 13.

[11] The PRC has signed some seven UN treaties on human rights. In 1998 it joined the two main UN treaties on human rights: the International Treaty on Civil and Political Rights and the International Treaty on Economic, Social, and Cultural Rights, but has not ratified them.

[12] These conferences led to publications, such as CASS Law Department 1992 and Huang, Chen, and Dong 1993.

[13] Press Bureau of the PRC State Council 1991 and Dong and Liu 1991.

[14] For a discussion of the White Paper, see Hintzen 1992.

[15] According to the dictates of democratic centralism, once a matter has been officially settled, it is forbidden to openly disagree with it. Of course, in internal publications, establishment intellectuals may offer different views.

a universalist view within the official theory of human rights. After all, as one veteran Chinese lawyer put it, human rights may be seen to constitute the very 'nature of man' (*renxing*).[16] Most officials and scholars, however, would reject such an interpretation.[17] In order to apply human rights, they could say, they have to be made concrete (*jutihua*). As is the case with all Chinese legislation, human rights must be fitted into the actual circumstances of society. Based on this materialist worldview, the most basic of all human rights are the rights to subsistence and development. After all, without these two basic conditions, there would not even be a society to exercise the rights in. The effect of human rights is therefore said to increase as society develops.[18] Human rights are thereby identified as a moral issue that is naturally derived from socio-economic development itself. In this sense, as long as the party-state rules in the interests of the people, it respects human rights. Human rights is primarily a moral, rather than a legal concept.

There is also an extremely important social dimension to the official view of human rights. This reflects a Chinese traditional default mode, that the ethical knowledge of social rules is what elevates man above the beasts.[19] Together these social rules form a social hierarchy into which every individual is fitted by virtue of a combination of birth and talents. In China, man has traditionally been man not because of his individuality, but because of his respect for and ability in social roles. Individuals are socialized to fit into a pre-ordained hierarchic network of social roles (the *sangang* or *wulun*), in which the correct role patterns that are internalized according to the specific social relations are of paramount importance.[20] Ideally, the greater one's abilities in acting out social roles, the higher one's status is

---

[16]Li 1992, pp. 3–15.

[17]See, for example, Liao Zuobin, 'Lun you Zhongguo tese de shehuizhuyi renquan' (On Human Rights with Chinese Characteristics) in Huang, Chen, and Dong 1993, pp. 31–46.

[18]This idea is repeated by Jiang Zemin in his political report to the 15th Party Congress: 'The more socialism develops, the more democracy will also develop'. It has been little noted that Jiang has not coupled the development of democracy to economic modernization, but to the far more elusive concept of the 'development of socialism'; see Jiang Zemin 1997, p. 3.

[19]See Mencius, Book IV, Part II, chapter 19, where *ren* and *yi*, that is knowledge of human relations and the appropriate behavior, are put forward as the human attributes that distinguish man from animals.

[20]Conversely, Chinese experience difficulties dealing with persons outside their network of relations and prefer to deal with such persons through a middleman, rather than directly.

deemed to be. Under Marxism-Leninism, this network of roles has been transplanted to a model of class contradictions, in which the traditional relations of father and son, man and woman have been largely suppressed, ultimately to strengthen the larger relation between the party-state (and in the end, Mao Zedong) and the masses.[21] By breaking away all individuals from their traditional relationships in smaller social units, such as the family, the Chinese communists hoped to strengthen the nation-state as a whole against perceived foreign aggression.[22] In this holist approach, the human rights of the masses are granted as civil prerogatives by the supremely powerful (*zhuquan*) party-state.[23] As Article 51 of the 1982 Constitution stipulates, these rights are only granted to be exercised in the general interest.[24]

In this way, the official view of human rights in the PRC is shown to be a dual one: external and internal.[25] There is one view of human rights that addresses external issues between China and the other countries of the world.[26] This view stresses both the sovereign right of China and its citizens to subsist and to develop as a collective nation-state and its claim to the discourse of modernity.[27] Another view of human rights focuses on the internal developments of civil rights as the politically, economically, and socially correct roles of the different groups and individuals within the party-state and society at

[21] This has also been one of the main themes of the famous May 4th Movement; see Chou 1960, p. 301.

[22] In the process, they have destroyed whatever autonomy society possessed and made the emergence of a civil society impossible.

[23] For an alternative to the theory of legitimacy that Westerners insist on finding in the Chinese system, see Hintzen 1998, Chapter Five. Chinese political discourse does not even have a word for legitimacy.

[24] Art. 51 of the 1982 Constitution states: Citizens of the PRC, when exercising their freedoms and rights, must not infringe upon the interests of the state, of society, and of the collectives, or upon the lawful rights and freedoms of other citizens. For a discussion of this important article, see Hintzen 1994, pp. 11–15.

[25] Lin Jiangong, 'Deng Xiaoping de renquan sixiang chutan' (Initial Remarks about Deng Xiaoping's Thoughts on Human Rights) in Huang, Chen, and Dong 1993, p. 22.

[26] This aspect forms an answer to the perceived aggression of the human rights policy of the USA; see for example, Huang Hong, 'Meiguo de renquan waijiao' (The Human Rights Foreign Policy of the USA) in Huang, Chen, and Dong 1993, pp. 270–289.

[27] The link between human rights and sovereignty is addressed in Lin Jiangong, 'Deng Xiaoping de renquan sixiang chutan', in Huang, Chen, and Dong 1993, pp. 23–24. The issue of modernity is put forward in Kong Youzhen, 'Lun fazhan quan' (On the Right to Develop) in Huang, Chen, and Dong 1993, p. 164, where the socialist view is placed above the bourgeois one.

large. If civilians adhere to these roles, it is thought, socio-economic modernization will be executed swiftly, stably, and smoothly.[28] These rights have been formulated as positive and programmatic items in the Chinese constitution and are theoretically balanced by – or even barely distinguishable from – duties. They are positive in that the legal stipulations that lay them down are considered to create them as a grant of rights by the state to society. Moreover, in the Chinese legal tradition, there has never been any theory about directly binding laws. All laws are programmatic and must be adapted to more concrete circumstances through a process of *jutihua* (concretization).[29] Therefore, without lower legislation and local regulations, no civil rights may be said to be concretely granted. On the other hand, the programmatic nature of civil rights and the lack of lower regulations allows for a grey area in which local officials may at their discretion decide which rights may be exercised.[30]

Unlike in the West, in China there has never been a legitimate theory that pitted society against the state. In fact, it is often overlooked that in the Chinese culture the scholastic notion of a general law, that lies at the root of Western legal thought, is absent.[31] The party-state has justified its leadership over the nation-state by its claim to a unique insight into the processes of historical development, as set out in the Chinese version of Marxism-Leninism. The official human rights theory of the PRC is incorporated into this vision by a smart appeal to the idea of the three generations of theories of human rights. Instead of viewing the political, economic, and Third World theories of human rights as incremental elements of a growing theory of human rights, Chinese scholars have embedded these theories into the objective process of Marxist-Leninist historical development. They have portrayed these theories as steps in a developmental process, in which each new stage effectively superseded the preceding

[28]Liu Han and Li Lin, 'Makesizhuyi renquanguan chulun' (A First Theory on the Marxist View of Human Rights) in CASS Law Department 1992, p. 135.

[29]Parts of China's civil legislation have also been 'concretized' in local regulations.

[30]Unlike in the political cultures of the West, such discretionary power is viewed as a positive traditional default mode in Chinese political culture. Recently, the introduction of 'rule by law' has led to criticisms of this discretionary power, but old habits die very, very hard.

[31]Berman's remark, that Western legal practices have formed the beginning of the Western conception of science, is illustrative in this respect. Chinese science denies that a law can be both generally true and practically applicable; see Berman 1983, p. 152.

one.[32] Like its socialism, which is portrayed as morally – and ultimately economically – superior to Western capitalism, the Chinese view of human rights is presented as a more comprehensive theory than the Western theory, and therefore as superior.

As has been the case with other new concepts of Western political philosophy, on the one hand, the term 'human rights' has been adopted by the Chinese political establishment as a sign of its modernity. On the other hand, aided and abetted by the traditional vagueness surrounding the contents of human rights in international law, the definition of human rights has been thoroughly redefined to suit the interests of the regime. One might say that the Chinese authorities simply decided to adopt the sign board of 'human rights' and to use it for something completely different. It is not unlike the change in meaning of the traffic lights during the Cultural Revolution, when for a short while the red light meant one could drive on. To a certain extent, China has reaped the benefits that accrue from the term, but has avoided its actual consequences. This is part of the holistic tradition of Chinese politics that stresses a comprehensive approach. In practice, it amounts to a situation in which the PRC tries 'to have its cake and eat it'.

The recent culture craze among China's establishment intellectuals

In spite of the official White Paper, debates about human rights have continued among Chinese establishment intellectuals. According to the dictates of democratic centralism, once the White Paper was published it was no longer possible to address the issue directly, but other less direct topics, nonetheless, were found to put forward views. These included such issues as the definition of culture, the exact nature of historical development, and social relations. All clearly touched upon different views of human rights.

Overall, there were three main clusters of views about human rights: ethical, Marxist, and legalist. Because the official view of human rights was linked to the Marxist-Leninist theory of socio-economic and political development, in order to 'place' the different views about human rights, it is perhaps expedient to give an overview

[32] Bai Guimei 1991, p. 1 and Chen Zhishang, 'Renquan yanjiu yao jiefang sixiang, shishi qiushi' (In Researching Human Rights We Must Liberate Our Thoughts and Seek Truth through Facts) in Huang, Chen and Dong 1993, pp. 5-6. This interpretation runs contrary to the UN assertion that all human rights ought to be viewed equally.

of the main differences in this field first. During the 1980s, an important political cleavage within the Chinese political elite emerged over the question of the nature of historical development. Was historical development a universal process, the rules of which applied in varying extents to all countries in the world, or were there different processes for each different country or culture? This issue was of great importance for such political issues as democracy and human rights. After all, orthodox Marxism indicated quite clearly that political emancipation had to take place at the same time as economic development. Conservative and mainstream intellectuals, no doubt supported by most officials, took pains to advance a different view. Briefly put, as long as the party-state ruled in the interests of the people, political reform could be limited to improvement in administrative efficiency and suppression of the worst excesses of official misconduct. Democracy and human rights would be postponed to a later date.

Non-Marxist views about human rights were also put forward. During the eighties, the monopoly of Marxism-Leninism had been successfully challenged in academic circles[33] and had received a severe blow from the spectacular collapse of the Soviet Union. Except for the Western ideas, many traditional Chinese theories made a comeback – sometimes in novel forms. He Xin's theory about the origins of the Chinese dragon underscored the growing popularity of traditionalist theories.[34] Inspired by the success of – supposedly Confucian – Singapore, a number of publications on Confucianism and Eastern culture started to appear. By the mid-1990s Confucian ethics constituted something of a vogue among groups of Beijing intellectuals[35] and Confucian literature was freely available.

From the late eighties onwards, there was a noticeable revival of Confucian 'culturalism'. Supported by some mainstream and conservative Marxist views of the 1980s, which claimed that China was following its own unique path to modernization through socialism with Chinese characteristics, re-born Confucianists started to point to the traditional basis of social relations which underlie Chinese culture.

---

[33] See Hu Sheng, 'Guanyu jiaqiang shehui kexue yanjiu de jige wenti' (On Some Problems to Strengthen Research in the Social Sciences) in Hu Sheng 1994, p. 346. In this speech, which was held in 1986, Hu conceded that theories other than Marxism-Leninism could contribute to scientific research and that in the future Marxist views should no longer be forced upon scholars.

[34] He Xin 1990.

[35] At Beijing University, I was told in 1996 that some scholars wanted their wives to stop working and remain at home according to Confucian ethics.

Unlike some of their predecessors in the late 1980s,[36] to varying extents today's Confucianists have sought to merge Confucianism with the mainstream of Marxism-Leninism. Without offering any clear reasons, for example, Li Zhengang proposed a traditional answer to a long list of problems of China's perceived 'spiritual disorientation' (*jingshen mishi*).[37] There was a loss of reference for moral appraisal, value trends were confused, all kinds of immoral practices proliferated, the control mechanisms of social morality were weakened, and moral education had turned out all wrong and become deformed (*niuqu bianxing*).[38] These problems, he believed, 'were seriously obstructing the development of the material and spiritual civilizations of socialism'. Pluralism was leading people to self-contradictory beliefs so that they 'no longer knew what constituted an ideal person' (*bu zhi ruhe zuoren cai shi lixiang de*).[39] Quoting an array of Confucian maxims, Li proposed to 'use old morals in service of modern life' (*yong gulao daode wei xiandai shenghuo fuwu*) and, amongst other things, to rectify (*zhengzhi*) the cultural market.[40] This new-found morality, moreover, would not have to limit itself to the outward relations and ideals, but would try to reach people's innermost psychological makeup. In slightly more Marxist terms, Chen Xianda basically stated much the same.[41] Pointing to the economic successes of those East Asian countries that had experienced the influence of Confucianism, he propounded that 'the main contemporary value of China's traditional culture is its value for us'.[42] Of course, Chen continued, any discussion of cultural values had to be based on the socialist essence (*shehuizhuyi xingzhi*) of the country. But, instead of Westernizing Chinese culture, Chinese had 'to be good at inheriting and spreading our traditional culture'.[43] Confucian values had to be applied to limit the egoism and immorality, that a market economy would foster if left unattended. It stressed a hierarchic social order of reciprocal duties (*fu ci, zi xiao, xiong you, di gong*) and such things as 'first worry about the worries of the world, then enjoy the enjoyments of the world' (*xian tianxia zhi you er you, hou tianxia zhi le er le*).[44]

[36]Yang Baikui rejected Marxist materialism altogether for a return to Confucian values; see Yang Baikui 1989, pp. 25 and 48–51.

[37]Li 1997, pp. 29–32.

[38]*Idem*, pp. 30–31.

[39]*Idem*, p. 31.

[40]*Idem*, p. 32.

[41]Chen Xianda 1997, pp. 161–165.

[42]*Idem*, p. 162.

[43]*Idem*, p. 163.

[44]*Idem*, p. 164.

In this way, social stability and harmony in interpersonal relations would be ensured.

A slightly different approach by Chinese culturalists is represented by establishment intellectuals who stress the differences in the way in which the Chinese and the Western cultures view the relationship between man and nature.[45] Whereas Western culture is uniformly portrayed as dividing man and nature, Chinese culture is said to search for unity or harmony between the two.

The Marxist critique of these Confucian views went a long way towards showing the extent to which the normative default mode of spiritual civilization, that the party-state proposed, had started to look towards tradition. At the same time, their views revealed how foreign the international debates on human rights issues remained to the Chinese Marxists.

The problem of the Chinese Marxists was that, ever since class struggle had been discarded as the main contradiction in society, they had been in search of a theory that could provide a theoretical basis for an ideal of interpersonal relations. Collectivism had so far failed to provide a satisfying social ethic, and patriotism was too general to be practical.[46] In this sense, Chen Xianda's traditionalist observation that China was 'disoriented' was not entirely beside the mark. Mao's destruction of the family, in favor of a chaotic populism around his person, has served to both demoralize and immoralize society. But, if class no longer determined who was good or bad, what element of man could do that? With the Confucianists, Huang was forced to agree that respect for (the new) social status provided a good alternative.

Human rights were only addressed explicitly by those establishment intellectuals who supported the establishment of a legal system. These scholars and officials were to be found both in the mainstream of the Chinese political elite and among pro-Western reformers. Both agreed to a view of law as a means to ensure that officials implemented policies effectively and correctly. To this extent, even parts of the Chinese mainstream were in favor of human rights legislation. An early instance of such legislation is formed by the stipulations on civil rights, such as personal honor and an identity, that have been laid down in the *General Principles of the PRC Civil Law.*[47] Later on, this resulted in laws on the right of assembly, procession, and demon-

[45]Chen Guoqian 1994 and Ye 1997, pp. 36–39.

[46]On collectivism, see Chen Laozhi 1984, pp. 17–25; on patriotism, see Zhang Jiangming 1992.

[47]See 'Zhonghua renmin gongheguo minfa tongze tiaowen chanshi' (Discussion and Explanation of the Articles of the General Principles of the PRC Civil Law) in Liu Yaping 1992, pp. 382–384.

stration,[48] on administrative appeal, and more recently in an entirely revamped criminal legislation. The rank and file of the political mainstream, however, viewed such legislation as an additional instrument in the hands of the authorities to implement sovereign policies and a means to harness the people in the interests of the party-state. Many believed that the ideological quality of cadres had to remain the most important guarantee for good government. Among mainstream intellectuals, therefore, the development of a legal system in the PRC was often portrayed as the result of the success of economic modernization, rather than as a means to restrain the party-state.[49] Legally defined human rights still constituted rights that were granted to citizens by a party-state that wanted to maximize its own political strength. State power and civil rights were viewed as two sides of the same coin. In this view, the inner stability and outward strength of the party-state were deemed more important than the rights of individual citizens.[50] Civil rights were granted under the condition that they were used in the general interest. This was recently exemplified by one official who implicitly attacked the traditionalist reliance on Confucian ethics. 'Believers in a faith', he remarked, 'must not merely read classics, but they must also know the law'.[51] Although the PRC guaranteed the individual freedom of faith, as a social phenomenon, religion had to be controlled and managed by law to fit the needs of the party-state.

Legalist reformers, by contrast, advocated an egalitarian conception of law that was far more reflective of the perceived moral rights of the people. Zhang Shuguang adopted this approach when he contrasted a dictatorial or despotic state with a democratic one. In the former people have no rights, whereas in the latter they enjoy ample freedom and rights.[52] Moreover, rather than inner ideals, they stressed the need for outward constraints. At the end of the 1980s, for example, Zhang Guicheng had already pointed out that formally human rights were protected in the PRC, but that officials failed to apply them to themselves.[53] If the state granted rights to its citizens, Zhang contended, it would have to be prepared to accept that in some cases these rights proved detrimental to its policies. More recently,

[48] For a detailed analysis of this law, see Hintzen 1994, pp. 43–68.

[49] See, for example, Jiang Lishan 1998, p. 13.

[50] Zhang Siqing 1998, p. 2.

[51] Ye 1998, p. 16.

[52] Zhang Shuguang, 'Geren quanli he guojia quanli' (Individual Rights and State Power) in Gonggong luncong 1995, p. 5.

[53] Zhang 1988, p. 12.

some other – mostly young – lawyers also voiced similar views.[54] Lü Taifeng has sought to stress the independence of the constitution and the legal system vis-à-vis the CCP and its organizational discipline. The exercise of people's power and rights 'only has to conform to the concrete contents and procedures, that the constitution and the laws have stipulated, to be acceptable' (*jiu xing le*).[55]

An additional remark is perhaps in order. In the past, with some notable exceptions, Western-educated and Japan-educated scholars have often been prone to voice more reformist views. With the growing openness of Chinese academic debate, this has probably become somewhat more even. Still, it needs to be pointed out that many scholars appear to be more reformist at the outset than later in their careers. A good example of this is the first holder of a Ph.D. degree in political science from Beijing University, Yu Keping. He first published an article commemorating the French Declaration of the Rights of Man and the Citizen in 1989, in which he set out a moral and quite 'Western' view of human rights. Some years later, however, he published 'a more Marxist view of human rights'.[56] As young scholars are socialized into the system, they tend to mold their views after the normative default mode.

Although it may not seem readily apparent, human rights issues are still debated amongst establishment intellectuals today. Within the Chinese elite, in fact, a search is still going on for the best ideal of man in a modern society. What ideally constitutes man? Confucians only see man as a part of a hierarchical network of social relations, from which he derives his identity and his value. So do the mainstream Marxists, although their view is somewhat different. Social relations, for example, are more equal than among Confucianists and they propose a rule by law. Both, however, stress the value of a personal ethic of social appropriateness and humility within a larger social framework. It is difficult to fit a clear view of human rights into this picture. Human rights, in fact, are solely viewed within the context of law. Lawyers, many of whom proclaim to be Marxists, quite naturally[57] tend to favor a more formal and superficial approach.[58]

[54]See, for example, Zhang Hengshan and Xu Xiangmin's views in 1996, as expressed in 'Yifa zhiguo...' (1996).

[55]Lü 1998, p. 143.

[56]Svensson 1996, p. 296 note 9. Yu's article is published in *Zhengzhixue yanjiu* 1989 (4) and not in the third issue, as Svensson notes.

[57]Within the Chinese elite, becoming a lawyer during the eighties in itself was already an indication of certain views. As law becomes more accepted, this may slowly change.

[58]As a recent article by Zhang Hengshan shows, however, the distinction is not that clear. There are also lawyers who set great store by a moral basis for rights.

Like other establishment intellectuals, however, many lawyers tend to view the power of the state and civil rights as two aspects of one and the same thing.[59] More civil rights, in this view, automatically mean less power for the state. This zero-sum view is related to the belief that civil rights are granted by the party-state.

Within the establishment, the group of officials and scholars, that advocate a view of rights that may be used to limit the party-state, is rather small. Most scholars and officials seem to adhere to a different set of positive values. Their belief is in a traditional default mode view of ideal man as an actor of social roles in hierarchical relations. The quality of one's performance ideally determines one's status and one's rights within society. Of course, since China is a 'people's republic', the elite seeks to 'stand in service of the people'. This may be interpreted to mean anything from overall rule in the general interest of the people (while individual casualties are justified for the sake of the collective) to a benevolent authoritarianism that provides everyone with a place within society, however humble. Importantly, the emphasis of this traditional default mode is on the value of personal ethics, rather than on exterior laws. In China, law is still generally viewed as coercive and therefore second-best to ethical or ideological values. Human rights, as a part of law, are also ranked below ethics.

So far, human rights issues have been viewed solely within the context of the PRC's elite. For obvious reasons, this is where human rights would be most visibly present in words. As I have attempted to show, in theory the culture of the Chinese elite is not particularly enthusiastic about human rights. But, what about society, what about the actual deeds? After all, many Western scholars seem to believe that – regardless of the authoritarian or paternalistic ethics of the elite – macro-economic modernization will necessarily lead to some form of rule by law and more general political participation. The first step towards such an open society would be the emergence of some form of 'civil society', that is forms of social organization that exist independently from the party-state. These, in turn, could lead to demands for a greater respect for human rights.

In search of civil society

Both the official redefinition of human rights and the recent debates among establishment intellectuals showed that the Chinese elite continued to believe that stable and harmonious social relations were of

[59]For an example, see Huang, Chen, and Dong 1993, p. 25 and Gonggong luncong 1995, pp. 5-6.

crucial importance for a fulfilment of the ideal nature of man. In this view, an opposition – even a loyal one – between the party-state and parts of society constituted a taboo. The party-state had the right to manage society in the general interest as it saw fit. In order to bring about human rights in Chinese society, order and stability had to accompany economic development, and society had to implement party-state policies. This meant that autonomous social organizations were automatically viewed as obstacles to the general interest.

Against this view, both Western and some Chinese reformist scholars have put forward the legitimacy of a public sphere. In the aftermath of the Tiananmen Incident, scholars started to look for such a sphere in Chinese society.[60] The large-scale, student-led protests were widely interpreted as the beginning of such a civil society. Economic development, it was believed, was leading to a social transformation in which, for the first time since 1949, society was separating from the party-state and asserting itself.

The instinctive reaction of the party-state to the beginnings of a more autonomous society, however, has been to try to reassert its control. This reflex has been strongly conditioned by the traditional default mode of the main perceived functions of the Chinese state: to order social relations and to manage society. By keeping the management of key organizations within its own power, the Party has admirably succeeded in retaining its control over all sectors of society. In so doing, it has maintained its social monopoly on power and the exclusive right to define and apply human rights as it sees fit.

In *In Search of Civil Society*, Gordon White and two other scholars have attempted to look for the beginnings of 'civil society by the beacons of social organisations'.[61] As detailed fieldwork on the trade unions and women's federation revealed, however, the Party still kept a tight leash on these organizations. In spite of ambitious reform proposals, mainly within the trade unions, to create a tripartite corporatist relationship in which the government would function as a mediator between the enterprises and the trade unions, the old

[60]Prominent among them were White, Howell and Shang 1996. In China, the informal social group around Deng Zhenglai, which published the bi-lingual *Zhongguo shehui kexue jikan/Chinese Social Sciences Quarterly* and related publications, was perhaps the most important promoter of the concept of 'civil society' in the PRC. See, for example, Deng 1994, pp. 50–60.

[61]White, Howell and Shang 1996, p. 98. Word has it that White and his group set out to map civil society in China and discovered that it still did not exist. Instead of something like *Civil Society in China*, they then decided to call their work *In Search of Civil Society*.

structure of the official Party-led interest groups was not called into question.

The establishment of professional associations was first proposed, it seems, by Yu Guangyuan in the late 1970s.[62] Yu was one of Deng Xiaoping's more senior advisors. At the time, the post-Mao leadership was busy re-establishing the entire academic framework of the pre-Cultural Revolution period. Research associations seemed a good way of bringing scholars from different academic institutions from all over the country into contact with one another. In spite of their academic character, however, these associations were uniformly set up as extensions of administrative organs.

My own recent research on the Chinese Association of Political Science (CAPS) may serve as an example for the way in which all such associations have been established.[63] CAPS was founded in December 1980 as the national association of political science. It was clearly a semi-official organization, because it could never have been set up without official approval. Moreover, organizationally, it was a part of the *xitong*, or organizational network of the Chinese Academy of Social Sciences (CASS). Under CAPS, a network of provincial level associations was partly established. The official character of these lower associations was even more marked than that of the national association: local officials attended the founding ceremonies and sat on their boards. CAPS itself soon became a battleground between propaganda and educational officials, who sought to use it as a conveyor belt to scholars for official policies on political science, and scholars, who wanted a more independent association. At the same time, CAPS provided an international platform from which the PRC sought to further its foreign policy with respect to Taiwan. By attempting to join the International Political Science Association (IPSA), it became an instrument through which the PRC attempted to isolate Taiwan even further on the international scene.

The official character of all academic associations like CAPS was underscored by the shadowy existence of federations of social sciences or *shelian*. These were official organs at the provincial level which sought to manage all the associations of social sciences at their level. Typically, they published internal magazines containing the main policy guidelines and research plans for the social sciences in

[62]Su 1996, p. 25.
[63]The following has been based on Hintzen 1998, pp. 120–130.

general.[64] Other professional associations also seemed to be managed through similar administrative organs.[65]

In general, such research-oriented academic associations reportedly made up the largest category of all social groups.[66] By the mid-1990s, some 38 per cent of all social groups at the provincial level were of this type. A further 29 per cent were specialist or expert associations and 10 per cent were federations and umbrella organizations. If one adds these up, a staggering total of 77 per cent of all social groups would belong to this category of semi-official, state-managed organizations. To quote a Chinese scholar, 'The Party knows from its own experience that it is possible to start a mass movement capable of overthrowing the government from just a small group of about a dozen people'. In other words, the organization has been set up in such a way that the power of the CCP is strengthened.

According to the same report, a remaining 23 per cent of social groups were trade-related. As early as 1980, Deng Xiaoping had issued directives for the separation of both Party and government and of government and enterprises. After urban reform started in 1984, the departments of industry and trade were ordered to transform themselves into independent professional or sectorial associations. Progress was slow, however.[67] In many cases, so-called professional associations and independent enterprises were autonomous in little more than name. Officially, many associations and enterprises have remained in 'a situation under which the old and the new structures exist side by side'.[68] Still, by the 1990s, many such business and trade associations have begun to develop real lobbying functions, thus reflecting the heightened status of the different enterprise sectors.

Another category of social group was that of the informal groups of semi-establishment intellectuals. Gu Xin's research on a number of such informal groups has shown clearly that these groups usually aspired to be coopted by the establishment. As a result, they tried to enlist patrons within the establishment and proffer ideas and publications which – at times – were slightly out of step with the official Party line. Since such groups aspired to be successful in their attempts to acquire an official status, they could hardly be considered to be a part of an emerging civil society.

[64] Personally, I have seen the *Beijing shelian tongxun*, but have heard of a similar publication in Shanghai.

[65] See Human Rights in China 1997, pp. 5-6.

[66] The following is taken from Human Rights in China 1997, p. 6.

[67] See Chen Yaoqi 1986, p. 27.

[68] Document Research Bureau of the CCP Central Committee 1994, p. 144.

In looking for an emerging civil society in China, a promising category of social groups was formed by the many urban-based, non-elite independent organizations that were mentioned in the report of Human Rights in China.[69] These small groups often performed social functions that would not directly involve them in an interaction with the authorities. They provided 'counselling, telephone hot-lines, and provision of advice of various kinds (and varying quality)' for such different groups as women, AIDS patients, homosexuals, religious and ethnic minorities, and workers.[70] These groups, however, were often subject to continuous oppression by the authorities. As one Chinese scholar observed, '[Party] control is vital. They feel they cannot allow any non-official group to gain ground in society for fear it will grow into a potentially threatening movement'.[71] Attempts at setting up independent groups on 'human rights, labor, migrant workers, and minority cultures' were generally nipped in the bud. The environmental pressure groups that existed were viewed with great suspicion.

Finally, the peasantry formed a group from which an embryonic civil society could emerge. As Liang Zhiping has pointed out, in reality the earliest agricultural reforms, that took place in the late 1970s, were forms of resistance against the Chinese authorities. Peasants, who were fed up with the constraints of the system of collective ownership, spontaneously started to take their fate into their own hands and reverted to family farming. The authorities were only later forced to accept a *fait accompli* or to crack down. They opted for reform. Still, changes did not stop here. During the 1980s, the position of the CCP in the countryside was gravely undermined. Cadres were often too old to work, out of touch with the times, and slow to recruit new members. As the economic reforms picked up speed, the centrality of the Party to the lives of hundreds of millions of peasants started to disappear. Suddenly, other ways to social status and wealth lay open. In the past fifteen years or so, there has been a re-emergence of much of traditional peasant society. Religion and secret societies have provided social frameworks for peasant resistance against the authorities.

---

[69] Human Rights in China 1997, pp. 9–11.

[70] Human Rights in China 1997, p. 10. The following enumeration is also from this page. Labor groups may try to tap the vast numbers of migrant workers and recent jobless state workers in the large cities who form a potentially volatile group.

[71] Human Rights in China 1997, p. 6.

As was the case with the urban population, the party-state concentrated primarily on measures of crowd control. In answer to its shrinking popularity, the Party has been forced to allow for a larger measure of political participation at the grass-roots level. Officially, this policy was clearly aimed at reimposing some form of effective control on large parts of the countryside. The village elections, that were carried out as a result of the self-governance system since 1988, displayed all the elements of the traditional rituals of a democracy that the communists have perfected. Actual elections, however, revealed the extent to which the Party had already lost influence and power in the countryside. In spite of carefully planned arrangements, Party candidates were voted out of office. It was obvious that many Chinese in the countryside were attempting to revert to a more traditional form of life, in which they shut the political system out of their lives as much as possible. Still, the revival of clan life and Confucian morality may hardly be viewed as the emergence of a civil society.

Civil society needs an open and autonomous public debate between truly independent groups that has so far been impossible in the PRC. By any standards, civil society as it is understood to have developed in the West could therefore not be said to exist in China.[72] Although some autonomous groups existed, they have by and large been marginalized or pushed into illegality. As a result, a number of Chinese scholars have begun to prefer the term 'corporatism' to describe Chinese state-society relations.[73] Although by Western standards this would not be very fashionable, one observer has gone somewhat further and has likened Chinese society to the south of Italy under fascism. Indeed, the authoritarian political system, the weakness of an open middle class, and the Mafia-like secret societies in rural areas may all be found in today's China. With the decline of Marxism-Leninism, other authoritarian ideas have received far more official support than their democratic alternatives.

To conclude, the overall socio-economic conditions for the development of human rights in China remain rather bleak. For any meaningful improvement in the human rights situation to take place, society would have to form much more of a counterweight to the party-state than it has done thus far. Conversely, the party-state continues to refuse to subject itself freely to the rule of law, democracy or human rights. On the contrary, it has successfully clung on to its monopoly

[72] The *locus classicus* on the emergence of 'civil society' in Western Europe is Jürgen Habermas 1962.

[73] Ding 1998.

of power. A vast machine of repression, which in itself forms an influential interest group within the establishment, continues to exist. By any standards, the party-state has remained extremely successful at destroying every form of larger, non-official social organization. There is a sociological reality behind the amorphous Chinese term of 'the masses of the people' because PRC citizens, who even try to form civil organizations, are extremely rare.

Additionally, the sheer size of China has constituted a much overlooked factor in most human rights discussions. The only social organizations that span the entire country are the party-state and its army. Their control is at once supreme and extremely weak. There is still no national economic network that could provide a counterweight. If it would emerge, it would still not automatically guarantee respect of human rights. As modernization continues to make progress, the political system will find itself increasingly forced to change its traditional role of crowd control. This is a change that it will find extremely difficult to bring about. Under this system, Chinese society remains elusive and – at best – extremely fragmented. Outside the country's elite, there is still no real 'Chinese nation' in the European nineteenth-century sense of the word, let alone a 'civil society'. Most Han Chinese still feel their strongest attachments to their county or their province. Although the UN and all other world states do not classify them as such, most minority areas continue to form *de facto* colonies. A Chinese state that respects human rights requires a vastly altered communist party-state, but perhaps most of all, a politically active society that wrests the necessary concessions from it.

Conclusion

In human rights issues, official China certainly wants to have its cake and eat it. Redefined by Chinese establishment intellectuals, the term human rights (*renquan*) in the PRC has been officially formulated to suit the needs of the party-state. As a term, it allows China to partake of the discourse of modernity. By attaching a new definition to this term,[74] it seeks to deflect the consequences of the term's older meaning. Externally, the collective redefinition is put to use in China's quest for wealth and power. All international documents on human rights may be interpreted according to this redefinition because the

[74]This is something that international law allows for.

collective approach imposes an implicit hierarchy. As Chinese knowledge about the international literature on human rights grows, increasingly refined collective theories of human rights will presumably be put forward.

It would be of benefit to the world community to make the Chinese authorities realize, that it cannot have its cake and eat it. The PRC must be made aware that human rights issues should not be used to redefine relations between states, but ought to be indicative of the treatment that states mete out to (groups of) individuals. Oddly enough, China's international fervor for the right to development either contradicts its stance of non-interference in domestic affairs or suggests a dangerous basis for military expansion. This is probably one of the most worrying aspects of the official Chinese White Paper.

Internally, the collective redefinition may serve as the basis for a long period of political tutelage and a form of Confucian nationalism. The social basis for a collective interpretation is much underrated in Western literature on human rights. Even if it wanted to, the political leadership would not be able to impose a more individual form of human rights on the country. The redefinition of human rights fits traditional default modes of Chinese political and social culture that have permeated society. Cultural control mechanisms, such as deference to authority and taboos of opposition, are not values that one can change at will. They lie at the base of the personal sense of identity and the social structures of hundreds of millions of people. A few Westerners clamoring for political freedom and human rights will not change that overnight. Moreover, the normative default mode on human rights of the present regime forms a serious obstacle to a clearer understanding of what human rights constitute in the West. The Chinese regime has successfully spread the idea that Western notions of human rights constitute deceitful instruments to keep the bourgeoisie in power at the expense of the rest of the population. Moreover, the idea of division of powers that is also implicitly present in our notion of human rights is anathema to the overwhelming majority of the Chinese elite, if not the Chinese population at large. A Chinese saying states: In a family only one can be the boss.

Other East Asian countries have shown that cultures displaying similar features to China's are perfectly capable of evolving legal systems and social practices internally that are much more respectful of human rights than the PRC's. Although, for instance, the Japanese constitution also stipulates that national and collective interests should go before individual interests, in practice the Supreme

Court has decided that the two can never conflict. In fact, China's theory of a hierarchy of interests is a surprisingly feeble one. The party-state and society are large enough and strong enough to overcome the perceived and temporary setback of an individual interest. Its authoritarianism is a vicious circle which keeps the people uneducated and unaware of the ways of the world while oppresses them for lack of such education and experiences. In fact, as Chinese reformers have pointed out, the communist theory about rule in service of the people offers a good starting-point for both a parliamentary and a presidential tradition not unlike the French 4th and 5th Republics.

The countries of the European Union stand to gain from a clear understanding of the implications of the Chinese redefinition of human rights. A consistent and principled European approach towards human rights issues is of crucial importance in convincing the PRC that Europe is sincere in its support for human rights. A more refined ideological approach would also offer better chances of avoiding Pavlovian reactions on the Chinese side. This would only involve overt ideological rhetoric on human rights or forms of boycotts in certain cases. In this way, international pressure – which is regularly successful – may be applied in an even more efficient way. Targeted support for local democracy, legal training, and social projects are long-term ways of improving the human rights situation. But, China is simply too large for fast and ready-made solutions.

European Union members should seek to make clear to the Chinese in words as well as in deeds that their support for human rights is not aimed at destabilizing or breaking up Chinese society. They should complain much more energetically, for example, about the distorted and unfriendly representation of official Chinese accounts of human rights theories and practices in Western Europe.[75] Karl Marx's accounts of the Industrial Revolution are now between 100 and 150 years old. It is time the Chinese communists started to give due credit to contemporary European conditions. A more diverse and balanced representation in China of European history would contribute to a more positive view of human rights among the Chinese population.

[75] China complains in much the same way about Japanese accounts of the Second World War.

References

Chinese

– (1996), 'Yifa zhiguo jianshe shehuizhuyi fazhi guojia xueshu yantaohui jiyao' (Main Points from the Academic Forum on Building a State that is Ruled by Socialist Law through [the Principle of] Ruling the State on the Basis of Law), *Faxue yanjiu*, No. 3, pp. 3–23

Bai, Guimei (1991), 'Lun xin yidai renquan' (On a New Generation of Human Rights), *Faxue yanjiu*, No. 5, pp. 1–6

CASS Law Department (1992), *Dangdai renquan* (Contemporary Human Rights), Beijing: Zhongguo shehui kexue chubanshe

Chen, Guoqian (1994), 'Guanyu huanjing wenti de zhexue sikao' (Philosophical Reflections on Environmental Problems), *Zhexue yanjiu*, No. 5, pp. 32–37

Chen, Laozhi (1984), et al. (eds), *Gongchanzhuyi daode jianghua* (Talks on Communist Morality), Jilin: Jilin renmin chubanshe

Chen, Xianda (1997), 'Zhongguo chuantong wenhua dui jiaqiang shehuizhuyi jingshen wenming jianshe de zuoyong' (The Role of China's Traditional Culture in Strengthening the Construction of Socialist Spiritual Civilization), *Zhongguo shehui kexue*, 1997, No. 2, pp. 31–41

Chen, Yaoqi (1986), 'Guanyu chengshi zhengfu jingji guanli jigou gaige de ruogan wenti' (Some Problems Concerning the Reforms of the Economic Management Structure of Urban Governments), *Zhengzhixue yanjiu*, No. 3

Deng, Zhenglai (1994), 'Zhongguo fazhan yanjiu de jianshi – jian lun Zhongguo shimin shehui yanjiu' (A Review of Chinese Research on Development – as well as Research on China's Civil Society), *Zhongguo shehui kexue jikan*, No. 8 (Summer), pp. 50–60

Document Research Bureau of the CCP Central Committee (1994), *Sanzhong quanhui yilai de zhongda juece* (Important Policies since the Third Plenum), Beijing: Renmin chubanshe

Dong, Yunhu and Liu, Wuping (1991) (eds), *Shijie renquan yuefa zonglan* (An Overview of the World's Human Rights' Treaties), Chengdu: Sichuan renmin chubanshe

Gonggong luncong (1995), *Shichang luoji yu guojia guannian* (*Res Publica*, The Logic of the Market and Views of the State), Beijing: Sanlian chubanshe

He, Xin (1990), *Long: shenhua yi zhenxiang* (The Dragon: Mythology and Truth), Shanghai: Renmin chubanshe

Huang, Dansen; Chen, Zhishang and Dong, Yunhu (1993), *Dangdai Zhongguo renquan lun* (On Human Rights in Contemporary China), Beijing: Dangdai Zhongguo chubanshe

Hu, Sheng (1994), *Hu Sheng wenji 1979–1994* (Collected Works of Hu Sheng 1979–1994), Beijing: Zhongguo shehui kexue chubanshe

Jiang, Lishan (1998), 'Zhongguo fazhi gaige he fazhihua guocheng yanjiu' (Research on Reform of China's Legal System and the Process of Transformation to Rule by Law), *Zhongguo faxue,* 1997, No. 6; reprinted in *Xinhua wenzhai,* 1998, No. 2, pp. 7–13

Jiang, Wenzan and Duan, Rongkui (1991) (eds), *Renquan minzhu ziyou zonghengtan* (Free Talks about Human Rights, Democracy, and Freedom), Beijing: Zhongguo renmin gongan daxue chubanshe

Jiang, Zemin (1997), 'Gaoju Deng Xiaoping lilun weida qizhi, ba jianshe you Zhongguo tese shehuizhuyi shiye quanmian tuixiang ershiyi shiji' (Raise High the Glorious Banner of Deng Xiaoping Theory, Comprehensively Push the Building of Socialism with Chinese Characteristics towards the Twenty-First Century), *Fazhi ribao,* 22 September, p. 3

Li, Buyun (1992), 'Lun renquan de sanzhong cunzai xingtai' (On the Three Forms of Existence of Human Rights), CASS Law Department, pp. 3–15

Li, Zhengang (1997), 'Xiandai Zhongguoren mianlin de daode kunjing jiqi bujiu' (The Moral Straits That Contemporary Chinese Are Facing and Their Redress), *Zhongguo renmin daxue xuebao,* 1997, No. 1; reprinted in *Xinhua wenzhai,* No. 6, pp. 29–32

Liu, Yaping (1992) (ed.), *Xinbian Zhonghua renmin gongheguo changyong falü tiaowen chanshi* (A Newly Compiled Discussion and Explanation of Articles of Frequently Used Laws of the PRC), Beijing: Zhongguo jiancha chubanshe

Lü, Taifeng (1998), 'Xianfaxue jichu lilun yanjiu de ruogan sikao' (Some Reflections on the Research of the Basic Theories of Constitutional Studies), *Faxue yanjiu,* No. 3, pp. 141–145

Press Bureau of the PRC State Council (1991), *Zhongguo de renquan zhuangkuang* (Human Rights' Conditions in China), Beijing: Zhongyang wenxian chubanshe

Su, Shaozhi (1996), *Shinian fengyu* (Ten Years of Upheavals), Taibei: Shibao chubanshe

Yang, Baikui (1989), '"Wusi" sichao zai lunli daode wenti shang de pianshi' (The One-Sided Views of the 'May Fourth' Currents on Matters of Ethics and Morality), *Tianjin shehui kexue,* No. 4

Ye, Jun (1997), 'Rentianguan: Renti kexue he shehui shengtaixue de zhexue' (Views on Man and Nature: The Science of the Human Body and Philosophy of Social Ecology), *Yantai daxue xuebao*, No. 4; reprinted in *Xinhua wenzhai*, No. 12, pp. 36–38

Ye, Xiaowen (1998), 'Zongjiao yu pufa' (Religion and the Common Law), *Zhongguo zongjiao,* 1997 (Winter); reprinted in *Xinhua wenzhai*, 1998, No. 2, pp. 14–16

Zhang, Guicheng (1988), 'Lun quanli' (On Rights), *Zhengfa luntan (Zhongguo zhengfa daxue xuebao)*, No. 1, pp. 6–10

Zhang, Jiangming (1992), 'Aiguozhuyi shi Zhonghua minzu ningquli de hexin' (Patriotism is the Core of the Cohesive Strength of the Chinese Nation), *Renmin ribao*, 24 December, p. 1

Zhang, Siqing (1998), 'Xuexi Deng Xiaoping minzhu fazhi sixiang jianshe shehuizhuyi fazhi guojia' (Study the Thought of Deng Xiaoping on Democracy and the Legal System to Establish a Socialist State Ruled by Law), *Fazhi ribao,* 18 February; reprinted in *Xinhua wenzhai,* No. 5, pp. 1–3

Other languages

Baehr, P.R. (1998), *De rechten van de mens. Universaliteit in de praktijk* (Human Rights. Universality in Practice), Amsterdam: Boom

Berman, H.J. (1983), *Law and Revolution. The Formation of the Western Legal Tradition*, Cambridge (MA) and London: Harvard University Press

Chou, Tse-tung (1960), *The May Fourth Movement. Intellectual Revolution in Modern China*, Cambridge (MA): Harvard University Press

Ding, Yijiang (1998), 'Corporatism and Civil Society in China: An Overview of the Debate in Recent Years', *China Information,* Volume XII, No. 4 (Spring), pp. 44–67

Geertz, C. (1973), *The Interpretation of Cultures*, New York: Basic Books

Gu, Xin (1992), *Zhongguo qimeng de lishi tujing* (Historical Prospects of China's Enlightenment), Oxford: Oxford University Press

Gu, Xin (1998), 'Non-Establishment Intellectuals, Public Space, and the Creation of Non-Governmental Organizations in China: The Chen Ziming – Wang Juntao Saga', *The China Journal*, No. 39 (January), pp. 39–58

Habermas, J. (1962), *Strukturwandel der Öffentlichkeit. Untersuchungen zu einer Kategorie der bürgerlichen Gesellschaft* (Changes in the Structure of Public Space. Research into a Category of Civil Society), Marburg: Hermann Luchterhand

Hintzen, G. (1992), 'The Right to Differ', *Tian'anmen*, Vol. 3, No. 1 (October), pp. 1–5

Hintzen, G. (1994), *Protest Your Loyalty. An Analysis of the Right of Assembly, Procession, and Demonstration in the People's Republic of China*, Leiden: CNWS Publications

Hintzen, G. (1998), *Imagining Political Science. The Formative Influence of Political Science in the Establishment of the PRC's Political Science (1980–1989)*, Leiden, Ph.D. dissertation

Human Rights in China (1997), *China. Social Groups Seek Independence in Regulatory Cage*, New York and Hong Kong: Human Rights in China

Svensson, M. (1996), *The Chinese Conception of Human Rights. The Debate on Human Rights in China, 1898–1949*, Lund: Lund University Press

White, Gordon; Howell, Jude and Shang, Xiaoyuan (1996), *In Search of Civil Society*, Oxford: Oxford University Press

4

A Criminal Justice System for a New Millennium?

*Jianfu Chen**

1996 and 1997 saw some major revisions being made to the Criminal Procedure Law (CPL) and the Criminal Law (CL) of the People's Republic of China (PRC) respectively.[1] Although both laws had undergone many changes since their initial promulgation in 1979, the recent revision was comprehensive, aiming at a fundamental overhaul of the laws for the coming millennium.

In the case of the CPL, seventy out of the original 164 articles were revised, 2 two articles abolished and sixty-three articles added, thus making the CPL much more comprehensive and precise. The importance of the revision lies, however, not in the total number of articles revised, but in that, to some extent, certain fundamental 'due process' principles have been, for the first time, incorporated in the CPL.

* The author would like to acknowledge the financial support provided by an ARC Small Grant for the research of this paper. The author also gratefully acknowledges that some earlier materials on criminal procedural law and on criminal law were published in *Journal of Comparative and Chinese Law* and *China Perspectives*, with the kind permission from Butterworths Asia and the French Centre for Research on Contemporary China respectively.

[1] Both the Criminal Procedure Law and the Criminal Law of the People's Republic of China were first adopted by the 5th National People's Congress on 1 July 1979, effective since 1 January 1980. The CPL was revised by the Decision Concerning the Revision of the Criminal Procedure Law, adopted by the 8th National People's Congress at its 4th Plenary Session, 17 March 1996. A comprehensive revision to the Criminal Law was adopted on 14 March 1997 at the Fifth Plenary Session of the 8th NPC.

Similarly, the CL of 192 articles has now been expanded to include 452 articles in total. The categorization of crimes has been overhauled with many new offenses being identified to meet the prevailing circumstances for the orderly development of a socialist market economy. Certain fundamental principles of justice, e.g. *nullum crimen, nulla poena sine lege* (and the consequential abolition of the provision on analogy), equality before the law, and proportionality, are now for the first time expressly incorporated into the Criminal Law.

It is the view of the present author that the revision of CPL is a moderate step towards improving the criminal justice system in China, but the outcome is mainly a result of major compromises with opposing views and arguments among scholars, officials and different forces in the Chinese legal system. The revision of the CL, however, is a major disappointment although it is officially heralded as 'a major and significant measure to improve the criminal law and criminal justice'.[2] This chapter will first provide an overview of the major deficiencies, both at face value and in their implementation, of the CPL and CL before their revision, and criticisms they had attracted since their adoption in 1979. It will then analyze, in detail, specific problems in the original CPL and CL and major changes made in 1996 and 1997 respectively. It will conclude by pointing out potential difficulties in the actual implementation of the laws and the continuing deficiencies in the Chinese criminal justice system.

An overview of the 1979 Criminal Law and Criminal Procedure Law

The Criminal Procedure Law

The CPL, based on drafts prepared in the mid-1950s and early 1960s,[3] was one of the first seven major laws enacted in post-Mao China.[4] The purpose of its enactment was twofold: to elaborate the constitutional provisions regarding the division of powers and responsibilities among the people's courts, the people's procuratorates and the

[2] *People's Daily*, 4 April 1997.

[3] In particular, it was based on a draft prepared in 1963. See Wang, Wang and Wang 1981, pp. 50–52.

[4] The other six laws include a substantial criminal code, an organic law for local people's congresses and local governments, two organic laws for the people's courts and people's procuratorates respectively, and a law on Sino-foreign equity joint ventures.

public security organs, and to provide working procedures for criminal adjudication. Although the CPL was supposed to be a comprehensive code, its provisions were short, vague and, in many instances, ambiguous. Its deficiencies, both on the face of it and in actual practice, soon became apparent and, thus, attracted severe criticisms, particularly from Western human rights organizations.[5] Fundamentally, many important 'due process' principles, such as the presumption of innocence, judicial independence, adequate right to legal counsel, etc., were absent from the CPL and many other provisions in the CPL were far short of minimum requirements for the administration of justice.[6]

The deficient law was made even worse by many decisions of the NPC's Standing Committee, issued during various anti-crime campaigns,[7] and by the inability or unwillingness of the law enforcement organs to act within the law. Indeed, no sooner than the implementation of the CPL began came the realization of the judicial inability to handle criminal cases according to the law. In February 1980 – one month after the CPL came into effect – the NPC's Standing Committee had authorized the standing committees at the provincial level to approve extensions of time limits for handling criminal cases as prescribed by the CPL.[8] Such authorization was again granted by the Standing Committee in September 1981 for handling criminal cases during the period of 1981-83.[9] Thereafter, no less than twenty revisions (in the form of Decisions and Supplementary Provisions) concerning criminal and criminal procedure matters were made by the NPC's Standing Committee alone by the end of 1995.[10] Many of these provisions had serious implications for the protection of human rights and the administration of justice in China. Some of them, such as the Decision of the Standing Committee of the NPC on the Pro-

[5]There are many reports on human rights violations in relation to criminal processes in China by international human rights organizations. For some more recent and comprehensive reports, see e.g. Amnesty International (1991), Amnesty International (1992), Amnesty International (1996), Lawyers' Committee for Human Rights (1993), and Reports of the Australian Human Rights Delegation to China (1991 and 1992).

[6]By minimum requirements, I mean those provisions embodied in the Universal Declaration of Human Rights (1948) and the International Covenant on Civil and Political Rights (ICCPR) (1966).

[7]See 'Note' 1985; and Townsend 1987-88.

[8]See Decision of the Standing Committee of the NPC Regarding the Questions of Implementation of the Criminal Procedure Law (12 February 1980).

[9]See further discussions in Leng and Chiu 1985, p. 87.

[10]Huang Shengye 1996, p. 30.

cedures for Rapid Adjudication of Cases Involving Criminal Elements Who Seriously Endanger Public Security (1983), were criticized by Chinese scholars as being a blatant violation of the Chinese Constitution.[11]

With these supplementary provisions, many of them issued specifically for anti-crime campaigns with *ad hoc* policy orientation, the deficiencies of the CPL were no longer its vagueness and ambiguities, but internal contradictions and confusion. Together with the inability or unwillingness of the law enforcement organs to act within the law, the practical consequences for society were serious abuses of human rights, including the widespread application of the so-called administrative sanctions, prolonged detention without trial, and the disregard for minimum procedural protection. Thus, fundamental concerns about human rights in China can easily be traced to the structure and functioning of the PRC's criminal justice system.

Gellat, writing on behalf of the Lawyers' Committee on Human Rights, provided the following overall assessment of the CPL and its implementation before the 1996 revision:

The 1979 CPL is a detailed document that provides procedures for the criminal process which were completely absent during the PRC's first thirty years. Nevertheless, the procedure law contains numerous defects that on the face of it violate international standards of fair judicial process. In addition, the authorities frequently violate the provisions of the procedural law. They take advantage of ambiguities in the law or simply disregard the legal protection that exists in the formal criminal process. They also commonly circumvent such protection by use of administrative, 'non-criminal' sanctioning methods. These abuses occur perhaps most frequently and egregiously in political cases, but also in ordinary criminal cases.[12]

With the development of legal research and the 'open door' policy which brings in foreign influences, Chinese scholars soon recognized the deficiencies in their law and began to argue for the inclusion of many Western criminal procedural principles into the CPL.[13] Many problems in the implementation of the CPL also came to the attention

---

[11] Cui 1995, p. 96.
[12] Lawyers' Committee for Human Rights 1993, pp. 9-10.
[13] Chen Guangzhong 1989a, pp. 5–14 and 1989b, pp. 1–8.

of scholars and officials.[14] Thus the issue of revising the CPL soon became a topic of academic discussion and official consideration.[15]

The first formal forum to discuss the revision of the CPL was held in January 1991 in Beijing, organized by the Legislative Affairs Committee of the NPC's Standing Committee. A report on the forum was prepared and submitted to the Central Committee of the Chinese Communist Party. Several seminars were later held in various locations among Chinese scholars. In September 1993 it was officially announced by the Director of the Legislative Affairs Committee, Mr. Gu Angran that a formal decision had been made by the Standing Committee to include the revision of CPL in the legislative agenda of the NPC.[16] Thereafter, the Legislative Affairs Committee formally entrusted the drafting work to Professor Chen Guangzhong of the China University of Political Science and Law, who then organized a group of scholars and Ph.D. students to carry out the drafting work. The drafting work was efficiently completed in about six months. Thereafter, many more symposiums were held to discuss the revision of the CPL, either organized by scholars or by the Legislative Affairs Committee. In October 1995, the Legislative Affairs Committee issued a draft Bill and Explanations on Several Major Issues Concerning the Revision of the CPL. These two documents then formed the basis for further academic discussions.[17] At the same time, the draft Bill was twice submitted to the Standing Committee of the NPC for deliberation.[18] Thus it can be said that the revision of the CPL was the product of major joint efforts by scholars and law-makers.

---

[14] One Chinese scholar described the problems in the criminal process in the following way: 'Those (laws) that have been published are not implemented; and those not published are enforced', 'those who see the patients do not give prescription and those who give prescription do not see the patients – the separation of hearing from decision'. See Zhao 1990, pp. 380–384.

[15] As early as mid-1985, the Legislative Affairs Committee of the NPC's Standing Committee had indicated that the revision of the CPL was already under consideration. See Gu 1989, p. 206. One of the major academic gatherings to discuss the 'perfecting' of the CPL was the 1986 Guangzhou Conference, at which over 100 procedure law specialists came together to discuss a wide range of issues concerning the improvement of the CPL. See Zhao 1990, pp. 373–375.

[16] Cui 1994, p. 92.

[17] See Wei 1996, p. 89.

[18] Gu 1996, p. 85.

The Criminal Law

The CL of 1979 was initially drafted in the 1950s and 1960s and based mainly on the 33rd draft of 1963. Although supposed to be a comprehensive code following a European continental model, it consisted of only very general, ideology-ridden, vague and ambiguous principles in 192 articles, with a strong Soviet influence.[19]

As with the CPL, major deficiencies in the 1979 CL soon became apparent when implementation of the law began. To start with, provisions in the 1979 CL were soon found to be too vague and general and lacking in precision for actual implementation. Second, various anti-crime campaigns launched in China since the early 1980s have required the imposition of severe punishment for targeted crimes (e.g. rape, murder, smuggling, drug trafficking etc.). Third, the deepening of economic reform also led to certain economic crimes that were not anticipated in the 1979 CL.[20]

To deal with the above deficiencies, major changes and additions were made. Barely a year and half after the implementation of the 1979 CL, the Decision Regarding the Handling of Offenders Undergoing Reform through Labor and Persons Undergoing Rehabilitation through Labor Who Escape or Commit New Crimes, and the Provisional Regulations on Punishment of Crimes of Servicemen in Violation of Duty were issued by the NPC's Standing Committee on 10 June 1981. Thereafter, numerous 'Decisions', 'Provisional Regulations' and 'Supplementary Provisions' were issued by the NPC's Standing Committee, amending or supplementing the 1979 Law.[21] Many new offenses were also created by various non-criminal statutes issued by the NPC, its Standing Committee or even the State Council.[22] Clearly, the CL had become too fragmented and unsystem-

[19]The 1979 Law was a mixture of the Soviet Criminal Codes of 1926 and 1960, and China's own innovations. The German influence was second-hand through the Soviet codes. See Berman, Cohen and Russell 1982.

[20]Wang Hanbin 1997, p. 670.

[21]By the time of the 1997 revision, twenty-two such Decisions, Provisional Regulations or Supplementary Provisions had been issued. See Wang Hanbin 1997, pp. 670–680.

[22]By the time of the 1997 revision, more than 130 provisions contained in various non-criminal statutes had provided criminal liabilities. See Wang Hanbin 1997, p. 671. These provisions created no less than 103 criminal offenses. See Lin and Jia 1997, p. 80. Together with the supplementary provisions, no less than 230 offenses had emerged since 1979. See Chen Xingliang 1997, p. 60.

atic. Further, certain supplementary provisions violated the principles of the 1979 CL. For instance, the 1982 Decision of the Standing Committee on Severely Punishing Criminals Who Gravely Endanger the Economy and the 1983 Decision of the Standing Committee on Severely Punishing Criminals Who Gravely Endanger Public Security of Society clearly took retrospective force, whereas the 1979 CL prohibited the retrospective application of the criminal law (Art. 9 of the 1979 CL).

Further, provisions on analogy, counter-revolutionary crimes and the death penalty have attracted severe criticism from many intellectuals and human rights organizations.[23] Chinese scholars also questioned the wisdom of including provisions on analogy and counter-revolutionary crimes and the extensive application of the death penalty.

Under these circumstances, the need to comprehensively revise the 1979 CL requires little justification. Although various ideas for revising it were advanced by Chinese scholars, ranging from a complete overhaul to the rejection of any comprehensive revision,[24] the guidelines for the 1997 Revision apparently offered an easy path. First, the revision was to incorporate various Decisions and Supplementary Provisions issued by the NPC's Standing Committee since 1979. Second, the revision was to ensure continuity and stability of the Law; thus provisions without 'major' problems would not be revised. Third, general and vague provisions were to be elaborated and clarified.[25] In short, the revision was to rationalize, systematize, clarify and elaborate the 1979 Law.

Principal revision of the Criminal Procedure Law

Preliminary Detention and 'Shelter and Investigation'

The CPL divided the criminal processes into four stages: pre-trial, trial, appeal, and execution. The pre-trial stage included three steps: filing a case (*li'an*), investigation, and institution of prosecution. These three pre-trial steps concerned mainly two principal acts –

[23]See Lawyers' Committee for Human Rights 1993, and numerous reports by Amnesty International and Asia Watch.

[24]Ma and Ding 1995.

[25]Wang Hanbin 1997, pp. 671-672.

detention and arrest,[26] and investigation – and were carried out by the public security organs and the people's procuratorates.

The Chinese pre-trial process was very different from that in the West; it was a process during which the investigatory organs would have completed investigation of the defendant's crime, and complete and reliable evidence would have been collected (Art. 100 of the 1979 CPL). In order for the investigatory organs to complete the above tasks, the CPL provided very generous time limits for each stage of the investigation. Under the 1979 CPL, a public security organ could detain a person if he/she was suspected of preparing to commit a crime, was committing a crime, was discovered immediately after committing a crime or other activity which undermined work, production or social order (Art. 41 of the 1979 CPL). If a public security organ considered it necessary to arrest the detained person, it should, within three days of the detention, submit a request to the people's procuratorate for review and approval. Further time limits (ranging from two months to an indefinite period under some special circumstances) are then defined by the CPL (Arts. 48, 92, 93, 97 and 99 of the 1979 CPL) and extended by the Supplementary Provisions Regarding the Question of the Time Limits for Handling Criminal Cases (1984).

Apparently, the maximum duration of detention before trial as provided by the 1979 CPL was a far cry from any international standard for preliminary detention[27] and the matter was even made worse in practice by the Chinese 'ingenious' distinction between 'administrative' and 'legal' sanctions. Put simply, administrative sanctions are those penalties provided by administrative regulations and administered and executed by administrative organs.[28] Limited judicial supervision was only possible until the promulgation of the Administrative Litigation Law in 1989 and the Administrative Penalties Law in 1996. The most notorious and widely used form of administrative sanctions was the so-called Shelter and Investigation (*shourong shencha*).

Although Shelter and Investigation, first established in 1961 and intended as a form of preventive detention, not as a punishment, was as widely used as alternative measure by the public security organs

[26]The CPL distinguished two kinds of detention: detention (*juliu*) and arrest (*daibu*). The former referred to preliminary apprehension of a suspect by the public security organs and the latter formal arrest upon approval of the procuracy. See Arts. 39 and 41 of the 1979 CPL.

[27]For more detailed discussions, see Chen Jianfu 1997.

[28]*Chinese Encyclopedia – Law* 1984, pp. 670-671.

to detain people and thus to bypass the procedures for arrest and detention as provided in the Regulations of Arrest and Detention (1979) and the 1979 CPL, its precise legal nature was unclear and it had been a very controversial institution for many years.[29]

Several serious problems were identified by Chinese scholars. Chen Weidong and Zhang Tao, from the Department of Law of the People's University and the Law Institute of the Chinese Academy of Social Sciences, for instance, provided some excellent analyses on the theoretical and practical problems associated with the institution of Shelter and Investigation.[30] They doubted whether Shelter and Investigation could be defined as an administrative measure, as opposed to a criminal sanction. They further questioned whether the scope of application was controlled. Finally, they outlined several major problems in the use of Shelter and Investigation, which included how widespread this use was; detention which exceeded time limits, poor management of the system, and unlawful practice of investigation involved in the application of Shelter and Investigation.[31] Strangely, however, they believed that Shelter and Investigation should continue to be available to the public security organs, but that the system should be improved through legislation.

Those who opposed the use of such an extra-legal form of sanctions also questioned its nature and legal basis, constitutionality and legality, scope of operation, and abuse in practice, emphasizing the importance of the protection of individual rights.[32] They made it very clear that Shelter and Investigation should be abolished because 'Shelter and Investigation itself is a serious violation of citizens' rights as provided for by the Constitution'.[33]

Whatever the nature of this extra-legal form of detention, the public security organs preferred Shelter and Investigation to the two mechanisms for detention as provided in the CPL.[34] Further, Chinese scholars agreed on the following explanation for the widespread use of this institution: the time limit provided for arrest by the CPL

[29]In every large and medium-sized city in China, there were several Shelter and Investigation centres and, annually, hundreds of thousands of people were detained under this institution. See Amnesty International 1991, pp. 6-7.

[30]Chen and Zhang 1992 and 1993.

[31]For more detailed discussions, see Chen Jianfu 1997.

[32]See e.g. Wang Xinxin 1993.

[33]Wang Xinxin 1993, p. 380.

[34]Such was the widespread practice described by Chinese scholars as 'those (laws) that have been published are not implemented; and those not published are enforced'. See Zhao Zhenjiang 1990, p. 380.

was too short to fulfill the task of clarifying crime facts in order to have the suspect arrested.[35] Officials too were concerned and now openly admitted that such an institution of prolonged detention administered solely by public security organs violated the CPL provisions and lacked supervision and control.[36] With this common understanding, it was not surprising to note that major reforms in the revision concerning preliminary detention involved redefining the requirements for arrest, extending the duration for detention, and abolishing Shelter and Investigation.

Under Art. 40 of the 1979 CPL, one of the requirements for arrest approval was that 'major crime facts should be clarified'. This, as discussed above, was said to be one of the major reasons that caused the prolonged detention and the use of Shelter and Investigation. Art. 28 of the Decision Concerning the Revision of the Criminal Procedure Law now stipulates that 'evidence of crime is required'. 'Clarification' of crime facts and adequacy of evidence are now matters to be inquired into and dealt with during the trial process. The revision also strengthens the preventive institutions, thus making detention and arrest the last means of coercive measures. Hence, Art. 26 of the Decision adds eight articles to the CPL to strengthen the measures of obtaining a guarantor or bond and thus allows a suspect to await trial out of custody, and allows a suspect to live at home under surveillance. Further, duration of preliminary detention by public security organs, in major cases where the persons are suspected of committing crimes in various places, or repeating crimes or committing crime in a group, has been extended to one month, thus allowing the investigatory organs sufficient time to complete their investigation. With these provisions in place, Shelter and Investigation is formally abolished.[37]

The presumption of innocence

The presumption of innocence is defined by the *Chinese Encyclopedia* as 'one of the principles of criminal procedure law in some bourgeois countries, which means that a defendant should be deemed as an inn-

[35] Cui 1996, p. 6; Lawyers' Committee for Human Rights 1993, pp. 13-14.

[36] Gu 1996, p. 86.

[37] As discussed above, Shelter and Investigation is not a measure provided by the CPL; therefore the revision of the CPL would not affect the operation of this form of administrative detention. The abolition of Shelter and Investigation was therefore announced in the 'Explanations on the Revision of the CPL of the PRC', delivered by Gu Angran at the 4th Plenary Session of the 8th NPC, not in the Decision Concerning the Revision of the Criminal Procedure Law.

ocent person before he/she is found guilty in accordance with law'.[38] This principle, according to the *Encyclopedia*, was initiated by the bourgeoisie during periods of revolution to oppose the feudalist presumption of guilt. It has thus played some positive and 'progressive' roles in the struggle against autocratic feudalism. In short, it was a bourgeois principle which had once been progressive in the evolution of society. The ambiguity is apparent: as a bourgeois principle, it should be rejected by a socialist legal system; yet, as it had played some positive and progressive roles, arguably it may still have some positive elements that a socialist legal system could adopt. Indeed, this ambiguity has spurred hot debates on the presumption of innocence in the 1950s and since the 1980s.

Although Chinese scholars assert that presumption of guilt is a feudalist criminal practice, they are also able to locate many legal provisions from the ancient codes of law to support the assertion that certain elements of presumption of innocence, in particular the emphasis on evidence and lenient treatment in cases of doubt, existed in traditional China.[39] However, as a criminal procedure principle, it was first codified by the Kwomintang Criminal Procedure Code (1935), a piece of legislation largely borrowed from Continental European and Japanese legal systems. That law, together with all KMT laws was abolished when the PRC was founded in 1949. When serious legal efforts resumed after the 1954 Constitution was adopted, there were academic debates on many theoretical and practical issues, including the presumption of innocence. Those debates were, however, short-lived as the 1957 Anti-Rightists Movement was soon to denounce those who advocated bourgeois theories as 'rightists' and to silence all serious theoretical debates.[40]

Legal reform in the 1980s created a more receptive environment for 'bourgeois' theories and practice, but the 1979 CPL did not adopt the doctrine. Instead, Art. 4 of the CPL, reflecting the Party policy of 'seeking truth from facts', provided that in conducting criminal proceedings, the people's courts, the people's procuratorates and the public security organs must rely on the masses and 'must take facts as the basis and law as the criterion'. This provision, according to Chinese officials, did not support nor reject any 'presumption'. In reality, people were presumed guilty until proved innocent.[41] Nevertheless,

[38] *Chinese Encyclopedia – Law*, p. 625.
[39] See e.g. Ning 1986, p. 99.
[40] Gellat 1982, pp. 267–281; and Thieme 1984, pp. 278–283.
[41] Lawyers' Committee on Human Rights 1993, p. 14.

theless, an ambivalent attitude, characterized by some Chinese scholars as 'empty talk', leaves room for academic debate. Thus, after more than twenty years of silence, the debate on the presumption of innocence resumed in the 1980s.

The debate resumed even before the promulgation of the CPL in 1979. The *People's Daily* led the way by publishing an article advocating the inclusion of the presumption of innocence into the CPL which was then being drafted.[42] Thereafter, many academic articles have been published on the topic, either advocating or rejecting the doctrine or trying to find a third position on the controversial principle to accommodate some elements of the doctrine.[43]

The third position seeks to avoid the controversy of a wholesale adoption or a total rejection of the doctrine. It advocates critical adaptation of certain positive elements of the doctrine. Specifically, it argues for the limited adoption of the doctrine in the following sense: (1) no one should be deemed guilty until declared by a court of law; (2) when a person cannot be proven guilty, he/she should be treated as innocent; (3) in doubtful cases, legal interpretation should be made in favor of the accused.[44] This third position, characterized in Chinese as *zuiyi congwu* (presumption of innocence in doubtful cases) was proposed by some scholars as a compromise to be included in the revision of the CPL.

The third position seems to have triumphed in the revision of the CPL. Art. 7 of the Decision Concerning the Revision of the Criminal Procedure Law adds a new provision to the CPL, which provides that 'no one shall be deemed guilty until a judgment passed by a people's court in accordance with the law'. This, according to Professor Chen Guangzhong who was in charge of drafting the revision, was designed deliberately to avoid the controversy of the doctrine.[45] Clearly, it is not a total endorsement of the presumption of innocence, but it is a significant improvement over the 1979 CPL provisions. Further, Art. 34 of the Decision designates a new term 'criminal suspect' to all persons suspected of committing crimes but before the institution of prosecution. The change of terminology reinforces the rejection of presumption of guilt, but does not necessarily support the adoption of the presumption of innocence.

---

[42] Tian 1979, p. 3.

[43] See Thieme 1984; Gellat 1982; Chen Guangzhong 1989b; Zhang, Zhang and Wang 1991; Chen Jianguo 1994; and Fan, 1994.

[44] Chen Guangzhong 1989b, p. 3; Tang 1980; Liao Zengyun 1980; Chen Guangzhong 1980.

[45] Chen and Yan 1995, p. 107.

With this compromised arrangement in the revision, it can well be expected that the principle of the presumption of innocence will continue to be controversial in China. However, if the essence of this principle is to afford better protection to the accused against over-eager prosecutors or police officials who find it easier to intimidate the accused on the basis of presumption of guilt,[46] then the practical significance of this revision will depend on the reform of other aspects of the procedure law, such as the law on evidence and the trial process. Indeed, other reforms in the revision, to be discussed further, seem to indicate a good understanding among Chinese reformers on this fundamental 'due process' principle.

Exemption from prosecution

Art. 101 of the 1979 CPL provided that '[i]n cases where, according to the provisions of the Criminal Law, it is not necessary to impose a sentence of criminal punishment or an exemption from criminal punishment may be granted, a people's procuratorate may grant Exemption from Prosecution (*mianyu qisu*)'. To grant Exemption from Prosecution, three requirements had to be met: (1) crime facts should be clear; (2) evidence should be sufficient and certain; (3) no criminal punishment is necessary or an exemption from criminal punishment might be allowed according to the Criminal Law.[47] This is what the Chinese scholars called a 'unique Chinese institution' of Exemption from Prosecution.[48] Its origin, according to a Chinese authority on CPL, could be traced to the Decision on Dealing with Detained Japanese War Criminals from the Sino-Japan War, issued by the Standing Committee of the NPC on 25 April 1956, which for the first time granted the people's procuratorate the power to exempt people from prosecution.

A decision by a people's procuratorate to exempt a person from prosecution is different from a decision not to prosecute. Art. 104 of the 1979 CPL provided that when any of the circumstances provided in Art. 11 of the CPL applied, the people's procuratorate should make a decision not to prosecute. Circumstances provided in Art. 11 include: (1) if the circumstances were clearly minor, the harm was not great, and the act was thus not deemed to be a crime; (2) if the period of limitation for prosecuting the crime had expired;

[46] Leng and Chiu 1985, p. 96.
[47] Wang, Wang and Wang 1981, pp. 213-214.
[48] Chen Guangzhong 1989b, p. 5.

(3) if an exemption from criminal punishment had been ordered in a special amnesty decree; (4) if, according to the Criminal Law, a crime was to be handled only upon complaint and there had been no complaint or the complaint had been withdrawn; (5) if the defendant was deceased; or (6) if other laws or decrees provided for exemption from investigation of criminal responsibility.

The difference between a decision to exempt someone from prosecution and a decision not to prosecute is that the person exempted from prosecution was guilty of a crime but was exempted from punishment whereas in the latter case, the person was not guilty of any crime or the law would not pursue any criminal punishment on specific legal grounds.[49] The problem was then clear, as pointed out by Gellat, the public prosecutor rendered a decision on guilt, usurping the role of the courts and acting before the suspect was legally entitled to counsel.[50] Further, in cases where the investigation was conducted by the procuracy, the people's procuratorate assumed all three functions – investigation, prosecution, and adjudication – which were clearly required by the CPL to be divided among the three law enforcement organs: the public security, the procuratorate and the court (Art. 5 of the 1979 CPL). The Exemption from Prosecution also lacked supervision, which then led to its abuse when it was employed to exempt persons from prosecution or to record an Exemption from Prosecution for innocent people which had severe repercussions on their lives.[51]

For these reasons, calls to abolish such a practice had been aired and debated in China for some time. The debate was heated but inconclusive.[52] Opponents of the abolition arguments asserted that such a practice was a reflection of the judicial policy of 'combining punishment with leniency (*chengban yü kuanda xiangjiehe*)', that it was only an exercise of discretionary power by the procuracy and it was economically efficient.[53] Similar to the debate on the presumption of innocence, a compromised solution was proposed during the revision process. This solution involved the abolition of the Exemption from Prosecution and, at the same time, the expansion of

---

[49]Wang, Wang and Wang 1981, p. 215.

[50]Lawyers' Committee for Human Rights 1993, p. 21.

[51]Cui 1996, p. 6; Shi 1995, p. 33; and Lawyers' Committee for Human Rights 1993, pp. 24-25.

[52]Chen Guangzhong 1989b, p. 5; Xu 1989; Song and Wu 1992; Wang Mingyuan 1992; Shi 1995; Wang Hongxiang 1994; Cui 1994.

[53]See Chen Guangzhong 1989b, p. 5; Cui 1995, p. 95; Huang Taiyun 1996, pp. 36-37.

the scope of decisions not to prosecute.[54] Again, the compromised solution was adopted. Articles 58-61 of the Decision Concerning the Revision of the Criminal Procedure Law have now abolished the Exemption from Prosecution. The scope of decisions not to prosecute under Art. 104 of the 1979 CPL has now been expanded to include cases 'where the circumstances of crime are minor and, according to the Criminal Law, where it is not necessary to impose a sentence of criminal punishment or criminal liability'(Art. 58 of the Decision Concerning the Revision of the Criminal Procedure Law).

Although the abolition is a step forward, the compromised solution is not without fundamental problems. The major problems with the Exemption from Prosecution identified by the NPC's Standing Committee include, first, the fact that the practice of Exemption from Prosecution violated principles of Rule of Law as a person was deemed guilty without adjudication by a court; and second, the fact that innocent persons were given Exemption from Prosecution which then violated lawful rights of the persons concerned, while others who deserved criminal punishment were exempted from prosecution.[55] Under the new provision, a person whom the procuracy decides not to prosecute can nevertheless be seen as being guilty of minor crime and this guilty verdict is not delivered by a court. Further, the phrase 'where the circumstances of crime are minor' is subject to interpretation in practice. There is then no guarantee that 'persons who deserve criminal punishment' will not escape from prosecution. Thus, the actual operation of the new provision may easily defeat the original intention of the revision of the law in this regard. It may also severely undermine the new provision on the compromised provision on the presumption of innocence.

Right to counsel

The 1982 Constitution provides for an ambivalent right of defense. Art. 125 states, 'All cases handled by the people's courts, except for those involving special circumstances as specified by law, shall be heard in public. The accused has the right of defense'. Literally, it is unclear in the Chinese language (*youquan huode bianhu*) whether such a right of defense includes a right to counsel, although it does in practice. More importantly, it is unclear whether such a right is only limited to trial in court or also allowed during pre-trial investigation.

---

[54] Huang Taiyun 1996, p. 37; and Cui 1995, p. 95.

[55] Gu 1996, p. 89.

More detailed rules regarding the right of defense were provided in the CPL. Art. 8 of the 1979 CPL repeated the above constitutional clause but further added that 'the people's courts have the duty to guarantee that defendants obtain defense'. The right to counsel – a lawyer, or relative or other citizens – was specifically provided for by Art. 26 of the 1979 CPL. However, the 1979 CPL was again silent on whether the defendant had a right to counsel in pre-trial processes; the 1979 CPL only provided that the court was required, seven days before the opening of the court session, to deliver to the defendant a copy of the bill of prosecution and to inform him/her that he/she might appoint a defender, or, when necessary, to designate a defender for the defendant (Art. 110). Although a right to counsel before trial was not guaranteed by the law, it is difficult to see any technical barrier to defenders' participation in pre-trial investigations. Chinese scholars, however, interpreted Art. 110 to mean that defenders were only allowed to enter into criminal process seven days before the trial.[56] It is clearly a usual practice that defense lawyers are only involved in criminal process several days before the trial.[57]

The inadequate protection for timely access to a defense lawyer has long been a concern to Chinese scholars.[58] Although the issue has been hotly debated in recent years, the controversial point was not whether lawyers should be allowed earlier participation in the criminal process, but how much earlier they should be allowed.[59] Not surprisingly, the major opposition to lawyers' early participation came from investigatory organs. They argued that early participation of lawyers in the criminal process would unduly interfere with investigatory conduct, particularly the secretive investigation.[60] In response to such a concern from the investigatory organs, a compromise was proposed: lawyers should be allowed early participation, ideally, immediately after the initial questioning of the accused by the public security officials, but such participation should be limited to providing legal assistance and collecting materials for defense. Further, certain supervisory powers should be granted to the public security organs in controlling the defendants' access to lawyers.[61]

[56]Zhang Wei 1994, p. 39; Chen and Xiong 1995a, p. 92.

[57]Leng and Chiu 1985, p. 92; Lawyers' Committee for Human Rights 1993, pp. 29-30; and Zhang and Chen 1990, p. 43.

[58]Chen Guangzhong 1989a, p. 13.

[59]Chen Guangzhong 1989a, p. 13; Hong 1996, p. 15; Huang 1996, p. 34; Zhang and Chen 1990, p. 43; Zhang Wei 1994, p. 39.

[60]See Lawyers' Committee for Human Rights 1993, pp. 36-37.

[61]Chen and Xiong 1995, p. 93; Li Baoyue 1994, p. 100; and Xu 1996, p. 92.

Again, the NPC decided to accept the compromised solution. Art. 41 of the Decision Concerning the Revision of the Criminal Law adds a new provision, as Art. 96 of the revised CPL, which provides: 'After the first questioning or the imposition of coercive measures, a criminal suspect has a right to appoint a lawyer to provide him/her legal consultation, to present petitions (*shensu*) or complaints (*konggao*) on his/her behalf. When a suspect is arrested, the appointed lawyer may apply for bail (obtaining a guarantor and awaiting trial out of custody, *qubao houshen*) on his/her behalf. When the case involves state secrets, the appointment of a lawyer by the suspect must be approved by the investigatory organs'. This article further provides: 'The appointed lawyer has a right to inquire about the charges against his client with the investigatory organ and may interview the suspect under detention to acquaint himself/herself with the circumstances of the case. When interviewing the suspect under detention, the investigatory organ may, according to the circumstances and the needs of the case, have representatives present. When the case involves state secrets, the interview of the suspect by a lawyer must be approved by the investigatory organ'. To strengthen the right to defense counsel, Art. 16 of the Decision adds a new provision to Art. 26 of the 1979 CPL as the new Art. 33 of the revised CPL which provides, 'In a case of public prosecution, a criminal suspect has a right to appoint a defense counsel when his/her case is transferred [to the people's procuratorate] for review and prosecution. The accused in cases of private prosecution may appoint a defense counsel at any time'. This revised article also imposes an obligation on the people's procuratorate to inform the accused of his right to appoint a defense counsel in cases of public prosecution within three days of receiving the case from an investigatory organ and an obligation on the people's court to inform the same in cases of private prosecution within three days of accepting the private prosecution. The rights of a defense lawyer are provided in the new Art. 36 (revising Art. 29 of the 1979 CPL): 'When the people's procuratorate begins to review and prosecute a case, a defense lawyer may consult, abstract and copy prosecution materials and other expert and technical assessment materials in relation to the case. He/she may also interview and correspond with the criminal suspect. Other defense counsels may also, with the permission of the people's procuratorate, consult, abstract and copy prosecution materials and other expert and technical assessment materials in relation to the case, and interview and correspond with the criminal suspect.' This article also provides similar rights for defense counsel after the court has accepted the case for adjudication. Two more articles (Arts. 37 and 38 of the revised CPL) are added by Art. 20 of the Decision which empower the defense lawyer to collect relevant materials from witnesses, crime victims and their relatives and other persons and impose an obligation on the defense lawyer not to help the crime suspects or the accused to conceal or destroy evidence or to obtain or alter evidence by threat or inducement or any other activities which interfere with judicial proceedings.

The above provisions apparently try to distinguish the roles of the defense lawyer during investigation and after prosecution, and limit the scope of activities of the defense lawyer during investigation. The rationale, according to Chinese scholars, is to strike a balance between the protection of citizens' rights and the prevention of interference with criminal investigation.[62] However, a range of discretionary powers have been granted to the investigatory organs, such as the presence of personnel from investigatory organs in interviews and the approval of appointment of lawyers in cases involving 'state secrets'. The question which then remains is the extent to which these powers will be exercised in good faith.

The trial process

The trial process, both on paper and in practice, had been flawed since it was re-institutionalized by the 1979 CPL. Its problems ranged from the passive role of lawyers to the lack of judicial independence, starting from the preliminary examination to the making of judgments. A Chinese scholar recently criticized the trial process thus:

> Many shortcomings of the criminal trial process have been documented. For instance, the practice of judges reviewing, examining and discussing the case based on materials supplied by the procuracy before the trial has led to prejudice of judges and the consequence of 'verdict first, trial second' (*xian ding hou shen*). The discussion and decision by the judicial committee and the practice of first instance court seeking instructions from higher court have caused the problems of 'trial judges not making decisions and decision-makers not trying the case' (*shenzhe bu pan, panzhe bu shen*) and 'higher court deciding and lower court delivering' (*shangpi xiapan*). Because judges are required to present evidence to prove the guilt of the accused, there is the phenomenon of 'non-separation between adjudicature and prosecution' (*kong shen bu feng*) and 'the *ultra virus* of adjudicature' (*shenpan yuewei*), etc. All

[62] Huang 1996, p. 35.

> these practices weaken, or even diminish the function of defense, thus rendering court trial a formality only.[63]

Some Chinese scholars thus describe the trial process as a process of legitimizing the conclusion which had already been drawn before the trial.[64] Such a practice then led to a judicial reality: the presumption of guilt.[65]

These problems are deeply rooted in the fundamental political system (e.g. the lack of judicial independence) and the lack of established legal tradition (e.g. the minimum role played by lawyers in society and litigation). However, the majority of Chinese scholars blamed the inquisitorial system for causing such problems. According to them, the inquisitorial system China adopted was an 'extreme' one in which judges played an extremely active and powerful role both in preliminary examination and in the actual trial process.[66] Thus the debate on reforming the trial process had been centered on merits and shortcomings of inquisitorial and adversarial systems and the comparison between the two.[67] Though there were scholars advocating a wholesale adoption of the adversarial system and those strongly resisting such a move, many scholars soon agreed that adopting certain elements from the adversarial system was an appropriate approach in the reform of the trial process.[68] This approach was then adopted by the NPC.

Four major changes are made by the revision. First, under Art. 108 of the 1979 CPL, a court would open a session and adjudicate the case only if, after preliminary examination of the case initiated by the public prosecution, the court had decided that the facts of the crime were clear and the evidence was complete. If the principal facts were not clear and the evidence insufficient, the court might remand the case to the people's procuratorate for supplementary investigation. It is these requirements that led to the practice of 'verdict first, adjudicate second'. Now the new provision, Art. 150 of the revised CPL, provides that a court shall open its session and adjudicate the case if the bill of prosecution contains alleged crime facts, a list of evidence,

[63] Zhang Zhiming 1995, pp. 94-95; see also Li Jianmin 1995, p. 85; Huang 1996, p. 37; Xie 1996, pp. 10-11; Leng and Chiu 1985, Chapter Five; and Lawyers' Committee for Human Rights 1993, pp. 38–60.

[64] Chen and Xiong 1995b, p. 85; Hong 1996, p. 56.

[65] Li Xuekuan 1995, p. 94.

[66] Xie 1996, p. 11; Zhang Zhiming 1995, p. 94.

[67] Chen Guangzhong 1993; Li Jianmin 1995; Zhang Zhiming 1995; Wang Shaonan 1995; Zhang Xiu 1996.

[68] Zhang Zhiming 1995; Wang and Liu 1996; Xie 1996; Chen and Xiong 1995b.

names of witnesses and copies or photos of principal evidence. This provision then substantially reduces the extent of preliminary examination by the court; the question of sufficiency of evidence is now a matter for debate and determination during a court session. Further, supplementary investigation is not to be initiated by a court. An application is to be made by the procuracy for which approval has to be given by a court during court session. The maximum period allowed for supplementary investigation is limited to one month (Arts. 165 and 166 of the revised CPL). Second, the functions of the collegiate panel and the judicial committee are redefined. Under the original CPL, cases other than minor criminal matters were required to be adjudicated by a collegiate panel consisting of judges and people's assessors (Art. 105 of the 1979 CPL). However, judicial committees have been established at all levels of the people's court (Art. 11 of the 1979 Organic Law of People's Courts). Their functions were vaguely defined as that of 'summing up judicial experience and discussing important or difficult cases and other issues relating to the judicial work'. Under Art. 107 of the 1979 CPL, all major and difficult cases were to be submitted to the judicial committee for discussion and decision and the collegiate panel must carry out the decisions of the committee. Other than this, the CPL was silent on the relationship between the collegiate panel and the judicial committee. In reality, many courts relied on the judicial committees to discuss and decide cases regardless of the importance of the cases concerned and sometimes before a trial by court.[69] Under Art. 149 of the revised CPL, after deliberation a collegiate panel must render a judgment. Only when the collegiate panel decides that it is unable to make a decision in difficult, major or complex cases may it request the president of the court to transfer the case to the judicial committee for discussion and decision. In other words, cases will not be decided by a judicial committee before trial and difficult, major or complex cases will no longer be automatically submitted to the judicial committee for deliberation and decision. This provision then is supposed to resolve the problem of 'trial judges not making decisions and decision-makers not trying the case'.[70] Third, instead of the trial judge presenting evidence to the court and questioning the witnesses, the revised CPL now requires the prosecutors and defenders to present evidence to the court, and questioning and debating on the evidence and the alleged crime facts will be mainly left to the prosecutors and the defenders

[69] China University of Political Science and Law 1987, pp. 205-206.
[70] Cui 1996, p. 6.

(Arts. 155-161 of the revised CPL). In short, the trial judges will be taking a much more passive role, concerning themselves mainly with the maintenance of court order and orderly debate, thus leaving much more room for meaningful defense. Finally, a new summary procedure has been established to deal with minor criminal offenses (Arts. 174-179 of the revised CPL). This would allow the court to concentrate its human and other resources on the more adversarial proceedings which would certainly be more time-consuming and, perhaps, financially more expensive.

With these revisions being made, there is little doubt that the quality of trial will improve considerably. However, a crucial issue relating to the quality of court trial has not been addressed, that is the issue of judicial independence – the 'most glaring deficiency in the PRC's trial process'.[71] Judicial independence has been a subject of debate since the 1950s in the PRC.[72] The 1954 Constitution – the first Constitution in the PRC – provided: 'people's courts shall conduct adjudication independently and shall be subject only to the law' (Art. 78 of the 1954 Constitution). However, advocating judicial independence was denounced as a Rightist thought and severely criticized in the late 1950s and during the Cultural Revolution. The 1975 and 1978 Constitutions thus abolished the 1954 provision. The present Constitution – the 1982 Constitution - stipulates an ambiguous principle: 'The people's courts shall, in accordance with the law, exercise judicial power independently and are not subject to interference by administrative organs, public organizations or individuals' (Art. 126 of the 1982 Constitution, also Art. 4 of the 1979 Organic Law of the People's Courts). On the other hand, the 1982 Constitution promulgates the so-called Four Fundamental Principles, among which is the upholding of the leadership of the Communist Party. This constitutional arrangement, particularly when compared with the 1954 constitutional provision, seems to suggest that judicial independence, if any, is subject to Party leadership. Indeed, Party control of the judiciary has been constantly asserted in China. Sometimes this involves the requirement of Party approval for specific cases,[73] despite the fact that a review and approval system by Party committee was officially abolished in 1979.[74]

---

[71] Lawyers' Committee for Human Rights 1993, p. 52.

[72] Cohen 1969; Koguchi 1987; Woo 1991.

[73] Chen Guangzhong 1989a, pp. 11-12; Bian 1995, p. 97.

[74] Leng and Chiu 1985, p. 99. The Party Review and Approval System was abolished by the Instruction of the Central Committee of the Chinese Communist

The 1979 CPL was silent on the issue of judicial independence. Scholars thus proposed that the 1954 constitutional provision be inserted into the revised CPL.[75] The NPC, however, opted to repeat the 1982 constitutional provision in the revision (Art. 5 of the revised CPL). With the issue of judicial independence unresolved, the effect of the reforms discussed above in the trial process is doubtful, as many of the problems identified by Chinese scholars are, in one way or another, linked with Party intervention in criminal adjudication, especially in politically sensitive cases and in rural areas.

Other revisions

A number of other revisions are also notable. The scope of cases to be directly investigated by the people's procuratorates has been narrowed (Art. 18 of the revised CPL). The status of crime victims is now defined and certain rights in the trial process provided (Arts. 37, 40-41, 82, 87-88, 145, and 182 of the revised CPL). Further, the function of judicial supervision in criminal process by the people's procuratorates is strengthened (Arts. 8, 87, 112, and 169 of the revised CPL). Finally, the 1979 Regulation on Detention and Arrest, together with the highly criticized Decision of the Standing Committee of the NPC on the Procedures for Rapid Adjudication of Cases Involving Criminal Elements Who Seriously Endanger Public Security (1983), and the Supplementary Provisions of the Standing Committee of the NPC Regarding the Question of the Time Limits for Handling Criminal Cases (1984), were abolished when the revised CPL came into effect on 1 January 1997.

Principal revision of the Criminal Law

An overview

Following the German model, the 1979 Criminal Law was divided into two parts: General Principles (*zongze*) and Specific Provisions (*fenze*). The General Principles define the purposes and scope of the Law' application as well as notions of crime and criminal liabilities. They also provide rules on sentencing, parole and statutory

Party Concerning the Full Implementation of the Criminal Law and Criminal Procedure Law.

[75]Cui 1995, p. 94.

limitations. The Specific Provisions then define and elaborate various crimes and offenses and their consequent penalties. This overall structure is retained in the 1997 revised Criminal Law.

The structure of the first part, the General Principles, is intact and revision to the provisions of this part is minimal. However, the incorporation of some fundamental principles of justice into the General Principles constitutes the most significant progress and development of criminal law since 1979.

Nullum crimen, nulla poena sine lege and the abolition of analogy

The 1979 CL did not expressly provide for the principle of *nullum crimen, nulla poena sine lege*; instead, Art. 79 allowed the application of the law by analogy subject to the approval of the Supreme People's Court. Many Chinese scholars and officials have, however, insisted that *nullum crimen, nulla poena sine lege* or its 'spirit' was one of the basic principles of Chinese criminal law.[76] The existence of analogy was said to be supplementary to the Law and represented a flexible application of the 'old and rigid' principle of *nullum crimen, nulla poena sine lege.*

This Chinese argument is, however, not convincing. As pointed out above, the 1979 CL was based on the 33rd draft of 1963, which itself was developed from various drafts completed in the 1950s and early 1960s. The principle of *nullum crimen, nulla poena sine lege* has been severely criticized since the Judicial Reform Movement in 1952 as one of the bourgeois legal principles that gave aid and comfort to the landlords and counter-revolutionaries at the expense of public interest and, as such, had to be rejected by socialist law.[77] The discussion on this principle did not resume until after the promulgation of the 1979 Law. Further, the use of analogy is conceptually inconsistent with the principle of *nullum crimen, nulla poena sine lege.*

Analogy was an ancient legal institution in China. According to Shen Jiaben, the founding father of modern law reform in China, the practice of interpreting the law by analogy started in the Han Dynasty (206 – 8 bc) and was sanctioned by law in the Sui Dynasty

[76]Wang Hanbin 1997, p. 672; Su 1994, p. 32; Huang and Teng 1997, p. 4; Ma and Ding 1995, pp. 31-32.

[77]Leng 1967, pp. 160 and 176; Cohen 1968, p. 330.

(589 – 618 ad).[78] However, as the conservatives who opposed the abolition of analogy had argued, the practice had perhaps started much earlier.[79] Meijer apparently agreed that the argument based on the *Li Ji* and the *Book of History* by the conservatives was more accurate.[80] It is clear, however, that analogy was codified in the earliest extant written code, the Tang Code (*Tang Lü Shuyi*, first published in 753 AD).[81] The long history of the practice of analogy is thus said to have created an 'analogy complex' in the Chinese mentality.[82] The nature and the actual use of analogy in traditional China, namely to create new categories of crimes retrospectively or simply to elaborate the 'most appropriate' punishment, are however disputed among scholars.[83]

In spite of strong opposition from conservative forces,[84] analogy was formally abolished and the principle *nullum crimen, nulla poena sine lege* introduced into Chinese criminal law during the law reform in the dying days of the Qing Dynasty.[85]

The Chinese communist justice system did not accept the principle of *nullum crimen, nulla poena sine lege*; the Statute of the Chinese Soviet Republic on Punishment of Counter-revolutionary Crimes – the first comprehensive legislation under the communist rule defining criminal acts – explicitly revived the application of law by analogy (Art. 38). The principle of analogy was reaffirmed by the first comprehensive criminal law in the PRC, the 1951 Regulations of the PRC on the Punishment of Counter-revolutionary Crimes (Art. 16).

---

[78] Meijer 1967, pp. 195-196. A similar view is also held by some modern scholars. See for instance, Buck 1993, p. 117.

[79] Meijer 1967, p. 94.

[80] *Idem*, p. 68.

[81] Buck 1993, p. 117.

[82] Chen Xingliang 1996, p. 40.

[83] Buck 1993, p. 117. One of the authorities on traditional Chinese penal law, Professor MacCormack, clearly holds the view that the reasoning by analogy employed by the imperial judicial officials was similar to statutory interpretation in the West and was not in conflict with the principle *nulla poena sine lege*. See MacCormack 1996, pp. 172–174.

[84] Meijer 1967, p. 94.

[85] Art. 3 of the Chapter on Rights and Duties of the Subjects of the Principles of Constitution (1908, never formally promulgated) for the first time in Chinese history provided: 'A subject shall not be liable to arrest, imprisonment or punishment except as prescribed by law'. The New Criminal Law issued by the Qing government in 1910 for the first time formally provided in a law the principle of *nullum crimen sine lege* (Art. 10 thus contained the principle of 'no offense, no punishment without previous legal provision'. See Meijer 1967, p. 71.) Art. 1 of the Criminal Code of the KMT issued in 1935 provided the same. See Chen Xingliang 1996, p. 39.

Abolition of analogy only began to be hotly debated in the 1950s and, again, in the 1980s.[86] Central to the debate were differing interpretations of the three major issues: the legal position and the trend towards the *nullum crimen, nulla poena sine lege* in the world's major legal systems, the possibility of the coexistence of *nullum crimen, nulla poena sine lege* with analogy, and preference in cases of conflict between *nullum crimen, nulla poena sine lege* and analogy.[87] Those who argued for the abolition of analogy believed strongly that *nullum crimen, nulla poena sine lege* was a universal principle upheld in all major countries under the Rule of Law, that *nullum crimen, nulla poena sine lege* and analogy were mutually exclusive and, thus, the upholding of *nullum crimen, nulla poena sine lege* necessarily required the abolition of analogy in criminal law.[88] Opponents were not convinced by these arguments, believing that the impossibility of making a perfect criminal code necessarily required the application of the law by analogy. They also believed that *nullum crimen, nulla poena sine lege* was not a principle in Common Law countries and its importance had decreased in all other countries.[89]

The final decision to abolish analogy was perhaps influenced by the fact that, first, the revised CL, after incorporating various supplements and decisions in the last eighteen years, would become relatively comprehensive and the coverage of the Law would be greatly expanded. Secondly, Art. 79 on analogy in the 1979 Law had been rarely used by courts. Thus it was deemed possible and necessary to abolish analogy and to incorporate *nullum crimen, nulla poena sine lege* into the revised law.[90]

According to Art. 3 of the revised Criminal Law, 'All criminal acts expressly stipulated by law as crimes shall be determined as such and punished according to the law; acts not expressly defined by law as criminal shall not be judged so and shall not be punished'.

---

[86] Up to the mid-1980s, scholarly discussion on analogy mainly concentrated on the justification and the proper use of analogy; there was only some isolated discussion on abolishing it. See Gao 1986, pp. 126–137; and Zhao and Xiao 1996.

[87] Zhao and Xiao 1996, p. 57.

[88] Zhao and Xiao 1996; Hu 1995; and Chen Xingliang 1996.

[89] Hou 1995.

[90] Wang Hanbin 1997, p. 672. According to Chinese scholars, in the eighteen years of implementation of the 1979 Criminal Law only a little more than seventy cases were decided by analogy and most of them concerned minor offenses. See Ma and Ding 1995, p. 7; Hou 1995, p. 64.

Equality before the law and Marxism-Leninism-Mao Zedong Thought as a guiding ideology for Criminal Law

Art. 4 of the 1979 Criminal Procedure Law which was issued at the same time as the 1979 Criminal Law provided: 'All citizens are equal in the application of the Law. No privilege whatsoever is permissible before the Law.' This principle of 'equality before the law' was not however provided in the 1979 Criminal Law.

The omission of this principle was perhaps attributed to the upholding of Marxism-Leninism-Mao Zedong Thought as the guiding ideology for criminal law (Art. 1 of the 1979 CL), which strongly emphasized the class nature of law. Under this ideology, criminal law was an important weapon for class struggle, aimed primarily at attacking counter-revolutionaries and other criminals who seriously undermined social order and socialist construction.[91] According to Mao's theory on correctly handling two kinds of social contradictions, i. e. contradictions between the enemies and the people and those among the people,[92] criminals are mainly enemies of the state who must be dealt with severely by criminal law. The 'people', though they may also be punished by the criminal law, must be treated differently from the 'enemies'. Under this ideology, it was not surprising that equality before the law was repudiated as an anti-Party bourgeois concept in the late 1950s and during the Cultural Revolution.[93]

Equality before the law as a legal principle re-emerged in the post-Mao era. However, there were also heated debates in the late 1970s and early 1980s as to whether equality before the law meant only equality in the application of the law or also included the making of law. Further, the major reason for upholding the principle was to prevent privilege being accorded to officials of all ranks; that is, the law was to fight tigers and flies alike. The emphasis was perhaps not as much on protection as on punishment.[94] Thus the principle was not included in the substantive law (the CL) but was incorporated into procedural (the CPL) or organic laws (the Organic Laws of the Court and the Procuratorate). The debate in the late 1970s and early 1980s also led to the reinstatement of the equality principle in the 1982 Constitution (Art. 33 of the 1982 Constitution).

---

[91] Cohen 1968, pp. 71–96.

[92] For Mao's theory, see his thesis on Problems Relating to the Correct Handling of Contradictions among the People, translated in Cohen 1968, pp. 83–88.

[93] Leng and Chiu 1985, p. 104.

[94] Office for Research Materials 1981; also Leng and Chiu 1985, pp. 104–108.

The new Art. 4 of the revised CL now provides: 'All are equal in the application of law. No privilege whatsoever is permissible beyond the law'. Like the previous equality provisions in other laws, the emphasis is on application of law and on the elimination of official privileges.[95] It is also important to note that Marxism-Leninism-Mao Zedong Thought as a guiding principle of criminal law has now been formally abandoned, which perhaps means finally burying the class nature of criminal law.[96]

Proportionality (Zuixing Xiang Shiying)

One of the guiding principles incorporated in the 1979 CL was the policy of combining punishment with leniency (Art. 1 of the 1979 CL), which meant 'leniency to those who confess and severity to those who resist' in the determination of sentence.[97] However the 1979 Law did not provide specific aggravating and mitigating circumstances to guide the court in sentence determination. Such an arrangement was to allow the law enforcement to adapt to the needs of the political situation of the time concerned.[98] Similar to the concerns regarding equality before the law, such a policy can provide, and has provided, loopholes in the law for officials in power to escape legal sanctions or avoid severe punishment.[99] Further, the emphasis on confession is also potentially in conflict with the presumption of innocence.

Similar to the fate of Marxism-Leninism-Mao Zedong Thought as a guiding principle, the principle of combining punishment with leniency has also been abandoned. Art. 5 of the revised Criminal Law now provides: 'The severity or leniency of punishment shall be proportionate to the crimes committed by the criminal and its consequent criminal liabilities [prescribed by law]'.

However, the revised CL continues to be weak in terms of elaborate and detailed provisions on aggravating and mitigating circumstances. Thus a proper application of the principle of proportionality will be a crucial point in the future operation of the CL.

---

[95] See Huang and Teng 1997, pp. 4-5.

[96] Chinese scholars have, however, insisted that, since the Four Fundamental Principles are constitutional principles, the CL issued under the Constitution would logically still include this principle. See Huang and Teng 1997, p. 1.

[97] Leng and Chiu 1985, p. 129.

[98] Leng and Chiu 1985, p. 129.

[99] Zhang Jun 1997.

'White collar' crimes – 'unit criminality' (danwei fanzui)

The development of the concept of corporations as legal persons in all legal systems has taken a long, difficult and slow path. A corporation as an abstraction is conceptually without its own mind or physical existence. The Chinese legal system is no exception. When the CL was enacted in 1979, it did not expressly provide for, nor absolutely exclude, criminal responsibility of a legal person. Some provisions seemed to hold only the individual liable (e.g. Art. 131); other provisions tended to hold both the legal person and the individual liable (e.g. Art. 121).

With the emergence of economic crimes committed by enterprises as a result of economic reforms, Chinese attitude and practice towards corporate criminality began to change. The judiciary led the way to affirm the criminality of legal persons when committing certain economic crimes.[100] The legislature followed suit.[101] Although legislative and judicial developments seemed to affirm corporate criminality, there was no law regarding a general concept of crime committed by legal persons nor general guidelines for the criminality of legal persons. Nor were there any procedural rules concerning the prosecution of legal persons. It was still unclear whether a legal person, in general, could be a defendant in criminal procedures.

The 1997 revised code now contains a new section, entitled 'Unit Crimes' (*Danwei Fanzui*) in Chapter One of the General Part. Art. 30 of the revised CL now provides: 'When companies, enterprises, institutions, state organs and social organizations commit crimes endangering the society, they shall assume criminal liability when prescribed by the law'. Art. 31 further provides: 'When a unit commits a crime, it shall be fined. At the same time, the person in charge of the unit and other directly responsible persons shall be punished by the criminal law unless otherwise provided by the Specific Provisions of the Law or by other laws'. Eighty-one articles in the Specific Provisions of the revised CL now mention unit criminality.[102] It should be pointed out that the revised CL uses the term 'unit crime' instead

[100] See the Resolutions of the Supreme People's Court and the Supreme People's Procuratorate Concerning Certain Questions on the Practical Application of the Law in the Present Adjudication of Cases of Economic Crimes (Trial Implementation) (1985).

[101] See Arts. 49 and 110 of the General Principles of Civil Law (1986); Art. 47 (3) of the Customs Law (1987), and many other national laws. By 1997, no fewer than thirteen Decisions and Supplementary Provisions had provided for corporate criminality; Lin and Jia 1997, p. 81.

[102] Based on my own calculation.

of 'corporate crime'. The reason is that many organizations are not necessarily corporations but may nevertheless commit a criminal offense; thus the term 'unit' encompasses not only companies, but also other unincorporated organizations.[103]

Crime and punishment

An overview

The Chinese CL defines any act which endangers state sovereignty and territorial integrity and security, divides the state, jeopardizes the political powers of the people's democratic dictatorship and socialist system, undermines social and economic orders, encroaches upon state property, collective property of the working masses or the privately owned property of the citizens, infringes upon the personal, democratic and other rights of the citizens, or any other act which endangers society and is punishable according to law, as a criminal offense, except those offenses which are obviously of a minor nature and cause negligible harm (Art. 13 of the revised CL).[104] Following this definition and according to Chinese jurisprudence, there are three basic criteria for determining criminality. First, a criminal offense is an act that endangers society. Second, such an act violates the criminal law. Third, such an act is punishable by the criminal law.[105] Chinese law also requires the existence of *mens rea* (either intention or criminal negligence); an act which results in harmful consequences due to unavoidable or unforeseeable factors rather than due to intention or negligence, is not a criminal offense (Arts. 14–16 of the revised CL).

These provisions defining the concept of crime are not substantially revised; nor are the original eight types of crimes stipulated in the 1979 CL substantially amended or supplemented.

While the structure of the law in stipulating crimes has not significantly changed, the Specific Provisions of the CL for these crimes has been vastly expanded through the incorporation of various decisions and supplementary provisions issued by the NPC in the last eighteen years or so. Thus, 'crime undermining the socialist market economic

---

[103] Liu Shengrong 1992.

[104] The original Art. 10 has been revised to abolish the more ideological terms (e.g. 'socialist revolution' and 'proletariat dictatorship' etc.) and to emphasize the protection of economic order.

[105] Huang and Teng 1997, p. 15; Leng and Chiu 1985, p. 124.

order' is further divided into eight sections dealing with eight subdivisions while 'crime disrupting social order and its administration' is subdivided into nine sections. Further, 'crime against marriage or the family' is now incorporated into 'crime infringing on the personal rights or democratic rights of citizens'. At the same time, the 'crime of bribery and embezzlement' is distinguished from malfeasance and becomes an independent category of crime. Finally, and of symbolic significance, 'counter-revolutionary crime' is now renamed as 'crime against state security'. 'Crime endangering the interests of national defense' and 'crime in violation of military duties' form a new category in the criminal law through incorporation of the NPC's earlier decisions.

While the revision has achieved the aims of rationalizing the structure, systematizing the fragmented code and expanding the scope to deal with various emerging crimes, there is major disappointment concerning the reform of 'counter-revolutionary' crimes, arbitrary distinction between administrative sanctions and criminal punishment, and the death penalty.

Counter-revolutionary crimes and crimes against state security

'Counter-revolution' has always been the primary targeted crime in the Chinese communist justice system. The provisions on 'counter-revolution' in the 1979 Criminal Law were vague and sweeping, reminiscent of the 1926 Russian Criminal Code.[106] In particular, Art. 90 of the 1979 CL contained a catch-all provision which defined 'crimes of counter-revolution' as 'all acts endangering the People's Republic of China committed with the goal of overthrowing the political power of the dictatorship of the proletariat and the socialist system'. Although this provision itself did not stipulate specific penalties, the 1979 Law contained twelve articles specifying punishment for various kinds of 'counterrevolutionary crimes'. Indeed, 'counter-revolution' attracted the most severe punishment prescribed in the 1979 Criminal Law. Sixty per cent of the provisions prescribe the death penalty, 45 per cent impose life imprisonment and 37 per cent stipulate imprisonment for ten or more years for the crime of counter-revolution.[107]

Although many of the subcategories of the 'counter-revolutionary crimes' may be seen as acts endangering social order and security, such as causing explosions, setting fires etc. (Art. 100), many other

[106] Berman, Cohen and Russell 1982, pp. 252-253.
[107] Lan 1982, p. 73.

'counter-revolutionary' acts were clearly aimed at political activities, such as organizing or leading 'counter-revolutionary' groups (Art. 98), and propagandizing for and inciting the overthrow of the political power of the dictatorship of the proletariat and the socialist system (Art. 102). Indeed, the essential element of all 'counter-revolutionary' crimes is the aim of 'counter-revolution', which clearly is a political, rather than a legal concept. As such it is not surprising that provisions on 'counter-revolutionary' crimes have attracted much criticism both in China and abroad. For this reason, many socialist countries, such as North Korea, Vietnam and the former Soviet Union all replaced 'counter-revolutionary crimes' with 'crimes against the state' or some similar term many years ago.[108]

In China, discussions on redefining 'counter-revolutionary crimes' began in the mid-1980s. One of the views emerging from these discussions on abolishing this category was the recognition that the concept blurred legal acts and political views and, thus, created difficulties in judicial practice. Further, it was argued that if 'counter-revolutionary crime' is not redefined as an ordinary crime, China would not be able to pursue criminals who have escaped abroad. More recently, it was recognized that the concept of 'counter-revolution' would not be compatible with the practice of 'One Country Two Systems' – a policy meant to be implemented for the unification of Hong Kong, Macau and Taiwan.[109] The first specific sign of the introduction of the concept of crimes against state security as a substitute for counter-revolution emerged in February 1993 in the promulgation of the Law on State Security. The law was intended to curb domestic and foreign activities that pose security threats, but it did not use the term 'counter-revolution' itself.[110]

The final revision in 1997 is, however, a major disappointment. 'Counter-revolutionary crime' is indeed redefined as 'crime endangering state security' and all reference to the term 'counter-revolution' has now been deleted from the law. Essentially, however, the revision is a matter of renaming, restructuring and supplementing; the majority of the previous provisions on 'counter-revolutionary crimes' have been retained.[111] Thus, acts of inciting the overthrow of political

---

[108] Berman, Cohen and Russell 1982, p. 252.

[109] Ma and Ding 1995, p. 8; Cao and Hou 1991; Zhang and Wang 1989, pp. 242-3; Gao, Zhao and Wang 1989; Zhang Sihan 1997; Lawyers' Committee for Human Rights 1993, p. 79.

[110] Lawyers' Committee for Human Rights 1993, p. 80.

[111] Although the total number of provisions in this chapter has been reduced from fifteen to twelve articles, this reduction has only been achieved by removing

power and the socialist system continue to be a major crime in the revised law (Art. 105 of the revised CL). The ambiguous provision on the crime of colluding with foreign states in plotting to harm the sovereignty, territorial integrity and security of the state remains, as does the vague provision on the crime of stealing, secretly gathering or providing state secrets and intelligence for foreign organizations or foreigners (Arts. 102 and 111 of the revised CL). The revised law also adds a provision to make it a crime for state personnel who desert their position and escape to foreign countries to engage in activities endangering state security (Art. 109 of the revised CL). Apparently, this provision is aimed at those who were sent to work or study abroad and then decided to stay by, for example, applying for refugee status in a foreign country. In China's own words, these provisions are aimed at acts of joint efforts to Westernize China.[112]

The punishment for these crimes continues to be very harsh. Offenders of the majority of the twelve crimes endangering state security face the death penalty. In addition, confiscation of property is applicable to all twelve crimes endangering state security (Arts. 102-113 of the revised CL).

Administrative sanctions versus criminal punishments

One of the major problems in the Chinese criminal justice system is its artificial and arbitrary distinction between administrative sanctions and criminal punishments. This distinction has caused many problems in human rights' protection as the imposition of administrative sanctions is beyond the control of due process and the supervision of the judiciary. Among the most criticized institutions of administrative sanctions are the previously discussed Shelter and Investigation (*shourong shencha*), and Re-education-through-Labor (*laojiao*). Shelter and Investigation was formally abolished in 1996. During the revision of the Criminal Law, suggestions were made by scholars to have the *laojiao* system reformed or abolished.[113] The *laojiao* system was first initiated by the Communist Party Central Committee as a measure to combine labor and education to deal with 'historical counter-revolutionaries' and other 'bad elements' of the society.[114] It

some provisions to chapters on crimes endangering public security and crimes against social order and administration. See Wang Hanbin 1997, p. 675.

[112] Zhang Sihan 1997.

[113] Tao 1995; Chen Xingliang 1997, pp. 56–60.

[114] Instructions on Completely Wiping Out Hidden Counter-revolutionary Elements, issued by the Central Committee of the Communist Party of China in 1955.

was then formally established by the State Council Decision relating to *Laojiao* Problems and regulated by the Supplementary Regulations of the State Council on *Laojiao*.[115] The regulations were implemented by the Ministry of Public Security through the Trial Implementation Measures on *Laojiao*, issued in January 1982. Under this regime of regulation, *laojiao* has been used to detain people whose offense is not serious enough to warrant criminal punishment yet too serious to be dealt with under the Regulations on Punishment for Social Order Administration. Although theoretically not a criminal penalty, a person can be detained for up to four years by a decision of a local *Laojiao* Administration Committee comprising representatives from the bureaux of civil administration, labor and justice, but in fact mainly administered by the local public security organs.[116] Clearly it is arbitrary to define such loss of freedom as administrative sanctions. The legality of such an institution was openly questioned in 1996 when the NPC adopted the Law on Administrative Penalties. Art. 9 of the Law provides specifically that all restraints of personal freedom must be prescribed by law. Art. 10 then adds that administrative rules and regulations can only prescribe penalties other than the restraint of personal freedoms. Since the State Council is only constitutionally empowered to issue administrative rules and regulations, the legal basis for *laojiao* is clearly questionable. Thus it was suggested that *laojiao* should either be abolished or be absorbed into the CL by establishing a new category of punishment, namely, police orders (similar to community-based orders in the West).[117] These opinions were ignored by the authorities, and the revision of the CL chose not to deal with the issue of *laojiao* at all.

The death penalty

Reflecting the idea of relying heavily on criminal punishment to maintain social stability and order, the death penalty was widely prescribed in imperial Chinese codes and frequently used in practice.[118] The reduction of the death penalty thus became one of the major aspects of criminal law reform at the turn of this century. The Qing reform managed to reduce capital offenses from more than 800 in total

[115]The Decision was issued in August 1957 and re-published in November 1979. The Supplementary Regulations were issued in November 1979.

[116]Tao 1995, p. 12.

[117]Chen Xingliang 1997, pp. 56–60.

[118]Davis 1987, pp. 306–308.

to about twenty.[119] The KMT governments continued the reform regarding the death penalty; the various criminal codes issued by different governments retained about twenty offenses, most of which related to violent crimes.[120] Communist justice began with a show of violence and frequent summary executions, especially against 'counter-revolutionaries'. This practice carried on long after the founding of the PRC as the campaign to eliminate 'counter-revolutionaries' continued, although Mao and the authorities from time to time called for caution in the application of the death penalty.[121]

According to Peng Zhen, the 1979 Criminal Law significantly reduced the capital offenses originally contained in the previous drafts.[122] Even so, the 1979 Criminal Law prescribed twenty-eight capital offenses in fifteen articles.[123] Chinese authorities obviously realized the severity of such a penalty, and thus the death penalty with a two-year suspension period was introduced from the very early stages of the PRC's justice system.[124] At the same time, a policy of cautious application was introduced.[125] However, this policy has rarely been translated into practice; indeed, Decisions and Supplementary Provisions by the Standing Committee promulgated during various anti-crime campaigns had, by March 1997, increased the application of the death penalty to no less than eighty offenses contained in over fifty criminal law provisions.[126] Some scholars thus argued that the

[119] Ma and Ding 1995, p. 115; Meijer 1967, pp. 28–35.

[120] Ma and Ding 1995, pp. 115-116.

[121] See Peng 1992, p. 151; Kang 1991.

[122] Peng 1992, p. 151.

[123] Ma 1996, p. 5. 60 per cent of the provisions prescribing the death penalty related to the crime of counter-revolution. See Lan 1982, p. 73.

[124] The death penalty with a two-year suspension period is a unique innovation of the PRC; it is said that the idea came from Mao Zedong and formed an important contribution to the Chinese justice system. See Zhang Youyu 1985, p. 25; Kang 1991, p. 32. This policy of suspension for two years was first explained by the *People's Daily* on 1 June 1951. See Davis 1987, p. 314.

[125] Peng 1992, p. 151.

[126] Shen, p. 28; Xing 1997, p. 50. No one knows the exact number of death penalties handed down in China each year as the number is treated as a 'state secret'. It is however clear that the number has been large and on the increase for many years. In 1992 alone, Amnesty International recorded 1,891 death sentences and 1,079 executions in China, cited in Lawyers' Committee For Human Rights 1993, p. 82. One of the most recent notorious cases that has attracted international condemnation was the one concerning workers Bian Hanwu, Xu Guoming and Yan Xuerong, who were arrested for allegedly setting fire to a train during demonstrations in Shanghai in 6 June 1989. They were charged on 11 June, sentenced to death on 14 June and executed on 21 June 1989 after an appeal on 20 June to the Shanghai High People's Court. The whole process took only two

incorporation of all capital offenses into the code would make Chinese Criminal Law a 'Death Penalty Code'.[127]

If the death penalty caused concern for the authorities, it has certainly been seen as one of the areas for reform by scholars.[128] However, few Chinese scholars advocate the abolition of the death penalty, the majority of them arguing for restrictions and restraint in its use. In their view, China's reputation and international trends were among the major considerations for restraint. Although some of them advocate the gradual abolition of the death penalty, their proposed timetable simply undermined their own argument.[129] Some have pointed out that, according to statistics from one province, 90 per cent of death penalties were imposed for crimes of murder, robbery, rape, serious bodily injuries, major theft, and that only ten offenses seemed to have attracted the death penalty frequently.[130] Some further pointed to the huge room for discretion in imposing the death penalty. For instance, it was pointed out that more than twenty offenses attracted penalties ranging from criminal detention to the death penalty.[131] Many of them clearly see the death penalty as an inappropriate form of punishment for economic crimes.[132]

However, these views were not accepted by the authorities. The policy on the death penalty in the 1997 revision was neither to reduce nor to increase the death penalty.[133] This confirmed the fear of some of the scholars, that the revised criminal law resembles a 'Death Penalty Code'. Among the 542 total Articles, seventy-six mention the death penalty. Further, many of these articles deal with more than one offense, and many offenses in the revised criminal law

---

weeks. See Lawyers' Committee For Human Rights 1993, pp. 83-84. A recent Amnesty International report recorded 3,152 death sentences with 1,876 already executed in 1997. This put the number of people executed in China higher than the combined total of the rest of the world. See 'Death penalty pressure', *The Australian*, 9 September 1998, p. 10.

[127] Chu 1997, p. 53.

[128] Ma and Ding 1995, pp. 105–124; Cui and Liao 1989; Wang Fengzhi 1995; Ma 1996; Chen Xingliang 1997; Jia 1997.

[129] For instance, one scholar argued that the death penalty should be gradually abolished, but that it would take about 100 years to do so. See Ma and Ding 1995, p. 120.

[130] Chen Xingliang 1997, p. 57.

[131] Chu 1997, p. 54.

[132] Ma and Ding 1995, p. 110; Cui and Liao 1989, p. 71; Ma 1996, p. 6.

[133] Wang Hanbin 1997, p. 679. The death penalty for those under eighteen years old was however reduced to life imprisonment in order to satisfy China's international obligation under the UN Convention on the Rights of the Child which was ratified by the Standing Committee in November 1991.

are punishable by the death penalty.[134] By any criteria, it is a major disappointment in the reform of criminal law.

Concluding remarks

Legal developments in China since 1978 can be assessed from two quite different perspectives: how far China has travelled towards a Rule of Law, and how much further it has to go to achieve this.

In assessing legal reforms in China, one should also bear in mind the constraints imposed by the present political system in China. As Gellat has pointed out, 'changes in many areas beyond the legal arena will be required to bring about substantial improvements in the human rights situation in the PRC. An overarching concern is of course the subservience of the legal system to the arbitrary dictates of the Communist Party, a problem that cannot by any means be resolved solely by reforms within the legal system. Without fundamental political changes there can be no independent judiciary or an autonomous bar – key elements of the rule of law.'[135]

Finally, one must also bear in mind that adjudication by an independent institution is a relatively new development in the modern legal history of China. There was no independent judiciary in traditional China; adjudicature was part of the administration. The first modern judicature system in the European style, independent from administrative organs, was only established at the turn of this century.[136] Although the old judicial system established by the Kwomintang Government was abolished in 1949, the new one continued to be based on the European system.

In this context, the present revision to the CPL, in my view, should be seen as very positive and encouraging, rather than as half-hearted measures.[137] The compromised revision of the CPL should be understood with this background in mind.

---

[134] Based on my own examination and calculation of the revised CL.

[135] Lawyers' Committee for Human Rights 1993, p. 85.

[136] Escara 1936, pp. 242–365; Pang 1922-24; Yung 1924-26, pp. 19–31, 77-87 and 117-134.

[137] Some of the conspicuous omissions in the revision are, however, very unfortunate. For example, the revised CPL continues to be silent on the legal validity of illegally-obtained evidence (such as confession through torture etc.), despite strong advocacy by scholars to address the issue in the revision. See Cui 1995, p. 94; Yang Duan 1994. Another issue not addressed is the absence of rules against self-incrimination.

The practical significance of these revisions will depend on the future endeavor of law enforcement agents and lawyers, as a Chinese scholar has rightly pointed out that 'a just law does not guarantee the justice of law'.[138] The adoption of many of the Western practices, e.g. the presumption of innocence, early participation by lawyers, elements of the adversarial system, etc., requires a change in the approach and thinking of judicial personnel. The strengthening of the role of defense in trial, the limitation of powers of investigatory organs, and the more adversarial trial process demand higher judicial and professional standards. Effective measures must be found to prevent interference in judicial work, including interference from the Party and administrative organs. It will be crucial whether lawyers will be able to limit the operation of various qualifications and limitations now existing in the CPL on the operation of the fundamental 'due process' principles. Clearly, these qualifications and limitations have a potential to be abused by the investigatory organs. The critical issue for lawyers is to argue strongly and forcefully in order to strictly limit these qualifications and limitations to address the concerns that were raised during the debates when the CPL was under revision; they should not allow such qualifications and limitations to be used as a backdoor or loophole in the CPL to circumvent the fundamental 'due process' principles now incorporated in the law.

However, the 1997 revision to the CL is also a major disappointment by any criteria. Although the revision strives to deal with, and has been quite successful in dealing with, a number of technical deficiencies (e.g. the fragmentation of the criminal law, the vagueness and ambiguities of the provisions, and disparity of punishment meted out for criminal offenses) in the criminal justice system, it fails to address some of the fundamental problems, chief among them being 'counter-revolutionary' crimes, the artificial distinction between administrative sanctions and criminal penalties, and the death penalty. The removal of counter-revolutionary crime as a legal category may be seen as a step forward. However, the retention of most of the counter-revolutionary crime provisions, although without the subjective label of 'counter-revolution', is a major failure. The concern is whether this actually legitimizes the punishment of political crimes (e.g. advocacy for changing the socialist system) as they are now treated as 'ordinary' crimes. The problem of the artificial distinction between administrative sanctions and criminal penalties is not addressed, nor is the question of the death penalty.

[138] Xie 1996, p. 13.

Now that the Chinese authorities are treating the implementation of the revised CPL and the CL as a priority, they should perhaps also start thinking about further improving the CPL and revising the CL again.[139]

References

– 'Criminal Law Called to Revise', *Beijing Review*, 24-30 April 1989, p. 7
– 'Death Penalty Pressure', *The Australian*, 9 September 1998, p. 10
– 'Note: Concept of Law in the Chinese Anti-Crime Campaign' (1985), *Harvard Law Review*, No. 98, p. 1890
– *Zhonghua renmin gonghe guo falü quanshu* (A Complete Collection of Laws of the PRC) (1989), Jilin: Jilin People's Press
Amnesty International (1991), *China – Punishment Without Crime: Administrative Detention*, ASA 17/27/91
Amnesty International (1992), *Torture in China*, ASA 17/55/92
Amnesty International (1996), *China: No One Is Safe*, ASA 17/01/96
Berman, Harold J., Cohen, Susan and Russell, Malcolm (1982), 'A Comparison of the Chinese and Soviet Codes of Criminal Law and Procedure', *Journal of Criminal Law and Criminology*, Vol. 73, No. 1, p. 238
Bian, Jianlin (1995), 'Direct Contesting and the Reform of Trial Process', *Zhongguo faxue* (Legal Science in China), No. 6, p. 96
Buck, Mary (1993), 'Justice for All: The Application of Law by Analogy in the Case of Zhou Fuqing', *Journal of Chinese Law*, Vol. 7, No. 2, p. 113
Butler, W.E. (ed.) (1983), *The Legal System of the Chinese Soviet Republic 1931-1934*, New York: Transnational Publishers Inc
Cao, Zidan and Hou, Guoyun (1991), 'On Redefining "Counter-revolutionary Crimes" "Crimes Endangering State Security"', *Zhongguo faxue* (Legal Science in China), No. 2, p. 9

[139] Indeed, revision to the CL has already taken place. On 28 August 1998, the Supreme People's Court issued an interpretation on certain provisions of the CL dealing with foreign exchange frauds. The document contained some very expansive interpretations to relevant provisions and hence effectively expanded the scope of the CL. On 29 December 1998, the Standing Committee of the NPC adopted a decision in a similar area. The Decision supplements the newly revised CL and creates a number of new offenses under the CL. These efforts seem to repeat the post-1979 practice of supplementing the existing law by creating new offenses to deal with *ad hoc* situations – precisely the same problem the 1997 Revision tried to deal with.

Chen, Guangzhong (1980), 'The Principle of the Presumption of Innocence Should Be Critically Adopted', *Faxue yanjiu* (Studies in Law), No. 4, p. 34

Chen, Guangzhong (1989a), 'Forty Years of the Chinese Criminal Procedure Science – Pt I', *Zhengfa luntan* (Journal of China University of Political Science and Law), No. 4, p. 5

Chen, Guangzhong (1989b), 'Forty Years of the Chinese Criminal Procedure Science – Pt II', *Zhengfa luntan* (Journal of China University of Political Science and Law) No. 5, p. 1

Chen, Guangzhong and Xiong, Qiuhong (1995a), 'Some Opinions on the Revision of the Criminal Procedure Law – Pt I', *Zhongguo faxue* (Legal Science in China), No. 4, p. 91

Chen, Guangzhong and Xiong, Qiuhong (1995b), 'Some Opinions on the Revision of the Criminal Procedure Law – Pt II', *Zhongguo faxue* (Legal Science in China), No. 5, p. 85

Chen, Guangzhong and Yan, Duanzhu (1995), *A Draft and its Explanation on the Revision of Criminal Procedure Law*, Beijing: China Fangzheng Press

Chen, Guangzhong, *et al* (1993), 'Market Economy and the Future of the Science of Criminal Procedure Law', *Zhongguo faxue* (Legal Science in China) No. 5, p. 3

Chen, Jianfu (1997), 'A Moderate Step in a Right Direction – The Revision of the Criminal Procedure Law in the PRC', *Journal of Chinese and Comparative Law*, No. 3, p. 120

Chen, Jianfu (1998a), *Legal Culture, State Orthodoxy and the Modernization of Law*, Occasional Paper C98/1, Leiden Beijing Legal Transformation Project, Van Vollenhoven Institute for Law and Administration in Non-Western Countries, Leiden University

Chen, Jianfu (1998b), 'Legalisme aux Couleurs de la Chine' (Legalism in Chinese Colors), *Perspectives Chinoises*, No. 50, p. 5

Chen, Jianguo (1994), 'The Principle of the Presumption of Innocence Should Be Written Into the Criminal Procedure Law', *Zhongguo faxue* (Legal Science in China), No. 5, p. 35

Chen, Weidong and Zhang, Tao (1992), 'A Research into Several Problems with Shelter and Investigation', *Zhongguo faxue* (Legal Science in China), No. 2, p. 82

Chen, Weidong and Zhang, Tao (1993), 'A Further Talk on Why Shelter and Investigation Should Not Be Abolished', *Zhongguo faxue* (Legal Science in China), No. 3, p. 113

Chen, Xingliang (1996), 'Nullum Crimen Nulla Poena Sine Lege in Modern Times', *Faxue yanjiu* (Studies in Law), No. 2, p. 11

Chen, Xingliang (1997), 'Dual Task for Criminal Revision: Change of Value and Adjustment of Structure', *Zhongwai faxue* (Beijing University Law Journal), No. 1, p. 55

Cheng, Rongbing (1994), 'Coercive Measures and the Shelter and Investigation', *Zhongguo faxue* (Legal Science in China), No. 5, p. 38

China University of Political Science and Law (ed.) (1987), *Research into and Discussions on Theoretical and Practical Problems of Criminal Procedure*, Beijing: Law Publishing House

Chinese Encyclopedia – Law (1984), (*Zhongguo dabaike quanshu – Faxue*) Beijing/Shanghai: Press of the Chinese Encyclopedia

Chu, Huazhi (1997), 'Criminal Law Revision and Criminal Law Policy', in *Zhongwai faxue* (Beijing University Law Journal), No. 1, p. 49

Cohen, Jerome Alan (ed.) (1968), *The Criminal Process in the People's Republic of China 1949-1963: An Introduction*, Cambridge, MA: Harvard University Press

Cohen, Jerome Alan (1969), 'The Chinese Communist Party and "Judicial Independence": 1949-59', *Harvard Law Review*, No. 82, p. 967

Cui, Min (1994), 'Abolishing the Exemption from Prosecution', *Zhongguo faxue* (Legal Science in China), No. 5, p. 44

Cui, Min (1995), 'A Summary of the Discussions on Revising and Perfecting the Criminal Procedure Law', *Xiandai faxue* (Modern Law Science), No. 1, p. 92

Cui, Min (1996), 'A Comment on the Major Changes to the Criminal Procedure Law', *Guangming ribao*, 28 March, p. 6

Cui, Qingsen and Liao, Zengyun (1989), 'On Limited and Cautious Use of the Death Penalty', *Faxue yanjiu* (Studies in Law), No. 2, p. 69

Davis, Stephen B. (1987), 'The Death Penalty and Legal Reform in the PRC', *Journal of Chinese Law*, No. 1, p. 303

Escara, Jean (1936), *Chinese Law: Conception and Evolution, Legislative and Judicial Institutions, Science and Teaching*, Peking (Beijing) and Paris (1936) (translated from the French by Gertrude R. Brown, and published by the University of Washington, Seattle, 1961)

Fan, Fenglin (1994), 'Several Thoughts on the Presumption of Innocence', *Zhongguo faxue* (Legal Science in China), No. 5, p. 36

Gao, Mingxuan (ed.) (1986), *Xinzhongguo xingfa yanjiu zongshu* (A Summary of Criminal Law Research in New China), Henan: Henan People's Press

Gao, Mingxuan, Zhao, Bingzhi and Wang, Yong (1989), 'A Review and Prospect of the Criminal Legislation in the Past Ten Years', *Zhongguo faxue* (Legal Science in China), No. 2, p. 66

Gao, Xinting (1997), 'Strengthen the Force and Secure the Implementation of the New Criminal Law', *Renmin ribao* (People's Daily; overseas edition), 2 July, internet edition

Gellat, Timothy A. (1982), 'The People's Republic of China and the Presumption of Innocence', *The Journal of Criminal Law and Criminology*, No. 73, p. 259

Gu, Angran (1989), *Shehui zhuyi fazhi he lifa gongzuo* (The Socialist Legal System and Legislative Work), Beijing: China University of Political Science and Law Press

Gu, Angran (1996), 'Explanations on the Revision of the Criminal Procedure Law of the PRC', delivered at the 4th Plenary Session of the 8th NPC on 12 March 1996, in *Zhonghua renmin gongheguo quanguo renmin daibiao dahui changwu weiyuanhui gonggao* (Gazette of the Standing Committee of National People's Congress of the PRC), No. 3

Hong, Bing (1996), 'Major Measures to Perfect the Criminal Procedure System', *Zhengzhi yu falü* (Politics and Law), No. 3, p. 13

Hou, Guoyun (1995), 'Nullum Crimen, Nulla Poena Sine Lege in a Market Economy and the Value of Criminal Analogy', *Faxue yanjiu* (Studies in Law), No. 3, p. 61

Hu, Yunteng (1995), 'Abolition of Analogy and the Scientific Nature of Criminal Law', *Faxue yanjiu* (Studies in Law), No. 5, p. 55

Huang, Shengye (ed.) (1996), *Lüshi shouce*, (A Lawyer's Handbook), Beijing: Press of the Economic Daily

Huang, Taiyun and Teng, Wei (eds) (1997), *Zhonghua renmin gongheguo xingfa shiyi yu shiyong zhinan* (A Practical Guide and Interpretation of the Criminal Law of the PRC), Beijing: The Redflag Press

Huang, Taiyun (1996), 'Major Reforms in the Criminal Processes – An Outline of the Major Revisions to the Criminal Procedure Law', *Zhongguo faxue* (Legal Science in China), No. 2, p. 29

Jia, Yu (1997), 'Reduction of Capital Offense – An Important Aspect of Criminal Law Reform', *Zhengzhi yu falü* (Politics and Law), No. 1, p. 7

Kang, Yunshen (1991), 'On Mao Zedong's Creative Contribution to the Marxist-Leninist Theory on the Death Penalty', *Zhengfa luntan* (Political and Legal Forum), No. 6, p. 29

Koguchi, Hikota (1987), 'Some Observations About "Judicial Independence" in Post-Mao China', *Boston College Third World Law Journal*, No. 7, p. 195

Lan, Quanpu (1982), *Sanshi nian lai woguo fagui yange gaikuan* (Thirty Years of the Development of Law and Regulations in Our Country), Beijing: Press of the Masses

Lawyers' Committee for Human Rights (1993), *Criminal Justice with Chinese Characteristics: China's Criminal Process and Violations of Human Rights*, New York: Lawyers' Committee for Human Rights

Leng, Shao-chuan and Chiu, Hungdah (1985), *Criminal Justice in Post-Mao China: Analysis and Documents*, Albany: State University of New York Press

Leng, Shao-chuan (1967), *Justice in Communist China: A Survey of the Judicial System of the Chinese People's Republic*, New York: Oceana Publications, Inc.

Li, Baoyue (1994), 'A Discussion on the Time When Lawyers Should Participate in the Criminal Process', *Zhongguo faxue* (Legal Science in China), No. 4, p. 98

Li, Jianmin (1995), 'Several Thoughts on the Reform of the Criminal Trial Process', *Faxue yanjiu* (Studies in Law), No. 1, p. 84

Li, Xuekuan (1995), 'Some Legal Considerations on the Functions of the Defense Lawyer in Our Country', *Zhongguo faxue* (Legal Science in China), No. 6, p. 90

Liao, Kuangsheng (1983), '"Independent Administration of Justice" and the PRC Legal System', Vol. XVI, No. 2-3, Chinese Law and Government, pp. 123–152

Liao, Zengyun (1980), 'Views on the Principle of Presumption of Innocence', *Faxue yanjiu* (Studies in Law), No. 5, p. 32

Lin, Yagang and Jia, Yu (1997), 'On the Characters of Special Criminal Laws and their Incorporation into the Criminal Code', *Zhongwai faxue* (Peking University Law Journal), No. 1, p. 79

Liu, Shengrong (1992), 'Corporate Crimes or Unit Crimes', *Zhongguo faxue* (Legal Science in China), No. 6, p. 77

Ma, Kechang and Ding, Muying (eds) (1995), *Xingfa de xiugai yu wanshan* (The Revision and Improvement of the Criminal Law), Beijing: Press of the People's Court

Ma, Kechang (1996), 'Strengthen the Reform Force, Revise and Perfect the Criminal Law', *Faxue pinglun*, (Law Review), No. 5, p. 1

MacCormack, Geoffrey (1996), *The Spirit of Traditional Chinese Law*, Athens and London: University of Georgia Press

Meijer, M.J. (1967), *Introduction of Modern Criminal Law in China*, 2nd ed., Hong Kong: Lung Men Bookstore

Ning, Hanling (1986), 'On the Presumption of Innocence', in *Faxue tanwei* (Enquiring into Legal Theories), Chongqing: Chongqing Press

Office for Research Materials, Law Institute of the Chinese Academy of Social Science (ed.) (1981), *Lun falü mianqian renren pingdeng* (On Equality before the Law), Beijing: Publishing House of Law

Pang, Chang I. (1922-24), 'History of Judicial Reforms in China', *China Law Review*, No. 1, p. 156

Peng, Zhen (1992), *Lun xinzhongguo de zhengfa gongzuo* (On Political and Judicial Work in New China), Beijing: Press of the Chinese Communist Party Documents

People's Daily Commentator (1997), 'A Major and Significant Measure to Improve the Criminal Law and Criminal Justice', *Renmin ribao* (People's Daily), 4 April (internet edition)

Reports of the Australian Human Rights Delegation to China, First Report, July 1991 and Second Report, November 1992, Canberra: Australian Government Publishing Service

Shen, Deyong, 'Our Criminal Law Should Establish a "Limited Use" Principle on the Death Penalty', *Zhongguo faxue* (Legal Science in China), No. 27, p. 28

Shi, Huifang (1995), 'An Opinion on Abolishing the Institution of Exemption from Prosecution', *Zhengfa luntan* (Journal of China University of Political Science and Law), No. 1, p. 33

Song, Yinghui and Wu, Jie (1992), 'A New Research into the Exemption from Prosecution', *Faxue yanjiu* (Studies in Law), No. 1, p. 24

Su, Huiyu (1994), *Xingfa xue* (Criminal Law), Beijing: China University of Political Science and Law Press

Tang, Guanda (1980), 'The Presumption of Innocence Should Be Concretely Analysed', *Faxue yanjiu* (Studies in Law), No. 1, p. 62

Tao, Jigang (1995), 'Some Thoughts on the Law on Re-education through Labor', *Zhongguo renmin jingcha daxue xuebao* (Journal of the China University of People's Policy), No. 3, p. 12

Thieme, G.V. (1984), 'The Debate on the Presumption of Innocence in the People's Republic of China', *Review of Socialist Law*, p. 277

Tian, Cai (1979), 'A Question Worth Investigating', *Renmin ribao* (People's Daily), 17 February, p. 3

Townsend, Deborah E. (1987-88), 'The Concept of Law in Post-Mao China: A Case Study of Economic Crime', *Stanford Journal of International Law*, No. 24, p. 227

Wang, Fengzhi (1995), 'Several Questions on the Abolition or Retention of the Death Penalty', *Zhengfa Luntan* (Journal of China University of Political Science and Law), No. 4, p. 23

Wang, Guo'ou, Wang, Yizhen and Wang, Cunhou (eds) (1981), *Xingshi susongfa gailun* (An Outline of Criminal Procedure Law), Beijing: Beijing University Press

Wang, Hanbin (1997), 'Explanations on the Draft Revision of the Criminal Law of the PRC', delivered to the 5th plenary session of the 8th NPC on March 6, 1997

Wang, Hongxiang (1994), 'Upholding and Perfecting the Exemption from Prosecution', *Zhongguo faxue* (Legal Science in China), No. 5, p. 42

Wang, Mingyuan (1992), 'Several Questions on the Exemption from Prosecution', *Zhongguo faxue* (Legal Science in China), No. 2, p. 75

Wang, Mingyuan and Liu, Donghua (1996), 'A Comment and Summary on the Study of Criminal Procedure Law', *Faxue yanjiu* (Studies in Law), No. 1, p. 51

Wang, Shaonan (1995), 'Establishing a Direction for the Trial Process Reform', *Faxue yanjiu* (Studies in Law), No. 1, p. 77

Wang, Xinxin (1993), 'Shelter and Investigation Should Be Abolished – A Discussion with Comrades Chen Weidong and Zhang Tao', *Zhongguo faxue* (Legal Science in China), No. 3, p. 110

Wei, Tong (1996), 'A Report on the Discussions on the Revision of the CPL', *Zhengfa luntan* (Journal of China University of Political Science and Law), No. 1, p. 89

Woo, Margaret Y.K. (1991), 'Adjudication Supervision and Judicial Independence in the PRC', *The American Journal of Comparative Law*, No. 39, p. 95

Xie, Youping (1996), 'Ideal and Reality: A Comment on the Revised Criminal Procedure Law', *Xiandao faxue* (Modern Law Science), No. 2, p. 9

Xing, Yan (1997), 'Criminal Law Revision: Minor or Major Revision or No Revision At All', *Zhongwai faxue* (Beijing University Law Journal), No. 1, p. 49

Xu, Yichu (1989), 'My Opinion on the Exemption from Prosecution', *Faxue yanjiu* (Studies in Law), No. 3, p. 74

Xu, Yichu (1996), 'Criminal Processes and Human Rights Protection', *Faxue yanjiu* (Studies in Law), No. 2, p. 89

Yang, Duan (1994), 'Appropriately Resolving the Issue of Validity of Illegal Evidence', *Zhongguo faxue* (Legal Science in China), No. 5, p. 41

Yung, Hon Kiang (1924-26), 'The Development of Modern Legal Institutions and Judicial Reform in China', *China Law Review*, No. 2, pp. 19–31, 77–87 and 117–134

Zhang, Jun (1997), 'The Three Basic Principles of the Criminal Law', *Renmin ribao* (People's Daily; overseas edition), 26 April, internet edition

Zhang, Lingjie, Zhang, Xun and Wang, Mingyuan (1991), 'On the Principle of the Presumption of Innocence', *Faxue yanjiu* (Studies in Law), No. 4, p. 34

Zhang, Sihan (1997), 'On Crimes Endangering State Security', *Renmin ribao* (People's Daily; overseas edition), 14 June, internet edition

Zhang, Tao and Chen, Weidong (1990), 'A Discussion of the Time for Defense Lawyers to Participate in the Criminal Process', *Zhongguo faxue* (Legal Science in China), No. 2, p. 43

Zhang, Wei (1994), 'Several Issues Regarding the Involvement of Lawyers in Criminal Procedure', *Zhongguo faxue* (Legal Science in China), No. 5, p. 39

Zhang, Xiu (1996), 'Choices for the Reform in the Trial Process for Public Prosecution Cases', *Faxue yanjiu* (Studies in Law), No. 2, p. 96

Zhang, Youyu (1985), 'Mao Zedong's Creative Contribution to the Development of Marxist Legal Theory', in China Law Society (ed.), *Mao Zedong xixian faxue lilun lunwen xuan* (A Collection of Articles on Mao Zedong's Legal Theories), Beijing: Law Publishing House

Zhang, Youyu and Wang, Shuwen (eds) (1989), *Zhongguo faxue sishinian* (Forty Years of the PRC's Legal Science), Shanghai: Shanghai People's Publishing House

Zhang, Zhiming (1995), 'A Further Thought on the Reform of the Trial Process', *Faxue yanjiu* (Studies in Law), No. 4, p. 93

Zhao, Bingzhi and Xiao, Zhonghua (1996), 'A Discussion on the Debate About the Abolition of Analogy in Criminal Law', *Faxue jia* (Jurists), No. 4, p. 54

Zhao, Zhenjiang (ed.) (1990), *Zhongguo fazhi sishinian* (Forty Years of the Chinese Legal System), Beijing: Beijing University Press

5

Development of the Shareholding Cooperative System and Property Rights in China

*Eduard B. Vermeer**

Over the past decade, the shareholding cooperative system (hereafter SHCS) (*gufen hezuo zhi*) has been put forward by national and local Chinese governments and entrepreneurs as a solution to ownership and management problems of rural industries. Its development in different regions has been very uneven, but by 1995, 12 per cent of all enterprises run by townships or villages (*xiangcun qiye*) had adopted this system. In the absence of adequate national regulations, many local forms have emerged. The introduction of the SHCS has been monitored in three experimental districts, giving rise to extensive political commentary and economic literature. Reflecting official promotional policies, almost all commentators have been very positive about its results, which makes one wonder why the SHCS is still the exception instead of the rule. Advocates claim that it is a mechanism that provides independence of management, financial responsibility, attraction of investment capital, incentives for employees, and profit distribution.[1] However, the evidence presented is biased and unconvincing. Moreover, its legal status is quite vague, a fact which is underlined by its omission from China's largest compendium of policies and regulations for management of

* I wish to thank the Dutch-Israeli Developmental Research Foundation for its support for a survey conducted together with Zhang Xiaoshan and Yuan Peng of CASS Rural Development Institute in Shandong and Hebei in 1995, and Zhang for his helpful comments.

[1]Tian Zhen 1993.

township and village enterprises (hereafter TVEs) (*xiangzhen qiye*).[2]

In this chapter,[3] the political and economic factors responsible for the development of the SHCS, its intended and perceived consequences for ownership and management of rural collective enterprises, and its effect on property rights will be considered. The analysis will be based on economic literature and a survey of thirty-six converted industrial enterprises in two districts in Shandong and Hebei.[4] First, some relevant aspects of ownership and management in China's TVEs in general will be outlined. Next, a history of the objectives for introducing the system and its local implementation and modification of regulations will be presented. We will show that its many forms and uneven spread – many inland areas have been very hesitant to adopt the SHCS – were due to several factors: differences in original ownership structures, choices by local authorities which reflected different economic circumstances or dominant political currents. Managerial preferences and evolution of ownership and management practices in rural areas also played a role. The name SHCS suggests, and Chinese scholars have claimed, that it is a combination of a *shareholding* company and a *cooperative*. It will be argued that the SHCS is a misnomer; at least in converted collective enterprises it is a hybrid form which lacks most of the attributes of both. Its viability is rather uncertain.

Subsequently, the conversion process of collective enterprises and its consequences for ownership and management will be described. Ownership and rights to benefits from the enterprise were changed by a new valuation of assets, allocation and/or sales of different types of shares, and new rules for decisions about profit retention and distribution. There appears to be considerable divergence between original policy intentions and eventual outcomes of the conversion to SHCS. This divergence is evident from employee perceptions of ownership and management under the SHCS, but also from shifts in managerial control. Finally, this chapter will try to establish the extent to which

---

[2] Fu 1993.

[3] A slightly different version of this contribution has appeared in Jean C. Oi and Andrew G. Walder (eds), *Property Rights and Economic Reform in China*, Stanford: Stanford University Press 1999, pp. 123–144.

[4] The survey included interviews with cadres and enterprise managers in Zhoucun county and Zunhua municipality, and questionnaire data from a manager, technician, workshop head, accountant and worker in each visited enterprise (all but three with more than seventy-five employees), yielding 159 effective respondents from twenty industrial enterprises in Zhoucun and twelve in Zunhua. For details, see Vermeer 1996.

SHCS has achieved a clarification of property rights, which was one of its intended goals. It is argued that the vagueness of the legal consequences of conversion to SHCS, including those regarding property rights, has contributed to its success in terms of local acceptance and spread. Such consequences have never been put to the test in an economic slow-down or crisis.

Background: the position of China's TVEs and some interpretations

In the 1980s, China's TVEs were disadvantaged in their competition with state-owned industries, lacking economies of scale; modern technology, easy credit from state banks, access to provincial and national markets, low-priced allocation of energy and raw materials, and many other forms of state support. Yet these factors were offset by some powerful advantages: the low cost of rural labor (with its low wages, flexibility, and absence of the welfare and pension burdens of the state-owned enterprises), lower tax rates, and the incentive of market-orientation. The result was that the TVEs continuously expanded and gained market share. After the demise of the people's communes, it seemed questionable whether there was sufficient economic reason and political support for a continued involvement of rural governments in running businesses. There was not much of an alternative to continuing *de facto* collective government ownership of the collectively-owned village-run industries: genuinely collective (that is, participatory) management or privatization was not supported or even accepted by the Communist Party and most Chinese villages lacked the necessary private capital and independent expert managers. However, the general political consensus which evolved was that ownership and management of enterprises should be separated because political interference was detrimental to economic efficiency and enterprise performance.

Why not transfer ownership of large collectively-owned TVEs to the state, and have them run by county government? According to Chang and Wang, the Chinese government feared that such action would create agency problems. Socialization of TVEs would result in similar soft budgetary constraints as those of the state-owned sector, increase wage costs and reduce efficiency. Township and village governments were best positioned to obtain the critical key resources (which include political support and bank loans), and its officials often commanded greater managerial experience than ordinary citizens. The rule that nominal ownership rests with local residents was maintained in order to guarantee that they would reap the main benefits rather than the state or township/village government. In order to keep rural governments from reaping excessive benefits and to prevent short-term profiteering behavior, explicit rules were laid down as to how much profit should be retained by the enterprise and how the remainder should be distributed.[5] One may add to this analysis that the state had neither the capital nor the managerial manpower to become involved in tens of thousands of small-scale enterprises. Thus, it left the rural sector to its own devices and capital inputs for developing a market-oriented industry.

Weitzman and Xu have tried to find an explanation for the paradox between strong economic performance and the absence of well-defined property rights in China's TVEs which they label as 'vaguely defined cooperatives'. They observed several features of TVEs which contradict the basic tenets of property right theory: (1) there is no owner, only a *de facto* owner: the community government, (2) there is no residual claimant in the traditional sense: residents cannot actively claim benefits. According to law, 60 per cent of profits must be retained by the TVE for reinvestment, and communal government is entitled to only a part of the remainder, which it must share with the workforce, and (3) assets cannot be transferred, sold, or inherited. Nevertheless, despite the predictions of property rights theory, TVEs have performed just as well as private firms. In spite of local support, they are subject to hard budget constraints because of heavy competition for funds within the community and between enterprises on the regional markets. The authors suggest that a solution to the paradox might be found in the cooperative culture of China. Admittedly, the term cooperative is misleading because the TVEs are not voluntary associations. Participation in a TVE is decided by residency and mandated by community government, e.g. by obliging residents or employees to invest.[6] Their analysis is useful because it suggests that shared, undivided property rights may be a stimulus to enterprise development and profitability. However, the dichotomy between 'collective' and 'private' rights is an over-simplification of the very intricate structure of rural property rights. Moreover, the questions of how vaguely defined these two rights are, and how functional that is for the achievement of different goals of the enterprise are not answered. This study of the SHCS will show that a number of different property rights have been formulated, belonging to the

[5] Chang and Wang 1994.
[6] Weitzman and Xu 1994.

collective community, the collective enterprise, the collective employees, managers as a cooperative or individual shareholders, individual employees, and outside individuals or organizations. Some of these rights (usually, the stronger and legally more defined ones) have been acquired voluntarily (by purchase or otherwise); other rights were forced upon village committees, enterprises, or employees and therefore are likely to be less strictly respected.

Usually, managers of enterprises have little recourse against local governments or Communist Party secretaries who exercise collective ownership rights, one reason being that they can be appointed and dismissed at will and are rotated frequently. However, predatory behavior of local government and CCP secretaries is restrained by regulations about retention of profits by the enterprise, and about their use for reproduction and collective welfare. Since liberalization, managers who contracted for an enterprise and brought in much tax and employment have improved their position. Still, their loyalty is not necessarily with their current enterprise, as they have a career to consider which is greatly influenced by township government or the Party, and are part of an often very strong village community. Thus, both managers and administrative cadres operate under restrictions imposed from above or moral obligations from below. Even if employees and ordinary members of the collective have little if any direct influence over the management of collective assets and allocation of benefits, in small communities their opinion counts.

The shareholding cooperative system is seen by some as the best way forward to help reduce the previously mentioned problems of ownership, management and distribution of benefits in TVEs. Others fear that stock capitalization and the concomitant external control will lead to market instability, employee insecurity and more, not less, short-term profit-seeking behavior. Some hold that genuine cooperativization (e.g. along the lines of Mondragon producers' cooperatives), for which they believe rural China offers favorable conditions, will boost TVE performance.[7] Since 1994 the SHCS has become the dominant model for the conversion of collective industrial enterprises. By tracing its history, this chapter will try to show how the very different origins of enterprises and different political currents have influenced the legal forms and adoption rates of SHC enterprises, and how they allow for different and even conflicting views on the function and effects of the conversion.

[7]Tsao 1995. Tsao overestimates the marketability of employee shares.

History of the SHCS: political objectives and local implementation

The Chinese term 'shareholding cooperative system' has developed over a decade and is applied rather loosely to very different enterprise organizations. The term is confusing because the system lacks many of the attributes of the ordinary shareholding company or those of a genuine cooperative. The State Statistical Bureau is unsure about how it should be categorized.[8] The 1994 law on shareholding companies does not apply to the SHC enterprises, and most larger ones are not voluntary associations. There are some superficial similarities with the American ESOP (Employee Stock Ownership Plan): both are usually adopted by small companies in order to increase their liquidity (by providing stock instead of cash wages or bonuses to their employees), enjoy certain tax breaks (notably for company savings), and foster employee cooperation.[9] However, the differences are much greater. China's SHCS are exclusively rural, often mainly or partly collectively-owned, most have issued employee shares only once, at the time they were established, most shares are purchased and carry voting rights, their tax breaks do not apply to sales of shares or deductibility of loans used to fund company stock but only to company profits. The SHC is a hybrid economic form, the product of mixed political signals from the central government and a range of local survival or development strategies of entrepreneurs and rural governments.

The CCP Central Committee espoused the idea that the shareholding system could have a definite function for TVEs in its 22 January 1987 decision 'On deepening the reform'. It believed it would contribute to the separation of government and enterprise and to the 'socialization of assets of private enterprises'. It noted that some private enterprises had already practiced methods such as employee shares, labor dividends, democratic management, and contributions to public funds which gave these enterprises a transitional character. However, a survey had revealed a lack of enthusiasm at the local levels of government, and some developed areas opposed it. Thereupon the State Council decided to conduct experiments on enter-

[8]The SSB includes many small SHC enterprises in 'rural partnerships' (*nongcun lianying qiye*), and larger ones in 'collective enterprises' (*qiti qiye*), but never in 'shareholding enterprises' (*gufenzhi jingji qiye*). The first belong to the private/cooperative economy, the second to the collective economy, the third (a product of the Company Law) is a category by itself. In 1994 the SSB began to distinguish *xiang-* and *cun-*managed SHC enterprises.

[9]Blasi 1988; John Case 1988.

prise ownership and management in three districts first.[10] The three were supposed to reflect different types of development and varying local experiences with shareholding: Zhoucun in Shandong, Fuyang in Anhui and Wenzhou in Zhejiang. Experiments were to focus on a number of questions: shareholder rights, asset management; profit distribution based on shares *and* labor, the authority of *xiang* and *cun* administrative organizations, responsibility for losses and in case of bankruptcy, and share markets. Local authorities should adopt model regulations based on their experiences. The Rural Experimentation Center under the Ministry of Agriculture and its provincial and local experimentation offices monitored these local experiments and summarized them. Soon, marketing of shares ran into political opposition and was called off.[11]

One of the reasons why the term SHCS came into use was that the word *he* ('common') was meant to be a bridge leading the private economy towards a public ownership system.[12] Thus, it reflected a 'left' policy of gradual collectivization of rural private enterprise. However, to independent entrepreneurs who ran into the legal limit of eight employees it offered a way forward, political protection and the favorable tax treatment of collective enterprises. The allocation of shares fitted well within the policy of providing more bonuses to workers. It could also be used to circumvent official regulations that income of directors of TVEs were not to exceed the average workers' wage by more than five times[13] and the new individual income tax, and (as in the capitalist world) distribute stocks to supplement managerial salaries. Possibly most importantly, the issue of shares provided new risk-bearing capital which village authorities and entrepreneurs badly wanted. Thus, different interest groups had different, even conflicting motives for supporting the SHCS.

The leftist political motive appeared most clearly in Wenzhou. In 1988, China's foremost 'capitalist model' city started with formally using the term 'Shareholding Cooperative System' and recognized it as a special economic form. Its objective was to contain privatization, and to lead individual and private enterprises down the road of the socialist collective economy. The Wenzhou regulations were adopted with minor changes in the national regulations of 1990. Reflecting the post-Tiananmen restrictive political climate, they expressed the

[10] Yuan Peng 1995.
[11] Liu 1994, pp. 500-501.
[12] Zhang and Wang 1993.
[13] 'Regulations on the contract management responsibility system in TVEs', issued by the Ministry of Agriculture on 4 April 1990, rule 19.

idea that collective interests should dominate over private interests, and labor over capital. The 1990 regulations, which still apply today, limited the rights of shareholders in many ways. In the disposition of enterprise profits, they must follow the rule for ordinary TVEs which stipulate that 60 per cent of profits after taxes should be retained and no more than 40 per cent be used for distribution. Distribution should be 'mainly on the basis of labor'. Generally, only a half should go to dividends, and the other half to collective welfare funds and bonuses; rates for each should be laid down by county, town and township enterprise bureaus.[14] Furthermore, they stipulated that voting should follow the cooperative principle of one-man one-vote, and not be based on number of shares. Shares could not be withdrawn in principle, and transfer was possible only with permission from the shareholders' meeting. Collectives could sell only a minority share of 30 per cent or less to management and employees. In the restrictive political climate of 1990-1991, some counties abandoned shareholding altogether and ordered rural cadres to return their shares and dividends, and dissolve SHCs.[15]

SHC enterprises were accorded the tax rates and preferential treatment of collective enterprises.[16] This constituted a considerable advantage over private enterprises, particularly because an SHC was permitted 'to include in its production management costs that part of its dividends which corresponds with the interest on savings'. The deduction of dividends from pre-tax enterprise profits, as if they were interest on loans, gives a sizeable advantage to shareholders, particularly in years of high inflation and interest rates. Moreover, SHCs paid lower management fees, viz. 0.5 per cent of turnover instead of 2 per cent. According to this and earlier surveys, without such favorable tax treatment many enterprises would have opted to remain private.[17]

In 1992, policies became more liberal again. The SHCS was allowed to diversify, without much attempt at standardization.[18] It covered a variety of different economic forms and sizes of enterprises, such as combinations of TVEs with state enterprises, township- or village-run enterprises with employee shareholders, and private part-

[14] Preliminary regulations for rural SHCs, issued by the Ministry of Agriculture on 12 February 1990, in *Nongyebu Zhengce Tizhi Gaige Fagui Si 1994*, pp. 73–79.

[15] *Nongmin ribao* (Farmers' Daily), 18 May 1992.

[16] Until 1989, Wenzhou maintained the 35% tax rate for private enterprises. Yu, Wen and Zhang 1994, p. 22.

[17] Yuan Peng 1995.

[18] *Zhongguo nongcun jingji*, 1992 No. 11, pp. 3–7.

nerships.[19] A fourth type which appeared in Guangdong, the 'community SHC' (*shequ gufen hezuoshe*), put all collective assets under the control of one company, whose shares were allocated to the resident population; it has the character of a *xiang-* or *cun*-run financial holding company rather than that of an enterprise.[20] The second group was by far the largest in terms of industrial output, employment and number of shareholders. In December, new directives dropped the minimum founding requirement of 'three or more working farmers' and the obligation to accept guidance by the state plan.[21] The SHCS was stimulated also by trials with the shareholding system for state-owned enterprises. Even if with few exceptions rural enterprises did not meet the requirements of the 1994 Company Law (e.g. a minimum share capital of 500,000 *yuan*, and a maximum of fifty shareholders), many of the regulations passed by *xiang* governments since 1992 were inspired by it. Several provinces set up experimental districts of their own, some of which defied the 1990 rules. For example, Mixian county declared, 'If shareholders really are masters of the enterprise, one should not have restrictive policies for profit distribution. So we allow enterprises to deviate from the rule of 60 per cent accumulation and 40 per cent distribution'. It accepted a minority share for the collective. While some areas had forbidden leading Party members and cadres to take shares, out of fear of corruption, Mixian actively encouraged them.[22]

The 1990 regulations were never revoked, but became increasingly obsolete. Local rules, practices and adoption rates have continued to diverge. Officials from the relevant departments recommended a flexible application of the rules on the size of the collective share, the distribution mainly according to labor, and the one-man one-vote. The SHCS should be suitable for all China. They expressed a major concern that the government and Communist Party had had ever since the contracting of TVE enterprises by their managers: 'an important objective of the SHCS is to solve the problem of "grey" privatization of the enterprise assets through appropriation by their present bosses'.[23] With this new objective in mind, political support for con-

[19]See, for example, Zhang and Wang 1993.

[20]The examples I visited in Dalian in 1996 had a strong collectivist character. For an interesting subdivision of such asset-holding companies see Mu and Tan 1993.

[21]Nongyebu, 'Guanyu tuixing he wanshan xiangzhen qiye gufen hezuozhi de tongzhi' (Ministry of Agriculture, Circular on promotion and perfection of SHCS for TVEs), in: Liang 1993, pp. 306–311.

[22]Zhou 1992.

[23]Yu, Wen and Zhang 1994, pp. 3–7 and 13–18.

version of TVEs to SHCs was stepped up in 1994, against widespread local resistance to the adoption of SHC for TVEs inspired by what came to be known as 'the three fears': township and village cadres feared the loss of power and profits, enterprise managers feared being restricted, and the people feared the risks. However, no uniform model of SHCS was intended, because of large regional differences.[24] This political support has not yet translated itself into national legislation, probably because of a lack of consensus about privatization of rural collective assets.

The very different adoption rates in different regions show the continued dependence of the SHCS on state propaganda for its spread. By the end of 1993, more than 20,000 of township- or village-run SHC enterprises had been established in Shandong and Zhejiang (where Zhoucun and Wenzhou were models) but less than 8,000 in Jiangsu, and less than 500 in Jilin, Shanghai or Shaanxi. In the interior regions, adoption rates were much lower than in the east.[25] In 1994, their total number increased by more than half from 133,000 to 204,000, i.e. to more than 12 per cent of all such enterprises. Their labor force increased from almost five million to eight million, that is, 13.6 per cent of the labor force managed by *xiangcun* enterprises.[26] By 1994, 49 per cent of the total share capital was owned by *xiang/cun* collectives. Managers and employees increased their holdings to 26 per cent, and other companies held 17 per cent. Foreign and state participation remained below 5 per cent each. The respective shares varied considerably between provinces. Collective ownership of shares was most common in Jiangsu and Shandong, individual ownership in Zhejiang, and foreign ownership in Fujian. Share ownership by 'legal persons', i.e. other units, was highest in Gansu, Guangxi, Sichuan and other western regions. Such differences in stock ownership can be explained by prior differences in the organization of rural enterprises and the political orientation of rural governments, and the relative strength of state enterprises in inner provinces, and are reflected in the various 'models'.[27] (See Table 1)

[24]Guo 1995.

[25]Guo 1995, p. 33.

[26]A comparison of aggregated national and provincial statistics on all SHCs with collective or private rural enterprises is not very useful, because no rigorous definition of SHCs is used and their sectoral composition is not given. The figures given here include only *xiangcun* SHC enterprises, most of which are converted collective enterprises.

[27]Average turnover per employee was 43,512 *yuan*, and profits *cum* taxes 4,077 *yuan*. These figures were 8,105 *yuan* and 1,152 *yuan*, respectively, above the average for all TVEs. *Zhongguo qiye guanli nianjian – 1994* (Yearbook of China

Table 1:
***Xiangcun* SHCs in China and six provinces, 1994 (year-end)**

	Number (1,000)	Labor (1,000)	Capital RMB bn	Percentage of stock owned by: coll.	indiv.	legal p.	foreign state
China	204.1	7,998	105.7	49	26	17	53
Hebei	13.3	554	7.8	47	28	16	64
Shandong	27.2	1,575	19.7	59	21	13	61
Jiangsu	14.1	1,056	14.8	65	17	14	41
Zhejiang	24.7	950	12.5	26	49	21	41
Anhui	7.9	318	3.3	39	29	22	73
Fujian	4.2	195	3.2	27	22	21	272

Source: *Zhongguo qiye guanli nianjian – 1995* (Yearbook of China Enterprise Management 1995), pp. 232-233, 362-363.

Paradoxically, the recent popularity of the shareholding cooperative system may be ascribed to the fact that it is a very useful vehicle not only for opponents of the often corrupting influence of government meddling with business, but also for those cadres who want to profit from privatization of collective assets. Which side will prevail, depends to a large extent on the force of existing local political representative institutions (that is, democratic and CCP control, the interests of which may run parallel here) and on control by shareholders through the Board of Directors (BoD). From our survey we got the impression that shareholder control is weakly developed. Although the SHC enterprise has a shareholders' representative meeting which should decide about all major issues and appointments, in actual practice the president of the BoD, the factory head and the managers are usually appointed by, and often are, local government and Party cadres, or, if they are large shareholders, are self-appointed.[28] The grey zone between administration and business, between collective and private varies between areas, but everywhere it tends to become larger. The initiative comes both from private entrepreneurs who further their business interests by 'wearing the red hat' of being manager of their 'collective' enterprise, and from local cadres who convert the government and collective institutions to 'companies' which are almost outside political control.

Enterprise Management 1994), pp. 253–255, and *idem – 1995*, pp. 232-233 and 362-363.

[28] Yao 1995.

'Neither donkey nor horse': the compatibility of a limited company with collective and cooperative ownership

Should the shareholding cooperative system be considered as a transitional form which will ultimately lead to privatization, or as a long-term viable system of its own which combines collective and private ownership and goals? If one argues the latter, as some Chinese economists do, one has to believe in the compatibility of its rules and in its proper combination of the interests of different types of shareholders. The charters of SHC enterprises never mention a future conversion to a private company. Other Chinese scholars are undecided about the nature of the SHCS, and while some believe that its lack of a definite form is a positive characteristic in times of rapid economic and institutional change, others doubt whether this hybrid could survive.[29] In this section, the conflicting ideologies and interests in various types of SHCs will be identified and it will be argued that the present SHC system cannot last because of fundamental contradictions and unclear collective ownership and management rights.

The conceptual and legal differences between shareholding companies and producers' cooperatives are well known. Disregarding specifically Chinese forms, we may contrast the main characteristics of the two types of organization as follows:

Item	Shareholding Ltd. Co	Producers' Cooperatives
Purpose	profitable capital use	profitable labor use
Ownership rights	transferable shares	partly indivisible
Profit distribution	based on shares	based on labor
Risks	limited to share	equal, limited if legal entity
Dissolution	sale of shares	withdrawal, with conditions
Decision-making	one-share one-vote	one-man one-vote
Management control	BoD, shareholders	democratic, workers

The SHCS has tried to bridge some of these fundamental differences in orientation and legal basis by devising compromise rules, and its proponents have allowed actual SHCS practice to diverge from ideology and regulations if found too restrictive. It has not marked itself off ideologically like Western cooperatives have. Western cooperatives consider their assets to be owned by individuals, and allow shareholders to return their shares, but not to transfer them to others.

[29] A synopsis of part of the debate may be found in *Zhongguo jingji kexue nianjian 1994* (China Yearbook of Economic Science 1994), pp. 158-159.

In China's SHC enterprises, ownership may be diverse and institutional, while returns or transfers of shares are either not permitted or are subject to restrictions. The ratio between income rewarded to labor and dividends has been a problem in both the West and China: dividends are either fixed or limited to half the profits (Italy) or below 6 per cent (France) or 8 per cent (Japan, USA), while the Chinese rules which limit dividend distribution to 20 per cent of the profit after taxes are no longer respected (Wenzhou put the limit at 25 per cent, Zhoucun at 30 per cent to 40 per cent and some areas apply no limits at all). Most SHCs have limited shareholder risks by guaranteeing dividends above the bank interest rates.

As for decision-making and control rights, Western cooperatives stress the equality of all their members. The Chinese SHC has the unique problem of a dominant third organizational element: the collective ownership and control exerted by township and village authorities. Partly because of their authoritarian collectivist ideology, the egalitarian premise of the SHCS as a genuine producers' cooperative did not have a chance to develop, and seems much less prevalent than in the West now. Only ten per cent of our respondents in Zhoucun said all categories of employees should have the same amount of shares, 78 per cent said they should not. In Zunhua, many ordinary workers evaded the question. Most felt that differences in shareholding should not be too large. Almost 80 per cent felt they should be less than triple the workers' share in the case of technicians and workshop heads (actual differences were mostly lower than that), and 40 per cent thought this should apply to managers as well.

The closed character of the Chinese village or township, both of which are strong economic units to which residents belong by birth, affects not only SHCs but *all* enterprises in the community. Individual and enterprise ownership rights are weak because of the pervasiveness of, and dependence on, the authorities which control allocation of resources – whether government cadres, CCP secretaries, clan elders or family heads. The dominant economic role of the rural authorities has enabled them to spread risks and guarantee stable dividend payments almost irrespective of enterprise performance to employee-shareholders; moreover, they are subject to considerable political and social pressures from the workforce. Our interview data show, and enterprise charters confirm, that in SHCs the shareholder rights to a predictable and often high income stream from their shares (risk-bearing or not) are substantial and secure. Because of their closed character, small size and strong informal control, the organization and economic behavior of many SHC enterprises seem more comparable with family firms than with the ideal-type shareholder-controlled limited company or producers' cooperative.

In this survey it is found that most managers and employees had mixed feelings about their ties with the township or village leadership. On the one hand, the close relationship between the enterprise managers and the local leaders of the *xiang* or *cun* was perceived as an advantage. The leaders were seen as instrumental in reducing transaction costs in dealings with the tax bureau, the police, the communications department, environmental protection bureau, banks etc. On the other hand, almost all managers of SHC enterprises indicated that adoption of the SHCS had shifted decision-making to the enterprise, away from government interference, and affirmed their independence. Managers emphasized that their enterprise had more freedom of management than other, non-shareholding enterprises, although half of the Shandong managers said the difference was not large. Most employees indicated that in order to improve management, more authority for the manager was still the top priority. They indicated that as shareholders they had little if any influence on management decisions, and the perceived threat was from above. To the question of whether the Township Economic Committee as a majority shareholder had the right to transfer assets from one enterprise to another, most managers said no, but four out of 27 said yes. They gave as reasons that the township needed the capital and that the SHCS enterprise belonged to it anyway. Apparently, not all followed proper procedures.

The lack of marketability and transferability of shares in most SHCs raises the question of their real value. Transfers to other partners occur in partnership-based SHCs; in SHCs converted from private companies, large shareholders can usually sell their share to outsiders, as long as the BoD agrees. Managers may try to resell their share to the collective. However, the vast majority of shareholders, the ordinary employees, are usually not permitted to sell, not even to other employees. None of our interviewed shareholders had ever transferred or sold shares. Seventy per cent stated they did not have the right to do so, and 83 per cent believed selling them to be unprofitable, and preferred to hold on to them. One might conclude that the real test about the employees' right to sell their shares is still to come. When, because of disappointing dividends, the demands to sell become stronger, one may doubt whether local authorities or enterprise managers will be able to uphold the enterprise statutes and withstand the pressure to sell.

One may conclude from this that the cooperative character of the SHC is not firmly rooted or strong enough to guarantee sustained development of an enterprise as a cooperative. Nor is its independence as a legal economic entity guaranteed. Its embedment in, and dependability on, an eroding rural power and ownership structure inherited from China's collective past hamper the development of rules and management practices of a shareholding company. If local authorities cannot back up their guarantees of dividends and shareholders demand to sell, the entire structure of the SHCS might collapse.

However, the SHCs have taken the thorny issue of how to combine the interest of the collectivity of the enterprise with that of the rural collective community (which is the theoretical owner of the collective shares) one step further. The SHCS has infused a new element in the simple dichotomy between 'closed' cooperative/collective and 'open' shareholding. Previously collectively-owned enterprises sold collective or individual shares to all employees collectively. Thereby they created or formalized a communality of interests between the employees of that enterprise who shared a common property separate from the *xiang*, *zhen*, or *cun* collective. Through the foundation of the SHC, individuals and collectivities of employees excluded the larger collective community from at least a part of its ownership rights. To the extent that share purchases were voluntary, employee action might be labelled as cooperative and risk-taking. If not, employees may have considered shares as just another form of bonus. In either case, they received ownership rights at the expense of the village or township community.

The effects of conversion of collective enterprises on the property rights of various stakeholders

From the beginning, clarification of property rights has been put forward by Chinese economists as a main reason for adoption of the SHCS in collectively-owned enterprises. The same claim is not made for the SHCS when applied in other types of enterprises: the SHCS has an ownership structure which is more complex than that of a partnership or private company because it introduces a collective stakeholder (and sometimes shareholder) whose rights (as we saw above) lack definition and legal restraint. Also, shareholders in a SHC do not enjoy the same protection as those in companies established under the 1994 Company Law. However, the SHCS is most often adopted in township- and village-run enterprises. They reduce the collective stake and express the remaining participation of *xiang* or *cun* authorities in terms of shares, the rights of which are defined in the company charter. The other stakeholders in the SHC and sometimes also new investors receive similarly defined shares. Thus, the conversion demands a change and consolidation of the property rights of all stakeholders.

Township and village authorities which want to raise cash (for a company, or other purposes) are not permitted to issue shares of their collectively-owned enterprises on the open market. They may sell a sizable share to one or more large investors from outside, whose participation will be noted in the company charter, or to a contracting manager. However, for legal and economic reasons, share sales are usually limited to the employees and managers of the enterprise. For that reason, the property rights of most SHC shareholders are restricted not only by official regulations and company charters, but also linked up intricately with their rights as resident villagers or employees, and their ability to effectuate these rights against village government, managers or other large shareholders.

Several questions deserve attention: did conversion make property rights clearer for those with a stake in the company? Has management improved and profit distribution become more accepted as a consequence? Did share issues go beyond a consolidation of existing stakes or did some existing or new stakeholders manage to capture a much larger share than others? Was the conversion beneficial to all, or have there been winners and losers in the process? In order to be able to answer these questions, we will consider four aspects: the valuation of assets at the time of conversion, the transaction price, the allocation of shares to different stakeholders, and the distribution of enterprise profits.

Valuation of enterprise assets

Once an enterprise has obtained approval from the collective government or village committee to adopt the SHCS, the first step is to have a valuation made of its assets. This should be done by an independent county accountancy office, but because of their limited capacity, it may also be performed jointly by the *xiang* economic committees and the enterprises concerned. Accounting practices have improved in recent years, but systemic problems such as administrative intervention, monopolies of accounting companies, and covering up of asset losses still remain.[30] Valuation may be based on age-related original value and net value, replacement cost, capacity to generate profits and other factors.[31] Inflation has rendered the traditional method based on historical price minus depreciation totally inadequate. Yet it was the preferred method in the districts surveyed.

As for fixed assets, the Fuyang accountants used a combination of book value and replacement value. Their guiding principle was that evaluation should be acceptable to both sides.[32] Zunhua did not take immaterial assets into account, and in Zhoucun it was highly unusual. Zhoucun used the method of historical price minus depreciation until 1993, and since then, also the actual price method, even if they admittedly were contradictory. The first method was mainly used for the SHCS because it depressed value and therefore favored the employees who purchased shares. Collective enterprises usually did not accept any valuation of immaterial assets. The eventually determined fixed asset value was the result of a negotiation process between the accountants and the enterprise.[33]

Evaluation of the financial assets is less problematic. Conflicting claims to ownership by different bureaus or collective levels are settled with the founding of the new SHC enterprise. The status of loans for working capital from the *xiang* or *cun* must be specified; under the SHC they will no longer be interest-free or subject to arbitrary withdrawal. Often, SHC charters stipulate that the previous collective owners are no longer responsible for their debts, which suggests that some debts were cleared before the conversion. Evaluation problems lie mainly in the assessment of the quality of loans and debts, the choice of interest rates, and the entitlement of money transfers immediately before the conversion. If evaluation is not performed by independent accountants, the *xiang* or *cun* authorities have great influence on its outcome.

Land may be an important part of the collective share in a company. It belongs to the *xiang* or *cun* unless stipulated otherwise by government. If ownership or use of collective land is transferred, a

[30] Luo and Xiao 1994.

[31] Asset evaluation rules, par. 4, Arts. 21-23, *Guowuyuan gongbao* (State Council bulletin), 15 November 1991.

[32] Yu, Wen and Zhang 1994, pp. 3–7, 13–18, and 23; Han, p. 30.

[33] Interviews with Zunhua Municipal officials and with Mr. Yun, Zhoucun Accountants' Affairs Office, September 1995.

price has to be set. Theoretically, this price should depend on its use; industrial land commands much higher prices than agricultural land. In practice, the government has allowed land to be leased to rural industries at the low agricultural price. Land which has been allocated to village or higher-level collective enterprises in the past can not be transferred at will, and is protected by law against usurpation by rural governments in the same (not always effective) way as other enterprise assets. SHCs have three options for the valuation of land: (1) the land may be considered as collective input into the enterprise, and take the form of a collective share held by village government; (2) the land lease (if cheaper than the market price) may be booked as an immaterial asset; (3) the land may be excluded from valuation and leased to the SHC under a new contract. The second option is hardly ever used, and the third is becoming more common as collective governments reduce their enterprise share. More often than not land is leased to the SHC at the old rate for agricultural land. Both undervaluation of land and cheap leases are hidden subsidies by *xiang* or *cun* to the SHC, which benefit its shareholders. By demanding more or less compensation for its input of land, the *xiang* or *cun* may manipulate its share in the SHC enterprise or its fixed production costs. One way or the other, local governments thereby influence the profits of the SHCs.

Thus, adoption of the SHCS presents an opportunity to the collective owner and new shareholders to reassess the value of its fixed, liquid and immaterial assets, including the price and utility of its land. This assessment has to be approved by independent accountants and is legally binding once establishment of the SHC enterprise has been approved. More importantly, employees and managers express their acceptance by taking shares. The partial privatization results in much more strictly defined ownership rights and virtual exclusion of any claims by non-shareholding employees or members of the collective.

Was the transaction price right?

Above, we noted an undervaluation of existing assets, which of course went at the expense of the original collective owner and benefitted the new SHC shareholders. The employees received undervalued shares, and investors a disproportionate share, because their new investment or technology was converted into shares at current prices, while existing assets were converted at lower historical prices or subsidized prices. National and provincial figures of total nominal value of SHC shares correspond fairly closely with the original value of their fixed assets, but are only weakly related to the value of their liquid assets.[34] This data demonstrates, and our survey confirmed, that in general total share value was put at par with total asset value.

However, the market value of an enterprise is only weakly related to its assets. Expected profits and cash flow are much more important; when discounted at expected rates of interest (plus compensation for the risk), they will yield an acceptable market value. National data on the profitability of SHCs in 1993 and 1994 show nominal capital returns on enterprises of about 20 and 26 per cent, much higher than bank interest rates and also higher than the rise in rural cost of living.[35] The initial conclusion from interviews, company founding charters, some balance sheets, and the above 1993-1994 national profitability data is that in a number of cases the collectives gave away or sold off part of their collective enterprises at prices considerably below market value. The frequent high dividends paid out immediately after the adoption of the SHC system point in this same direction.

The authorities may have felt justified to do so, for several reasons. Employees and managers held stakes in the enterprise which ought to be recognized by giving shares at low prices. Authorities could find comfort in the thought that as a majority shareholder and highest local authority, they could influence profitability and dividends, and thus reduce the value of the shares in the future. Most shares did not have a market value anyway because they could not be transferred or sold. Under traditional accounting rules, and because of subsidies such as free land and cheap loans, actual profitabil-

[34] See next note.

[35] In 1994, China's *xiang/cun* SHCs (excluding Guangdong) had fixed assets with an original value of RMB 113 billion and liquid (gross) assets totalling RMB 131 billion. If fixed assets are corrected for depreciation at 27 per cent (the percentage reported for all *xiang/cun* enterprises in 1993), and liquid assets reduced with 84 per cent of liabilities (*idem*), net value of fixed and liquid assets becomes RMB 83 bn + 21 bn = RMB 104 bn - only 5 per cent more than the reported total share value of RMB 99 bn. Reported 1994 profits were RMB 42.3 bn before taxes and RMB 25.6 bn after taxes, which gives an average return on shares of 25.7 per cent. Xiang SHCs gave lower returns (24 per cent) than *cun* SHCs (28 per cent). For 1993, data were given only for profits *cum* taxes; they were lower in 1993 (33 per cent) than in 1994 (42 per cent). However, when corrected for inflation with the rural costs of living index of 1.126 in 1993 and 1.234 in 1994, real yields declined from 8 to 2 per cent. *Zhongguo xiangzhen qiye nianjian – 1995* (Yearbook of Chinese TVEs), pp. 232–237, and *idem – 1994*, pp. 362-363 and 366-367.

ity of TVEs could not be determined accurately, and rapid growth and market fluctuations made extrapolation of past profits a risky business. Many collective governments wanted funds badly for new economic activities. Some colluded with contracting managers to enrich themselves through private purchase of undervalued shares. The relative weight of these considerations varied between the surveyed villages and townships, and needs further research.

Of course, governments and individuals considered profitability and risks before deciding to sell or invest. New investment capital, whether from managers, employees or outsiders has flowed into the TVEs which were considered the best buy. This is confirmed by the higher than average profitability of SHCs. This survey showed a very positive, even uncritical attitude among SHC employees towards buying more shares in their company if on offer; in Zhoucun 80 per cent and in Zunhua 57 per cent of the respondents, while only 8 and 23 per cent, respectively, said they would not buy more shares. Eighty-three per cent thought that selling their shares at face value would be unprofitable. They saw themselves as clear winners. This does not necessarily mean that the collectives lost. The *xiang* and *cun* managed to attract risk-bearing capital for their best-performing enterprises, though at a high price (through undervaluation or guaranteed high dividends) which was not only a recognition of vested interests of managers and employees, but also a function of the scarcity of capital during most of the past decade.

Shares: types, distribution and rights

When a collective owner converts its enterprise into an SHC, it defines its ownership in terms of company shares, and limits it to a definite percentage. Usually, shares are sold exclusively to managers and employees in the form of ordinary or preference shares. Sometimes other members of the local community can purchase shares as well. In rare cases the enterprise is put up for sale at an auction open to outsiders; then the new owners do not necessarily have obligations towards the employees. Preference, non-voting shares have occasionally been used to restrain collective government or village from interference in the enterprises. The employee share may come in any size: though districts and enterprises had stipulated a fixed percentage of distributed shares in advance, in many cases the eventual share depended on the employees' financial capacity and their willingness to buy. Enterprises may offer additional free shares as an incentive.[36] The rules state, and this survey confirmed, that the maximum number of shares which employees are allowed to buy is based on their employment record and position in the company. The record may go back to the 1960s, the founding of the company, or the introduction of household responsibility system. Distinctions in position may be made either between managers and all other employees, or between factory head, department head, workshop head, technician, ordinary worker, etcetera, each being entitled to a certain number of shares.

In the initial period, often SHC shares bore no risk because the collective guaranteed that in the case of losses they would retain their face value. Moreover, they guaranteed (and the company charter confirmed) that the interest on preference shares (and sometimes also on ordinary shares) would be increased according to rises in, and remain higher than, current bank interest rates for savings.[37] The enterprise statutes specify the different types of shares, their transferability (free, limited to other employees or to heirs only), duration (some shares may be bought back by the enterprise at face value after three or five years, but usually shares are sold back only when the employee leaves the company or retires), the rights of shareholders

---

[36]The different types of shareholders and shares in the SHC enterprise and their rights deserve some fuller explanation. Company statutes stipulate the amount and types. As for shareholders, the 1992 Circular No. 24 of the Ministry of Agriculture listed five types: (1) the *xiang*- or *cun*-held 'collective share'; (2) the 'enterprise share', based on its accumulated assets. Part of this could be distributed to individual employees based on their contribution to the enterprise as 'employee preference shares', which are non-transferable and non-inheritable; (3) shares held by other units, so-called 'social legal person's shares', on the basis of a (past) investment; (4) 'ordinary individual shares', owned by employees (or outsiders, then called 'social individual shares') who have contributed capital, materials or technical skills; and (5) 'foreign shares'. More recently, the 'enterprise share' has been abolished and distributed to employees. There are two types of shares: 'ordinary (risk-bearing) shares' and 'preference shares'. The latter (sometimes called 'empty shares' (*xugu*)) have fixed dividends which come before any other distribution of net profits, and their claim to the residual comes before common shareholders, but they do not bestow any of the other rights of common shareholders, who have purchased their shares. See Zang and Cha 1995). Some company charters have ruled that preference shares may be converted into ordinary shares within a given period. In the early years, preference shares were sometimes given free to the employees. More recently, employees receive such shares only as additions to purchased shares. Shares may be sold at a discount or with a bonus preference share, but usually at face value.

[37]*Zhongguo nongye nianjian 1994* (China Agricultural Yearbook 1994) 1995, p. 129.

(decision on dividend, and voting), and often the guaranteed percentage of dividend.

The experimental areas adopted different methods of conversion of existing interests of stakeholders into shares. There was, and is, no agreement over the entitlement of state or collective organizations which did not invest but contributed to the enterprise by preferential policies, such as tax remission, repayment of loans before taxes, or free loans.[38] Fuyang converted all assets which had resulted from state investment, tax exemptions, low-interest bank loans, and state preferential policies into non-voting preference shares with fixed dividends. Wenzhou, with its strong tradition of private entrepreneurship, was afraid that such state shares would go at the expense of the employees' share, and converted them into a non-interest bearing 'state support fund'. The guiding principle for Wenzhou was that only the actual investor who was the owner should reap the profits. For the same reason, unlike most other areas it allowed transfers of shares.[39]

In Zhoucun, the collectives divested only 30 per cent of their enterprise ownership at first, allocating it to the employees on the basis of employment record, basic wage, and position. Most enterprises in Wangcun township applied a ratio of 40:50:10 for these three factors, reserving the 10 per cent for 'managing cadres'.[40] Another township was less egalitarian: it allocated 60 per cent of the shares on the basis of employment record, 28 per cent for cadres and 12 per cent for achievement. In 1993 and 1994, Zhoucun lowered the required majority for the collective share to 51 per cent, leaving this decision to the township and village level. Sales were partly forced: some of the interviewed employees still resented the obligatory purchases of shares, but indicated that their position would have suffered if they had refused. Wangcun sold 80 to 90 per cent of its collective share, a minor part to outsiders. The proceeds were invested in better infrastructure and new enterprises.[41] Other townships in Zhoucun followed suit.

---

[38]Han Yuanqin *et al.* 1994 assert that such valuation of state policies are incorrect. A report by the Production Office of the Structural Reform Committee, *Zhongguo Tigai Yanjiuhui Yanjiu Baogao*, no. 5, 20 June 1995 notes the dilemma but does not take a stand.

[39]Yu, Wen and Zhang 1994, pp. 3–7, 13–18, 23; Han, p. 30.

[40]Yu, Wen and Zhang 1994, pp. 148-149.

[41]Interview with Bi Jinxian, head of Wangcun *zhen* government, 29 August 1995.

The Zunhua municipal government only started promoting the SHCS in 1993. It left considerable room for different practices, but ruled that shares should be distributed to employees only against payment and without obligation to buy. The collective share might be kept entirely in the hands of the collective, or subsequently sold in parts (in 1995, it recommended 40 per cent) to the employees.

Share ownership appeared to be widely spread among SHC employees by 1995. Three-quarters of our respondents owned shares; more than 80 per cent of the managers and workshop heads, and 60 to 75 per cent of the technicians and accountants. Among the latter group, share ownership was slightly more common in Zhoucun than in Zunhua. With ordinary workers the difference was significant: in Zhoucun 70 per cent held shares, but in Zunhua only 33 per cent. Two explanations may be offered for the difference: the political priority given to employee shares in Zhoucun, and the more recent date of conversion to SHCs in Zunhua (after some early cooperative ideals had faded). A more fundamental cause may lie in the weaker position of rural industrial workers in Zunhua, where economic growth and labor demand are not as strong as in Zhoucun.

In Zhoucun, 40 per cent of the respondents owned both ordinary ('cash') shares and preference shares, 55 per cent owned only ordinary shares and 5 per cent only preference shares. There was some indication that workers more than any other category had been obliged to purchase shares in order to obtain employment. Although this was mentioned fairly often, responses to the question 'why did you buy shares?' were ambiguous. 22 per cent of the Zhoucun workers said it had been necessary in order to obtain employment; 39 per cent chose the answer 'I imitated others' and 17 per cent the idealistic answer 'in order to become an owner'. The last two answers do not mean pressure was not exerted to get people to buy shares. Only 22 per cent gave a genuine financial reason: the wish to invest, or to obtain free shares.

We noted considerable differences in shareholding between sampled respondents, with a minimum of RMB 100 and a maximum of RMB 170,000 in Zunhua and RMB 70,000 in Zhoucun. Average holdings per employee in Zunhua were RMB 17,060, i.e. two and a half times larger than in Zhoucun (RMB 6,880). The more equal distribution of shareholdings in Zhoucun (in spite of its being economically more developed and wealthier than Zunhua) reflects the stronger political direction and collective ideology in Zhoucun's controlled implementation of the SHCS, and its earlier date of adoption.

Most employees felt that differences in shareholding between ordinary employees and managers should not exceed a ratio of one to three, but actual differences were larger than that.[42] Most managers stated that the incentive effect of shareholding could be noted only among employees who held sizeable numbers of shares, not with the other employees. Changes in the actual distribution of share ownership in rural China should give an important indication of the future direction of the SHCS, but there is no such data.

The conversion from a collectively-owned enterprise to an SHC enterprise and further privatization have clarified property rights to a certain degree only. Several questions remain unsolved. First, usually the collective maintained a dominant share, and the question whether collective government or village committee is the owner of the collective share or only the agent of all community residents was not solved. Second, because the required valuation of the enterprise assets at the time of conversion has often been incomplete, the ownership status of assets which had been omitted (such as immaterial assets, bad debts, land leases) has not been determined. As long as the collective government or village remains the majority shareholder, it is free to interpret its ownership rights and those of others according to its own interests. Third, separation between collective government or village and enterprise remained incomplete and ill-defined, particularly the power relations between the township economic committee (or the *cun*), its asset management company, and enterprise management. For instance, it is generally reported, and this survey confirmed, that if the collective holds a dominant share, the township economic committee or village party secretary continued to appoint managers and approve contracts. Fourth, the creation of additional nominal owners, the rights of whom were not always well defined or equal (shareholders whose shares may be bought back by the enterprise at face value within three or five years probably having the weakest position), added to the complexity of relations between

[42] Average holdings of managers and common workers differed by a factor six in Zunhua (RMB 35,800 and RMB 6,000, respectively) and a factor four in Zhoucun (RMB 14,170 and RMB 3,540, respectively). In Zunhua, workshop heads, technicians, and accountants formed an intermediate layer of stockholders, with averages between RMB 10,000 to RMB 12,000. In Zhoucun, these three categories owned little more than the common workers; technicians and workshop heads averaged less than RMB 5,000 and accountants about RMB 6,500. It should be noted that some of the largest shareholder-managers (one of whom possessed over RMB 1,000,000 of shares) refused to be included in our sample. Because of our small sample size, the few large shareholder-managers had a great effect on the Zhoucun and Zunhua averages.

owners and agents. The institution of multiple ownership may be divisive, or not acceptable to all interested parties, and fuel internal conflicts over property rights which had been dormant. Fifth, even after the collective has lost its majority stake in a company, its powers may be so extensive, and the interdependence of rural entrepreneurs, shareholders and local officials so great, that formal rights cannot be realized. Civil law litigation is inaccessible and rare, and contributes little to clarification of ownership rights of shareholders.

On the positive side, the SHCS's primary contribution has been the demarcation of property rights of employee shareholders and managers (at the expense of the theoretical rights of all members of the collective), that is, of *non-governmental* owners *within* the enterprise. It has done less to limit the self-proclaimed rights of government and other outside agencies. Its second main contribution has been the clarification of rights to residual income through the establishment of an explicit mechanism of distribution of dividends.

The further development of ownership in the SHC enterprise is a matter of grave concern and serious dispute for many Chinese economists and politicians. Some hold that the collective ownership share should remain dominant (as required by the 1990 regulations);[43] some even deny that private shares are privately owned;[44] others believe that collective dominance can be maintained without formal share ownership, and that a 10 per cent or 20 per cent share will do. Some continue to defend traditional ideas about the collective and cooperatives. 'According to regulations, the collective should own half of the shares... Some places convert the collective assets at current market value to create a share fund, and allow employees to buy shares. This belies the principle of one-man one-share. Other places distinguish two types of allocated shares, one on the basis of capital and another per person. This is wrong, too... The SHCS is characterized by the equal combination of labor and capital, and should have one share per employee in order to stimulate the workers.'[45] Only a few dare to advocate the creation of a strong share held by the employees collectively – this might create a well-

[43]'Under the condition that the collective ownership form is not changed, rural collective enterprises may absorb investment which is put into shares.' State Council Rules on Rural Collective Enterprises of the PRC, 3 June 1990, Art. 6.

[44]'Because individual shares cannot be sold, transferred, mortgaged or circulated, they are not ordinary private property, but a form of socialist private property.' Shi 1995a.

[45]Shi 1995b.

organized opponent of village government and threaten its control over collective assets.

Such debates are fuelled by ideological differences, and may also reflect growing disparities between regions, enterprises and employees. From an economic management point of view, it stands to reason that differences in type and size of enterprise and different needs for capital and incentives may lead to different conclusions about optimizing the capital structure of SHC enterprises. This requires more study than can be presented here. However, one may assume, and recent history shows, that local and sectoral variations will increase when economies grow apart and government does not pass proper legislation.

Profit distribution and dividend policy

The shareholders of the TVEs which have adopted the shareholding cooperative system have only limited rights of disposition of the enterprise profits. As noted above, the government has set rules for profit retention and distribution in TVEs, and its sequence,[46] which also apply to SHC enterprises. However, in many districts SHC enterprises no longer follow the regulations on distribution (which stipulate 6:2:2 or 5:3:2 ratios for collective accumulation, welfare, and pay-outs to employees). Zhoucun ruled that 50 to 60 per cent of profits should be retained by the enterprise for reproduction, 10 per cent go to welfare, and 30 to 40 per cent be distributed as dividends (to a maximum of 20 per cent of the nominal share value). Malanyu *zhen* (in Zunhua) ruled that this ratio should be 4:2:4. Zunhua county had ruled that about 25 per cent should be retained, 30 per cent should be distributed as cash dividend, 30 per cent as stock dividend, and 15 per cent be allocated to employee bonuses and welfare. In both counties rules were indicative rather than strictly enforced.[47] Wenzhou ruled that 15 per cent should be retained in the public accumulation fund, 50 per cent should be distributed in stock dividends, 10 per cent should go to welfare, and a maximum of 25 per cent to cash dividends (including interest). Some places in Wenzhou allowed share

[46]The sequence of profit distribution, after compensation of losses, is as follows: (1) 10 per cent of after-tax profits to the public accumulation fund, as required by law; (2) the common welfare fund for collective employee welfare; (3) priority shareholders; (4) public accumulation fund, according to company regulations and the decisions of the shareholders' meeting; (5) ordinary share dividends. Zang and Cha 1995, pp. 6 and 257–259.

[47]Interviews with Zunhua municipal officials, September 1995.

capital to be paid back to investors before taxes (which was at the expense of tax revenues). In some other places cash and stock dividends amounted to 30 to 50 per cent or more, even up to 100 per cent.[48]

Such differences in pay-outs demonstrate the evolution of the shareholding system. Of course, different types of enterprises require different levels of profit retention. However, as local regulations apply to all their SHC enterprises, the main explanation for growing differences should be sought in local economic policies. To the extent that the rule of retention of 60 per cent of profits was devised to protect and enlarge the collectively-owned assets, it hardly made any sense after the collective had sold off most of its assets. To the extent that it was devised as a correction to the old practice of artificially boosting profits, it had to be revised as profit calculations became more realistic. However, the high dividend payments which we discussed earlier represent a transfer from the collective to the private sector and speed up the process of privatization. Partly because of artificially boosted profits, share dividends have usually been as high as 20 to 30 per cent per year in the past few years, in some cases even higher. Even loss-making enterprises may give dividends.[49] During the spiralling inflation of 1992-1994, only guaranteed high dividends on shares could persuade employees or outside investors to take part in shareholding schemes. To the extent that such high dividend rates have been included in the company charters, established a custom or raised expectations, there is a real danger now that inflation and interest rates have come down, the financial position of SHC enterprises will be affected by pay-outs that are too high.

Pressure to exercise the right of shareholders is more likely to come from managers with controlling interests than from below. Asked whether they had any influence on the size of the dividend, 87 per cent of the shareholding respondents said they had not. The few positive answers came mainly from managers, but even of them a majority (62 per cent) gave a negative answer. Those who gave positive answers indicated that the decision about dividends was taken by the Board of Directors (60 per cent), by the majority shareholder (13 per cent) or at the shareholders' meeting (27 per cent). Almost all laborers and

[48]Yu, Wen and Zhang 1994, pp. 3-7, 13–18, 23; Han 1994, p. 30; Zhoucun interviews.

[49]Without profit, in principle dividend should be passed. However, shareholders may decide to distribute a maximum of 6 per cent of the nominal share value from the public accumulation fund, as long as it does not drop below 25 per cent of the registered capital. See Zang and Cha 1995.

technicians said that they did not have any influence. Only 28 per cent of all respondents believed that shareholders should exercise their right to speak at the annual meeting of shareholders. One effect of the SHC has been, for better or for worse, to take the profit distribution issue out of the political arena, but as yet the SHC has provided neither shareholders nor employees with a level playing field to contest issues concerning dividends or wages.

Conclusion

Introduced as an experiment in China in 1987, the SHCS has diversified and now taken hold in a significant percentage of rural industrial enterprises. Its spread is uneven and the system has taken many different forms. It was used to convert private partnerships, collectively-owned and collectively-managed industries and enterprises contracted by their managers, as well as for newly established enterprises. Motives and objectives varied. Most collective enterprises wanted to attract new capital, and create formal independence from local political leadership at the same time. Private enterprises, and those dominated by their contracting managers, saw the SHCS as a means to obtain political protection and draw profits in the form of dividends. Large rural enterprises used the SHCS for its tax advantages, or as a quasi-limited company, because they were not qualified to operate under the new Company Law.

Different stakeholders in collective enterprises wanted different things from the SHCS: the *xiang* and *cun* leadership wanted to divest collective property, improve economic performance, or push for employee ownership for political reasons. Adoption of the SHCS showed their willingness to respond to political signals from above which favored the SHCS. Moreover, it protected or created the enterprise's classification as collective property, which implied that its taxes and administration fees would be under collective control. Many areas classified their rural enterprises as an SHC, even if they had rudimentary forms of shareholding only. Government and CCP wanted more institutional control over profiteering managers. Managers appreciated the greater independence, the opportunity to procure material incentives for employees and themselves, and to legalize or cash in on their stake in the company. Employees were attracted by the high dividends, or wanted to keep their jobs. With such diverse motives, it may take some time and real exercise of shareholder rights before the different shareholders agree on the purpose and priorities of their enterprise.

The system developed in a controlled manner in three experimental areas, and more freely elsewhere. The 'left' national regulations of 1990 did not have much of a standardizing effect. After the 1992 liberalization, they became obsolete. Local authorities preferred to promote, or sometimes obstruct, the SHCS by rules of their own. While adoption of the SHCS has been very much policy-driven, we found that many enterprises do not comply with local rules. The new Company Law set an example of a formal management structure, but practices in SHCs continue to be influenced by the rules for collective enterprises, their small size and operation in a closed community. Many remain under collective control, particularly if local government is the largest shareholder. Even when managers own a majority of the shares, their enterprise still depends on the goodwill or active support of collective government for its external relations. Employee shareholders were not seen (and did not claim) to exert any influence on decision-making.

Formal separation between collective ownership and enterprise management, and partial privatization under the SHCS affected collective property rights in several ways. Some managers of SHC enterprises interviewed mentioned the complexity of the SHCS as a reason for not following the SHC regulations or attracting capital through share issues. Its obsolete and idealistic regulations limited its usefulness as a legal basis for combining the interests of capital, labor and management. In general, the new management structure and procedures under the SHCS did not change operation of the enterprises or appointment of its managers very much. This may have had to do with the small size of most companies, the limited mobility of labor (including managers) and capital, and also with the combination of functions in one person. Often, the village party secretary or township economic committee exerts ultimate control. Nevertheless, the conversion is appreciated positively by almost all managers and employees. Many reasons are given: greater financial and managerial independence, greater political support, perceived opportunities to influence the direction of the company, and more rational and accountable distribution of residual income through dividends. Also, the SHCS has a modern image, which was reinforced by the Company Law, and interviewed managers anticipated further processes of change.

The property rights of the SHC enterprise are not fully secure or unambiguous under present conditions. The question of the extent of privatization has several layers: how much of the collective property rights were transferred and to whom, which type of rights, and how well will they hold up in case of conflicts? The answers depend just as much on an evaluation of the scope of prior collective rights (against the claims of other stakeholders in collective enterprises) as on an analysis of the qualities of the SHCS. The simple conversion from a collectively-owned enterprise into an SHC with the collective as a majority shareholder does not constitute privatization *per se*. Below, the main answers found in this study are summarized.

1. The legal framework of the SHCS holds conflicting elements of cooperative, collectivist and capitalist ideas. Certain rules, such as those on profit distribution and one-man one-vote shareholder representation are held to be obsolete by most people, and therefore ignored in enterprise charters or not observed in practice. Other rules, devised to separate ownership from management, and to regulate or exclude collectively-held 'common' rights of the community or employees are only partially effective because the extent of and control over these rights have not been settled. Therefore, enterprise behavior may deviate significantly from its charter.

2. Individual share ownership is restricted to employees and, in rare cases, to members of the collective. Employee shareholders have a double dependency: on their employer, and on the authorities of their collective *xiang* or *cun*. This puts them in a position where they dare not and do not cooperate and enforce their own rights against institutional and managerial shareholders. Because their shares cannot be sold, they do not have exit rights, and the value of shares is unclear. Often, shares are little more than a component of employee salaries.

3. Dividends from SHC enterprise are a superior and accepted form of distribution of residual income. However, their usefulness for enterprise management is limited in two ways. Their size is restricted by the national standard of 60 per cent profit retention, irrespective of the investment needs of the enterprise. In many enterprises, dividends are a quasi-wage, and therefore less flexible than if they only represented risk-bearing capital.

4. Usually, ownership and management are not fully separated. If the *xiang* or *cun* have a majority share, or even a minority share, they may continue to control appointments and dismissals of managers, and command external resources which are vital to the enterprise's economic success. If the collective share is small or entirely absent, usually the contracting managers or a few partners are the major

shareholders. For that reason, the formal powers of the Board of Directors and annual shareholders' meeting are not of much use. If SHC is adopted by a private company or partnership, it introduces elements of collective ownership or claims in return for political and tax advantages which make its property rights structure more, not less, complex and fuzzy.

5. The SHCS gives formal recognition to the claims of various stakeholders in collective enterprises. Their conversion to SHC reduced some of the 'vagueness' described by Weitzman and Xu, by establishing the value of the enterprise and converting various stakeholders into a definite number of shareholders with rights which are summed up in the company charter. The SHC legitimized or checked 'grey privatization' by assessing the claims of contracting managers and employees and giving recognition in the form of a definite number of shares and entitlement to dividends. The charters of SHC enterprises in which these rights were recognized had to pass formal political approval, and constitute the legal basis for the solution of future disputes.

6. So far, the partial privatization under the SHC has met with little opposition, neither from the investors (because collectives sold their most profitable enterprises first) nor from the collective community (because political procedures were observed and the community has little independent voice). However, we noted that at the time of conversion, inadequate and incomplete assessment of asset value and earning capacity was quite common. Usually, employee-shareholders profited at the expense of the collective, and received high dividends. Contracting managers profited most, when they obtained large and legally protected shares. Because most enterprises did well, all parties seemed to be content with their share, but if the economic situation deteriorates, conflicts over ownership, share value and entitlement to residual income are more likely. In the light of current expectations, employee-shareholders may refuse to accept a cancellation of guaranteed returns, let alone loss of share value.

One might argue that particularly in small-scale enterprises, and in periods of enterprise expansion, a certain degree of fuzziness of property rights is functional. Owners, managers and employees are motivated by (not necessarily realistic) high expectations about their future share in earnings, and discouraged by a strict and limitative definition of their ownership or control rights. While this may be true, it is unlikely that the incentive of high expectations could be maintained in large companies and over a longer period, or in times of adversity.

Whether the SHCS will ever realize its pretence of cooperative management by employee-shareholders is highly doubtful. Rather, the SHCS has been moving in the direction set by the Company Law. Its strength lies to some extent in its weak conceptual and legal clarity, which makes it acceptable and profitable to the Communist Party, government, managers and employees and other stakeholders with widely divergent views, in a period of economic boom and creeping transition from collective to private ownership.

References

Blasi, Joseph R. (1988), *Employee Ownership: Revolution or Rip-off?*, Cambridge, MA: Ballinger

Case, John (1988), 'ESOPs: Dead or Alive?', *Inc.*, June, pp. 94–100

Chang, Chun and Wang, Yijiang (1994), 'The Nature of the Township-Village Enterprise', *Journal of Comparative Economics*, No. 19, pp. 434–452

Fu, Chunsheng *et al.* (eds) (1993), *Zhongguo xiangzhen qiye jingying zhengce fagui daquan* (Compendium of Policies and Regulations for TVE Management), Beijing: Zhongguo tongji chubanshe

Guo, Wei (1995), 'Lun nongcun gufen hezuozhi' (About the Rural SHCS), *Nongye jingji wenti* (Problems of Agricultural Economy), No. 5, pp. 33–38

Guowuyuan gongbao (State Council bulletin), 15 November 1991

Han, Jun and Zhang, Qingzhong (eds) (1993), *Zhongguo nongcun gufen hezuo jingji: lilun, shijian, zhengce* (China's Rural Shareholding Cooperative Economy: Theory, Practice, Policies), Beijing: Jingji guanli chubanshe

Han, Yuanqin *et al.* (1994), 'Nongmin gufen hezuo qiye yanjiu baogao' (Research Report on Farmers' SHCs), manuscript, CAAS, Agricultural Economy Institute

Liang, Yi *et al.* (eds) (1993), *Xiangzhen gufen hezuo qiye zujian yu yunzuo* (Establishment and Application of Township and Village SHC Enterprises), Beijing: Zhongguo jingji chubanshe

Liu, Jiang (ed.) (1994), *Zhongguo nongye quanshu: Shandong juan* (Compendium of China's Agriculture: Shandong Volume), Beijing: Zhongguo nongye chubanshe

Luo, Ning and Xiao, Mingdi (1994), 'Zichan pinggu zhongzai de wenti jiqi duice' (Existing Problems and Remedies in Asset Evaluation), *Jingji yanjiu cankao* (References for Economic Research), No. 175, pp. 46–49

Ministry of Agriculture, 'Guanyu tuixing he wanshan xiangzhen qiye gufen hezuozhi de tongzhi' (Circular on Promotion and Perfection of SHCS for TVEs) in: Liang, Yi *et al.* (1993), pp. 306–311

Ministry of Agriculture, 'Preliminary Regulations for Rural SHCs', issued on 12 February 1990, in Nongyebu Zhengce Tizhi Gaige Fagui Si (ed.) (1994), *Nongye fa quanshu* (Complete Documentation of Agricultural Laws), Beijing: Zhongguo nongye chubanshe

Mu, Yongtai and Tan, Wei (1993), 'Laiyangshi gufen hezuozhi de shijian yu qishi' (Practice and Inspiration Drawn from the SHCS in Laiyang Municipality), *Zhongguo nongcun jingji* (Rural Economy of China), No. 7, pp. 47–51

Nongyebu Zhengce Tizhi Gaige Fagui Si (ed.) (1994), *Nongye fa quanshu* (Complete Documentation of Agricultural Laws), Beijing: Zhongguo nongye chubanshe

Oi, Jean C. and Walder, Andrew G. (eds) (1999), *Property Rights and Economic Reform in China*, Stanford: Stanford University Press

Production Office of the Structural Reform Committee (1995), *Zhongguo Tigai Yanjiuhui Yanjiu Baogao*, No. 5, 20 June

Shi, Yueqin (1995a), 'Guanyu Shenzhenshi Henggangzhen gufen hezuozhi de kaocha baogao' (Investigation Report of the SHCS in Henggang Town in Shenzhen), *Nongye jingji* (Agricultural Economy), No. 10, pp. 28-29

— (1995b) 'Dui nongcun jiti qiye tuixing gufen hezuozhi jige juti wenti de renzhi' (Understanding of Some Concrete Problems in the Promotion of the SHCS for Rural Collective Enterprises), *Nongye jingji* (Agricultural Economy), No. 11, pp. 23-24

Tian, Zhen (1993), 'Gufen hezuozhi: xiangzhen qiye gaige yu fazhandi biran xuanze' (The Shareholding Cooperative System: The Necessary Choice for Reform and Development of TVEs) in Han, Jun and Zhang, Qingzhong (eds), *Zhongguo nongcun gufen hezuo jingji: lilun, shijian, zhengce* (China's Rural Shareholding Cooperative Economy: Theory, Practice, Policies), Beijing: Jingji guanli chubanshe

Tsao, George K.Y. (1995), 'Reforming China's Township and Village Enterprises: A Feasibility Study on the Applicability of the Mondragon Cooperative Model', *Journal of Rural Cooperation*, Vol. 23, No. 1, pp. 31–65

Vermeer, E.B. (1996) 'Experiments with Rural Shareholding Cooperatives: The Case of Zhoucun District, Shandong Province', *China Information*, Vol. 11, No. 2, pp. 75–107

Weitzman, Martin L. and Xu, Chenggang (1994), 'Chinese Township-Village Enterprises as Vaguely Defined Cooperatives', *Journal of Comparative Economics*, Vol. 18, No. 2, pp. 121–145

Yao, Zhiji (1995), 'Dui xiangzhen qiye zhidu gaige de sikao' (Thoughts about the TVE System Reform), *Nongye jingji* (Agricultural Economy), No. 3, pp. 39-40

Yu, Guoyao, Wen, Tiejun and Zhang, Xiaoshan (eds) (1994), *Jiushi niandai chanquan zhidu de duice yanjiu: Zhongguo nongcun gufen hezuo jingji zhuanji* (Research of Policies Regarding the Property Rights System in the Nineties: Special Collection on China's Rural SHC Economy), Beijing: Zhongguo shangwu chubanshe

Yuan, Peng (1995), 'Gufen hezuozhi yu xiangzhen qiye zhidu zhuangxin' (SHCs and Renewal of the TVE System), *Zhongguo nongcun jingji* (Rural Economy of China), No. 12, pp. 48–52

Zang, Rihong and Cha, Zhenxiang (eds) (1995), *Nongcun gufen hezuozhi qiye kuaiji hesuan yu caiwu guanli* (Accounting of Budgets and Financial Management in Rural SHC Enterprises), Beijing: Zhongguo nongye chubanshe

Zhang, Luoxiong and Wang, Qiang (1993), 'Nongcun gufen hezuo qiye de fazhan qingkuang ji zhengce jianyi' (The Development of the Rural SHC Enterprises and a Policy Proposal), *Zhongguo nongcun jingji* (Rural Economy of China), No. 6, pp. 8–13

Zhongguo jingji kexue nianjian 1994 (1994) (China Yearbook of Economic Science 1994), Beijing: Zhongguo tongji chubanshe

Zhongguo nongye nianjian 1994 (1994) (China Agricultural Yearbook 1994), Beijing: Zhongguo nongye chubanshe

Zhongguo qiye guanli nianjian – 1994 (1994) (Yearbook of China Enterprise Management 1994), Beijing: Zhongguo Qiye guanli chubanshe

Zhongguo qiye guanli nianjian – 1995 (1995) (Yearbook of China Enterprise Management 1995), Beijing: Zhongguo Qiye guanli chubanshe

Zhongguo xiangzhen qiye nianjian – 1995 (1995) (Yearbook of Chinese TVEs), Beijing: Zhongguo nongye chubanshe

Zhou, Jianqiu (1992), 'Gufen hezuozhi shi shixian he fazhan gongyouzhi de zhongyao xingshi' (SHCS is an Important Form for Realizing and Developing a Public Ownership System), *Zhongguo nongcun jingji* (Rural Economy of China), No. 12, pp. 36–41

6

Law as Instrument: The Process of Direct Investment Authorization in China

*Jan Holthuis**

Section 18 of the Chinese constitution[1] legitimizes foreign investment in China. The first paragraph of section 18 states:

> The People's Republic of China permits foreign enterprises, other foreign economic organizations and individual foreigners to invest in China and to enter into various forms of economic cooperation with Chinese enterprises and other Chinese economic organizations in accordance with the law of the People's Republic of China.

In China, foreign investment is selectively directed to achieve economic objectives: to modernize China's economy,[2] to meet domestic market demands which cannot be satisfied by domestic enterprises and to contribute to China's foreign exchange balance. China's complex foreign investment approval system has been the crucial instrument in the pursuit of these policy objectives. It defines the scope and opportunities for foreign investment.

There is considerable confusion among foreign investors as to which authority is responsible for granting approval to a specific foreign investment project. Often local officials or government agencies claim approval authority which they don't have or they provide false information to foreign investors.

* The author wishes to express his gratitude to Dr. E.B. Vermeer of the Sinological Institute for his very useful contribution to this article.

[1] Adopted at the 5th Session of the 5th National People's Congress and Promulgated for Implementation by the Proclamation of the National People's Congress on 4 December 1982.

[2] By promoting the import of advanced technology and foreign capital.

The confusion has three main roots. First, the struggle of the local governments against China's central government which is a central theme in China's history. Regional self-interest to attract as much foreign investment as possible results in a cut-throat competition between local governments and a political struggle against Beijing. Second, local and the central governments have different priorities. Local governments push for rapid economic development while the central government aims to control inflation and to guide foreign investment towards the sectors in the Chinese economy it considers have the highest priority. Beijing wants to avoid costly duplication of investments which would reduce overall profitability and safeguard against sub-standard technology imports. Third, local governments are not always aware of the applicable approval procedures.

This contribution will set out the rules and regulations relating to foreign investment approval and elaborate on some methods which are used in practice to circumvent these rules and regulations.

Foreign direct investment laws in China

Foreign direct investment is regulated by various laws. There is a law or set of regulations for each type of China's foreign investment enterprises (FIEs): The Law of the People's Republic of China on Joint Ventures Using Chinese and Foreign Investment 1979 and the Regulations for the Implementation of the Law of the People's Republic of China Using Chinese and Foreign Investments 1983 (for Sino-foreign equity joint ventures), the Law of the People's Republic of China on Chinese-Foreign Contractual Ventures 1988 (for contractual joint ventures), the Law of the People's Republic of China on Foreign Capital Enterprises 1986 (for wholly foreign-owned enterprises), and the Provisional Regulations on the Establishment of Investment-Oriented Companies by Foreign Investors 1995 (for foreign investment holding companies).[3] With an eye to consistency, the Coordinating Committee for Foreign Investment was set up under the State Council in 1994. The commission is responsible for studying, coordinating and guiding foreign investment policies throughout the PRC. It does not have formal decision-making power but the advice of the commission can be implemented by the State Council and delegated legislative power.

Traditionally, an FIE is established by a Chinese party and a foreign party each contributing in cash or in kind to a newly

[3]The holding company serves the purpose of holding equity interests in subsidiary investment enterprises in China.

formed Chinese legal entity. Establishment of FIEs is subject to approval by the Ministry of Foreign Trade and Economic Cooperation (MOFTEC) or other authorized central government departments. The State Planning and Development Commission, the State Administration for Foreign Exchange and the State Economic and Trade Commission are the most important departments. Each has provincial and local representation.

In summary, approval is granted on the basis of a project proposal, a detailed feasibility study, a joint venture agreement, and the articles of association of the Chinese legal entity. The approval authorities look at the foreign direct investment project as a whole and consider its economic, financial, environmental and social implications. Special attention is paid to foreign currency arrangements to ensure that the investment project can independently sustain its foreign investment requirements.[4]

Foreign direct investment policy

China's initial foreign investment policy can, in general terms, be found in the respective national investment laws.[5] These provide for preferential treatment in industrial areas: energy development, machine manufacturing and electronics; and in remote areas such as agriculture, forestry and animal husbandry. In addition, local governments have considerable authority to approve foreign investment proposals and to formulate local law and policy on foreign investment as long as the latter do not conflict with higher government regulations.

Foreign investments in especially assigned geographical areas such as Special Economic Zones (the original experimental gardens for China's Open Door capitalist-oriented policies), Open Coastal Cities and Special Development Areas have reduced tax and fee structures for foreign investments. More recently, preferential treatment is given to foreign investments in other parts of China and to specific fields of industry.[6]

Central foreign investment approval policy is either interpreted differently by local governments or simply neglected.[7] It is therefore

[4] Art. 75 of the Joint Venture Regulations requires that joint ventures must in general maintain a balance between foreign exchange income and expenditure.

[5] See e.g. Art. 3 of the Joint Venture Regulations 1983.

[6] *China Economic News*, No. 22, 15 June 1998.

[7] See Wang 1993, p. 215: 'Since joint ventures and other ventures need to be approved by the Chinese government, the drafters of the law seemingly believed

possible that a deal can be made at the local level even when it is contrary to national law and policy. Foreign investors can find themselves in the uncomfortable situation where projects locally approved are not given approval or blocked by government departments at a higher level at a later stage after a considerable amount of money has already been spent.

Authorization of foreign investment

Depending on the total amount of investment involved, MOFTEC can entrust the people's governments in the relevant provinces, autonomous regions and municipalities directly under the central government or relevant ministries or bureaus under the State Council with delegated approval authority. However, the Chinese authorities designate most regulations or circulars relating to authorization of investment levels as internal (*neibu*) regulations. As they are not published, foreign investors are faced with an added confusion.

A foreign investment project totalling more than US$ 30 million requires approval from the central governmental level, MOFTEC, and the State Planning and Development Commission. Foreign investment projects above US$ 100 million require approval from the State Council, the highest authority in approving and supervising foreign investment. Provinces are authorized to approve foreign investment projects below US$ 30 million.[8] Projects up to US$ 10 million can be approved by local governments.

Embedded within these guidelines are multiple exceptions. In the event that a project involves foreign currency investments of more than US$ 5 million the provincial governmental departments remain the appropriate approval authority.[9] In addition, governmental departments have issued a large number of rules and regulations regarding foreign investment in specific industries and sectors of the

---

that enterprises with less advanced technology or which were oriented towards the local market might be denied approval automatically. Experience has proved this assumption to be wrong.'

[8]Before 15 September 1996 only certain provinces, cities and special economic zones were allowed to approve projects up to US$ 30 million. MOFTEC extended the right to approve projects under US$ 30 million that did not require substantial balancing to all its provincial departments, autonomous regions and municipalities with provincial status within the state plan. See the decision of the State Council of 20 August 1996, published in the 1997 yearbook of MOFTEC.

[9]Emerged from discussions at the Dutch Embassy and MOFTEC in Beijing in April 1998.

Chinese economy.[10] For instance, electric power projects are to be approved by the electric power administration of the State Council regardless of the amount of investment involved.[11]

In practice there are different methods to keep the investment project within the US$ 30 million investment limit in order to avoid central government involvement. The first method is to restrict the amount of investment although, from a commercial point of view, a more extensive investment would be preferred. However, the investment project may run into difficulty at the moment capital is needed to expand production. Increase of capital without approval is illegal (see the following).

Another method used is to divide the investment project into different phases.[12] Only the first phase is part of the feasibility study to be submitted to the authorities for approval. After approval has been granted, the project is divided into several different projects, each below a certain investment amount. In this way the parties involved 'escape Beijing's radar screen'. The approaches involve considerable risks if the higher authority is informed of the practice. Pursuant to Article 12 of the Interim Provisions (see below), the foreign investment project shall be cancelled.

Provisions 1986 and interim provisions 1995

As a result of complaints by foreign investors about the difficulty of penetrating the domestic market, in 1986 the State Council promulgated the Provisions[13] in order to restore foreign confidence. The measures aimed at reassuring foreign investors by removing the difficulties they had complained about[14] and to promote the industries of primary concern to China.

The Provisions gave preferential treatment to two kinds of industries, the 'export industries' (generating foreign exchange surpluses)

[10] For instance, MOFTEC and the State Administration for Industry and Commerce issued the Regulations on the Establishment of Sino-Foreign Enterprises in Advertising Industries in 1995. MOFTEC issued a Circular on Investment in BOT Form 1994 and the Ministry of Construction issued the Rules on Foreign-Invested Construction Companies 1995. The State Planning Commission and the State Administration of Foreign Exchange issued the Administration of Project Financing Conducted Outside China Tentative Procedures 1997.

[11] Art. 6 Electric Power Law, promulgated on 28 December 1995.

[12] The term used is 'phasing out'.

[13] Provisions for the Encouragement of Foreign Investment of 11 October 1996, a decree of the State Planning Commission, the State Economic and Trade Commission and MOFTEC.

[14] See e.g. International Bureau of Fiscal Studies 1995, p. 135.

and the 'technologically advanced industries' (developing new products or import-substituting products). These industries qualify for important tax and fee (e.g. land usage fees) reductions or exemptions. In addition, projects in these branches of industries are given preferential treatment in electricity and water supply, transport and telecommunication facilities.

In an attempt to further unify its policies and practices the State Planning Commission, the State Economic and Trade Commission and MOFTEC decreed in 1995 the Interim Provisions on Guiding Foreign Investment Direction.[15] Article 3 of the Provisions stipulates that:

> The State Planning Commission shall compile at regular intervals and revise in time and promulgate after approval of the State Council the Catalogue for the Guidance of Foreign Investment Industries according to these provisions and the development of the country's economy and technology.

The Interim Provisions classify investment projects according to three categories: 'encouraged', 'restricted' and 'prohibited' projects. The projects which do not belong to the three specified categories fall within the category of 'permitted' investment projects.[16] The liberties and restrictions pertaining to the different categories are set out in the Interim Provisions.

Projects introducing new agricultural technology, high technology, energy-saving and material-saving projects, projects which cater to a particular domestic demand not met by domestic supply, product development projects which improve the quality of products, projects that meet demands of the international market, and projects in the mid-west region are regarded as encouraged projects.[17] Imports related to encouraged projects enjoy exemption from import duties and VAT. In addition, foreign exchange balancing rules are relaxed.

Restricted projects are, among others, projects that involve technology for production capacity that meets the demand on the domestic market, project experiments in the state industries, projects for

[15] Approved by the State Council on 7 June 1995, and promulgated by the State Planning Commission and the Ministry of Foreign Trade and Economic Cooperation on 20 June 1995. Booklet issued by the State Planning Commission. According to a note on p. 9 of this booklet the English text is considered as the text of reference.

[16] Art. 4 Interim Provisions.

[17] *Idem* Art. 5.

exploring or mining mineral resources, and projects involving industries that need overall state planning.[18]

Prohibited projects are projects which endanger the safety of the state, pollute the environment, and occupy a lot of arable land or use the unique craftsmanship[19] or technology of China.[20]

The encouraged investment project is allowed to expand to related areas.[21] The restricted category is further classified into restricted Group A (slightly restricted) and Group B (highly restricted). Group A activities may be categorized as permitted activities if, for example, 70 per cent of the sale of the products is exported or if the state's needs to develop the middle and western regions are met.[22] Restricted foreign investment projects shall have the operational period of the enterprises agreed upon and the fixed asset investment by the Chinese party shall consist of the funds of the Chinese party's own assets.[23] This means that foreign investment in the restrictive category cannot operate indefinitely and the terms of the project must be clearly stipulated.[24] Further expansion of the foreign investment project in the restricted category is not allowed without additional approval. Projects listed under Group A are however exempt from this restriction. The authority to approve investment projects belonging to Group A or B cannot be delegated to lower levels than the provinces, autonomous regions, municipalities and municipalities directly under the control of the central government or cities planned by the state. Sub-delegation of projects falling within the restricted category is therefore not allowed.[25] The permitted category is not subject to matters such as the term of investment or the prohibition to sub-delegate approval authority. Foreign investment is allowed without preferential treatment or restrictions.

Violation of the Interim Provision 1995 leads to the cancellation of the foreign investment project, resulting in the invalidation of the contracts of association and the deregistration of the FIE.[26] Staff of

---

[18] *Idem* Art. 6.

[19] The list of prohibited projects also contains processing of green tea, handmade carpets, and other products which are not unique to China at all.

[20] *Idem* Art. 7.

[21] For example, foreign investors in highway construction and operation may be permitted to operate a retail gas station alongside the highway. See *China Law and Practice*, January/February 1998, p. 51.

[22] Art. 11 Interim Provisions.

[23] *Idem* Art. 9.

[24] Wang and Zhang 1997, p. 280.

[25] Art. 10 Interim Provisions.

[26] *Idem* Art. 12.

the examination and approval organs misusing their power or engaging in malpractices will face administrative sanctions and shall be prosecuted.[27]

Catalogues of 1995 and 1998

A detailed enumeration of industrial activities in each category can be found in the Catalogue,[28] which is an integral part of the Interim Provisions. The Catalogue may indicate sectors in which wholly foreign-owned enterprises are not allowed (e.g. construction and management of local railways, bridges and ferries,[29] non-ferrous metal industry)[30] or in which the state should have a holding or leading position (e.g. construction and management of a hydropower station[31] or assembly of motorcycles[32]).[33]

On 1 January 1998 the Catalogue was replaced by a new Catalogue.[34] This however did not affect the binding nature of the Interim Provisions. In case of inconsistencies between the Interim Provisions and other investment laws, the Interim Provisions prevail.[35] The Catalogue's items and priorities reflect new experiences and developments of the Chinese economy. The Catalogue 1995 restricted industrial sectors which were regarded as lucrative and to which the local governments had shown a more lenient approach in the past. Foreign investors were therefore disappointed by the restrictions spelt out in the Catalogue 1995.[36]

Similarly the Catalogue 1998 did not live up to their expectations. It was expected that the continuing efforts of China to join the WTO would open up new sectors of the economy, such as telecommun-

[27] *Idem* Art. 14.

[28] Catalogue for the Guidance of Foreign Investment Industries, promulgated on 20 June 1995 ('Catalogue 1995'), revised on 1 January 1998 ('Catalogue 1998').

[29] *Idem*, Encouraged Foreign Investment Industries, VIII, 5.

[30] *Idem*, Restricted Foreign Investment Industries (B), V.

[31] *Idem*, Encouraged Foreign Investment Industries, VI, 2.

[32] *Idem*, Restricted Foreign Investment Industries (B), VII, 1.

[33] Art. 4 Interim Provisions.

[34] The 1998 Catalogue was issued jointly by the SCP and MOFTEC on 31 December 1997.

[35] Wang and Zhang 1997, p. 297.

[36] It would be instructive to be reminded of the historical background of the 1995 Provisions: China had just devalued its currency by 40 per cent, abolished its preferential tax policies and suffered high inflation because of over-investment and a booming domestic demand. The devaluation was a stimulus to foreign investment, the inflation depressed it, and investors were confused as to how to react.

ications, wholesaling and retailing.[37] The investment restrictions in these sectors were not relaxed.[38]

However, the 1998 Catalogue aims not only to attract foreign investment but also to protect China's domestic industry[39] and restricting foreign investment is only one method to achieve this. The protection of domestic industries and services is deemed necessary by the Chinese government because many Chinese industries have idle capacity and have run up huge losses. Since 1996 foreign-invested companies have taken ever larger market shares and the Chinese government has tried to counter this development by introducing other methods like imposing limited market shares on Sino-foreign joint ventures and by favoring state-owned enterprises with cheap loans, lower tariffs, less stringent environmental demands, and lower social security requirements.[40]

The Catalogue 1998 restricted the encouraged category by making additional requirements e.g. concerning introduction of new technology for the sectors concerned. Furthermore certain minimum requirements on production capacity were introduced. Several items of the encouraged category (e.g. the shipping industry) and Group A (e.g. certain medical instruments) were shifted to Group B. These changes indeed reflect shifts of emphasis in developing China's economy.[41]

[37]The pilot establishment of equity or cooperative joint ventures in the retailing business in a number of designated municipalities and in the five Special Economic Zones was approved by the State Council in 1992. In November 1995 the State Council agreed that the Ministry of Internal Trade and MOFTEC could each approve the establishment of one pilot Sino-foreign equity chain store in either Beijing or Shanghai. The foreign party should be either a European, US or Chinese large multinational chain store.

[38]After 1995 there was some relaxation of the June 1995 Catalogue, especially in the service and financial sectors. At the end of 1996 RMB business was open for experiment and foreign insurance companies were allowed in Shanghai and Guangzhou (by the end of 1997 they captured 7 respectively 1.6 per cent of the local insurance income). In addition much retail commerce is not carried out by joint ventures but by other means such as domestic enterprises using foreign names and trademarks. Although real estate projects may formally only be owned by Chinese parties, they may be managed by foreign partners. Some foreign businesses lease and operate domestic shops (with only a fee to the Chinese partner).

[39]Which is understandable, keeping in mind the high rate of unemployment.

[40]Another method is to give export rebates to domestic producers or to allow state-owned enterprises to copy foreign technology without strict enforcement of copyrights. Over the past few years state-owned enterprises have recovered a third of their payments for such rights by selling them to other domestic companies.

[41]See *China Law and Practice*, January/February 1998, p. 52: 'Other additions are due to the development or popularization of new technology or phenomena.

The prohibited category remained substantially the same. Foreign investment projects in mass media, urban public utilities, weapon production and telecommunications remain prohibited. The Catalogue 1998 added some new definitions to the encouraged, restricted and prohibited items of the Catalogue 1995 to limit the possibility of different interpretations.

The Catalogue 1998 reflects China's growing interest in allowing foreign investments in terms of quality rather than quantity and improving international competitiveness. In view of the continuing devaluation of the Southeast Asian currencies and China's pledge not to devalue the Renminbi this seems a necessity.[42] New incentives to attract foreign investment are announced on a regular basis[43] and on 17 May 1998 Xinhua news agency, citing the Minister of MOFTEC, Shi Guangsheng, stated:

> With regard to the establishment conditions and market openness concerning restricted conditions or projects in which the ratio of foreign shares are limited, it is necessary to ease restrictions to some extent. The state will arrange a host of projects in agriculture, irrigation, transportation, energy, raw materials and environmental protection in central and western areas for foreign capital. ... It is necessary to encourage foreign-invested companies in eastern areas to re-invest in central and western areas. ... Trial openness areas and projects allowed by the state should proceed simultaneously in eastern, central and western areas in principle.

In the past the coastal provinces received almost all foreign investment, China now encourages foreign businesses to invest in central and west China.[44]

It should be noted that at the same time as the new Catalogue was issued, two other catalogues were produced. The first was the 'Catalogue of key sectors, products and techniques supported by

---

For example "electronic publication" was added to Class B clearly as a result of the wide use of the Internet in China.'

[42] *China Law and Practice*, January/February 1998, p. 53.

[43] See e.g. the October 1998 issue of China's Foreign Trade. The result of these initiatives in terms of attracting more foreign investment remains to be seen.

[44] *China Business*, 17 February 1997: 'Of the US$ 37.2 billion in foreign funds that China absorbed in 1995, 88 per cent flowed to its three centrally administered municipalities and nine coastal provinces. These same twelve regions are home to only 41 per cent of China's population and similarly dominate most key economic indicators, from GDP to personal income.'

the state at present'.[45] The guiding principle behind this list was present market demand, high technological content which should benefit economic efficiency, sustainable development of resources and revitalization of stagnant industrial sectors. The other catalogue was the 'Catalogue of foreign investment items which will not be granted tax exemption on imported goods'.[46]

Special approval instructions

On 5 November 1995 MOFTEC issued an opinion ('Opinion')[47] which provides further guidance on specific foreign investment vehicles. In Part One the Opinion further defines twelve sectors described in the Catalogue: road transport, commercial retailing, leasing, hotels, real estate, travel agencies, asset valuation organizations, translation, highways, ports and piers, railways and medical institutions. Part Two concerns the examination and approval of the following specific types of FIEs: (1) Joint Stock and Group Companies (MOFTEC will not approve increase of stock capital through allocation or issuing of shares unless the State Security Regulatory Commission has given approval); (2) Holding Companies (the total investment requirements are further defined); (3) FIEs that involve export licences (in principle only new projects in the form of equity and cooperative joint ventures in the encouraged or permitted category can be approved); (4) FIEs that involve granting of shares by an existing company to a foreign business.

Part Three of the Opinion relating to the approval instructions involving a transfer of shares from an existing Chinese enterprise to a foreign party and the approval policy on increasing the registered capital of an existing FIE will be further discussed below.[48]

---

[45] See the MOFTEC journal *International Economic Cooperation* (Guoji jingji hezuo), No. 1, 1998.

[46] We are not aware if this catalogue has ever been published.

[47] Directing of the Examination and Approval of Foreign Investment Enterprises Opinion, issued on 5 November 1996 by MOFTEC.

[48] On 25 December 1995 the State Council set the basic framework for the issue of B-shares in the Listing of Foreign Investment Shares inside China by a Company Limited by Shares Provisions. These provisions were followed by a number of rules and regulations affecting the issue of B-shares. Most recently, on 17 March 1998 the China Securities Regulatory Commission promulgated the Examination and Approval of Share Issue Procedures. The developments regarding the issuing of B-shares for capital increase by foreign investment share companies will not be dealt with in this paper since this subject alone merits extensive study.

Transfer of shares of an existing Chinese parent company to foreign investors

Recently a new phenomenon of foreign investment has appeared, i.e. buying into a state-owned enterprise by acquiring its shares and then amending the registration of the enterprise and transforming the enterprise into a foreign investment enterprise. In fact the foreign investor makes a capital contribution by buying shares into an existing company which involves no increase of capital.

The Opinion recognizes this foreign investment alternative and stipulates that the transformed enterprise should be approved by the provincial-level department of foreign economic relations and trade. The consideration related to the share transfer should be paid in one lump sum within one month of the enterprise receiving its business licence or, in special cases, the fee can be paid in monthly instalments over a period of one year. Until the fee is paid in full, no shareholder's rights can be transferred to the foreign investor.[49]

This venture bears considerable risks to do with the unknown debts and liabilities of the domestic Chinese parent company. The assets of the enterprise remain subject to the rules of evaluation of the State Administration of State-Owned Assets. The Opinion states that this form of foreign investment is easily influenced by changes in policy priorities, and since it involves a number of aspects which are more complicated than traditional joint ventures, it must be handled with care.[50]

FIE increase in registered capital contribution

In order for FIEs to grow and expand production, the FIE may seek to increase its capital. Part Three of the Opinion covers the principles and procedures related hereto. In summary all registered capital must be paid up within strict time limits, and the changes in shareholdings should not result in a controlling share by foreign investors if the Catalogue requires the state to have a leading position. The Chinese partner should have a majority shareholding in the case that the enterprise sells mainly to the domestic market. In case the foreign party shall obtain a controlling share the interests of the Chinese party must be protected by contract and no fundamental changes are to be made in the contract when the foreign party originally held 50 per cent or a minority shareholding.

[49] Opinion, Part Two, para. 4.
[50] *Law and Practice*, May 1997, p. 34.

The Opinion gives three instances where the FIE may increase its capital: (a) business reasons other than expansion of production scale; (b) in the case of expansion of production, which will not influence the balancing by the state, and if the venture does not fall within the restricted category; (c) in the case of expansion of production, which does influence the overall balancing of the state or if the venture is included in the list of restricted (B) projects. In general, the original authority shall approve the increase of capital if the total original and additional capital falls within the permissible limits attributed to the original approving authority.[51] The alternative (c) shall request central government-level approval.

The Opinion warns the approval officials that the method of increasing registered capital should not be used to evade industrial policy.[52] A dominant status of the foreign party in the stake capital of the FIE shall not be approved if a foreign party majority is disallowed in the respective industry. The principles laid down in the Opinion are expected to be further formalized in new regulations within the foreseeable future.

Conclusion

The Chinese foreign investment authorization procedures are used by the Beijing government to guide foreign investment towards specific geographical areas and to promote or restrict investments in specific Chinese industries. In addition, they are instrumental in controlling the expansion of business activities of foreign companies that are already active on the Chinese domestic market.

Local and central government priorities in attracting foreign investment contradict, resulting in a competition among local governments and against the central Chinese government policies. This situation gives rise to an ongoing struggle by the central government to control and supervise economic developments at the decentralized level and pursue a national foreign investment policy, and creates confusion with foreign investors.

The process of direct foreign investment authorization can therefore be characterized as a process of ongoing (re)definition which is dependent upon the status of China's domestic industry in relation to the outside world. This process is highly determined by the economic policy objectives of the central Chinese government.

---

[51] *Idem*, p. 35.

[52] This remark is evidence of how much the Chinese central government is aware of the practice of evading central policies and regulations by provincial and local officials.

References

External Services Department of the Economic Daily (1985), *Guide to Joint Equity Ventures*, Beijing: External Services Department of the Economic Daily

International Bureau of Fiscal Studies (1995), *Taxation & Investment in the People's Republic of China*, The Hague: IBFS

Joint Conference of Mayors of the Bohai Coastal Region (1991), *A Guide to the Economic. Development and Cooperation in China's Bohai Coastal Region*, Beijing: CITIC Publishing House

MOFTEC (ed.), *Almanach of China's Foreign Economic Relations and Trade 1997*, Beijing

State Planning Commission, *Catalogue for the Guidance of Foreign Investment Studies*

Wang, Chenguang and Zhang, Xianchu (1997), *Introduction to Chinese Law*, Hong Kong: Sweet & Maxwell Asia

Wang, Guiguo (1993), *Business Law of China*, Hong Kong: Butterworths Asia

Wang, Guiguo and Tomasic, Roman (1994), *China's Company Law*, Hong Kong: Butterworths Asia

List of Contributors

Jean-Pierre Cabestan is director of the French Centre for Research on Contemporary China in Hong Kong and chief editor of *Chinese Perspectives.*

Jianfu Chen is Senior Lecturer in Law and Legal Studies, La Trobe University, Melbourne, Australia.

Geor Hintzen is Guest Lecturer in Chinese Law, Catholic University of Leuven, Leuven, Belgium.

Jan Holthuis is managing partner at Holthuis International Lawyers, Amsterdam, specializing in Chinese law and practice. He is a frequent speaker on PRC legal and commercial issues.

Ingrid d'Hooghe is attached to the Documentation and Research Centre for Contemporary China of Leiden University, Leiden, The Netherlands and editor of *China Information.*

Yuwen Li is a researcher specializing in Chinese law at the Van Vollenhoven Institute for Law and Administration in Non-Western Countries, Law Faculty, Leiden University, Leiden, The Netherlands.

Jan-Michiel Otto is Professor of Law and Administration in Developing Countries at the Van Vollenhoven Institute for Law and Administration in Non-Western Countries, Law Faculty, Leiden University, Leiden, The Netherlands.

Eduard B. Vermeer is Senior Lecturer in Modern Chinese History and Head of the Documentation and Research Centre for Contemporary China, Sinological Institute, Leiden University, The Netherlands.